Silver Bullets

Second Edition

A Revised Guide to Initiative Problems,
Adventure Games, Stunts, and Trust Activities

Karl Rohnke

Project Adventure, Inc.

701 Cabot Street, Beverly, MA 01915 978-524-4500
PO Box 2447, Covington, GA 30015 770-784-9310

www.pa.org

KENDALL HUNT
PROFESSIONAL

Photo Credits

Most photos were taken by Karl Rohnke; exceptions listed here:
Front cover: Ryan McCormack, Project Adventure Staffing Coordinator and Trainer
Pages xiii, 17, 25, 48, 51, 61, 78, 83, and 101: Project Adventure, Inc.
Pages 1, 59, 111, and 165: istockphoto.com
Page 76: Carole Pouzar
Page 116: Nicki Hall
Page 118: John Guarrine
Page 140: Adrian Kissler
Page 173 (bottom two photos): Gloree Rohnke
Page 194: Yoav Daniel Bar-Ness

Thanks to Larry Beatty at Jumonville Christian Camp for application of his Photoshop skills and the use of the photos on the following pages: 14, 53, 162, and 183

Illustration Credits

Pages 13, 15, 19, 29, 33, 35, 37–39, 46, 54, 91, 102, 124, 132, 145–146, 150, 168, 170, and 175: Plynn Williams
Pages 62, 64, and 108: Bob Nilson
Pages 98 and 197: Project Adventure, Inc.
The author wishes to express his appreciation to Toshiyuki Morozumi for the illustrations found on pages:
    9, 23, 73, 115, 119, 155, 157, and 169.

For all activities that use the challenge course, Project Adventure standards for procedure and safety can be found in *The Guide for Challenge Course Operations: An Essential Reference for Challenge Course Practitioners* **by Bob Ryan, Project Adventure, 2005.**

To those thousands of Project Adventure workshop participants who said (or thought) "NO WAY"—and then found a way.

Contents

Adventure Games 1

Initiatives 59

Foreword

The first edition of *Silver Bullets* was published in 1984, and, in the years since, more than 200,000 copies have been sold, making it one of the top sellers in the adventure/experiential education field. Many teachers and counselors have discovered the power of experiential education through this book of activities and accompanying training clinics by Project Adventure and other organizations. And . . . the number of students who have experienced the activities in *Silver Bullets* in classes taught by those teachers and counselors, easily totals over twenty-five million.

"Bring the Adventure Home," a PA tagline off and on for the last 25 years, has been our way of saying that powerful experiential education can really happen, not only in a wilderness setting, but also in a physical education classroom in a gymnasium, in an academic classroom, and in a counseling session. There is now a strong consensus among our colleagues that the research, and curricula refinement based on that research, is still a needed and valuable component of the experiential model becoming truly the mainstream paradigm of education methodology. We at Project Adventure, and our colleagues, have increasingly refined the curricula and the research to validate this emerging educational paradigm.

And yet, there is a key variable in this facilities-based experiential curricula approach, a variable that really does make a huge difference: the activity itself. The design of activities matters, and matters a lot. The magic moments of insight and bonding that occur when these activities are effectively used are a major key to obtaining great educational outcomes. Here is how I described those magic moments in the preface to the 1984 edition:

"The name, 'Silver Bullets,' came to Karl and me as we were discussing this book and rambled into nostalgia on our youth. Remember . . . remember the games . . . remember the Ovaltine! There was a magic in those times, just as there seems to be a magic in these activities. The thrill of seeing a group of people come together quickly, build trust, begin to solve problems more efficiently—this thrill is reminiscent of early play. In both there is a spirit of playfulness and a flowing of creativity. The most enduring result is a kindred spirit and a feeling of bondedness that transcends words."

With *Silver Bullets, Second Edition*, you have a collection of very good, engaging, and fun activities that really work, that have the "magic." There are many new activities here, added by Karl, and the original writing has been refreshed to give it a more relevant context for today's world. You also have the security of knowing that these activities have been tested in many variable settings and curricula. Some of these classics from the original *Silver Bullets* have faded from modern usage but are jewels to be rediscovered. The activity, A-Frame, is a good example as this classic from the 70s and 80s was just reintroduced to the PA Training and Consulting staff, many of whom had not experienced it.

For those of you who do not know Karl Rohnke, he is the godfather of the evolution of activities that can be used effectively in a variety of curricula and situations that have social and emotional outcomes as their goal. He is truly one of the people of whom it can be said, "He is a legend in his own time." Through his experiential field work of over 45 years and his key roles at PA from 1971–99, Karl has been a prime mover in the evolution of activities and their role in facilities-based education. So, if Karl likes an activity, it means that it has a design that works well with people of all types.

For those of you looking for the original writing of some of the true classics of activities in our field, for those who are looking for a new activity to refresh a particular curriculum you are using, or for those who just enjoy Karl's writing and his engaging style and want to learn more of the history of the classic activities in our field, this book will be a valuable addition to your library of resources. Read, innovate, and enjoy!

Dick Prouty
President and Executive Director
Project Adventure, Inc.

Silver Bullets, Second Edition– The 25th Silver Anniversary Edition

In anticipation of this extensive 25th anniversary rewrite of *Silver Bullets*, and after reading through the first 15 pages of the 1984 edition, I couldn't help wondering why the original edit team of the PA staff and myself deemed it necessary to encumber the reader with so many preliminary announcements, caveats, statements of intent, and what seemed to be unnecessary justification for laying this in the reader's lap. Was a preface, foreword, introduction, statement of learning goals, benign caveat, blatant disclaimer, and diverse organizational comments necessary?

Absolutely, because we were asking readers to enter the terra incognita of untested and often esoteric theory and curriculum. Newly turned-on educators were not looking to *Silver Bullets* for entertainment, they wanted a piece of the educational excitement and personal fulfillment that an adventure curriculum had promised via workshops and preliminary testing. Readers needed justification for ploughing into a text filled with hoops, hollers, ropes, toys, and offbeat suggestions that had been unavailable and unheard of in their undergraduate training. Project Adventure was more than a new approach, it was a radical departure from the comfort of competition and teacher driven accomplishment. Catch phrases like "Bring the Adventure Home," "Full Value Commitment," and "Challenge by Choice" beckoned seasoned and battered educators (ready for retirement after ten years of traditional teaching) to try something new and exciting.

During the first decade since Project Adventure's inception at Hamilton-Wenham Regional High School in Massachusetts, the PA staff had become so used to being consistently "mis-ed" (misconstrued, misunderstood, misjudged . . .) that it became a necessary part of each staff person's job to act as an ambassador for adventure; to help define adventure as a unique educational approach rather than a proclivity for risky pursuits.

We have been beating the adventure/experiential drum since 1971, and the beat is obviously being heard and replicated, as literally thousands of adventure curriculum programs around the world subscribe to the comfortably portrayed hallmarks and documented material that identify an "adventure" approach.

And still I hear, "What is it you do?" So, welcome to this totally revised edition of *Silver Bullets*, including about 15 pages of absolutely necessary preliminary and introductory information.

What did you do to make the original Silver Bullets *different and better?*

- Took new photographs so that clothing looks more contemporary, less like the disco years. Is that an improvement? I guess it depends how much you like photos of guys in short shorts and long hair. Also, seeking some validity here, so that the photos better complement the text.
- Out-of-date games and activities have been deleted, including those activities that never seemed to catch on.
- Every game and initiative that was reevaluated and kept has been extensively rewritten, including additions and variations, to take advantage of 25 years of experience. Every effort has been made to maintain the unique and often zany writing style that tempted so many over the years to "just give it a try."
- Those activities that did not score well on Project Adventure's well-known safety survey have been either deleted or adapted to fit the programmed adventure paradigm, yet maintain the perceived risk aspect of curriculum design that has proved so valuable over the years.
- Approximately 14 somewhat new and REALLY NEW activities have been added to make up for the deletions, and to keep the book contemporary and programmatically useful. As much as I like and appreciate fun and enjoyment as applied to a facilitating style and repertoire of activities, I also appreciate the need for those based-in-theory pursuits that deliver.
- Peppered throughout the book are both "historical asides" and "boxed" vignettes specific

to the author's steel trap memory and proclivities related to instant recall, i.e., things that probably happened that have little to do with curriculum content and lots to do with <u>author</u>itative sharing.
- For *Silver Bullets, Second Edition* I dropped the four star evaluation system because in retrospect it seemed arbitrary and unnecessary. If I liked an activity enough to include it in a book, stars seemed superfluous.

- Plynn Williams created most of the original illustrations for *Silver Bullets,* and for other books I've authored. He had a feeling for "adventure" so I seldom had to explain more than once what I needed for an illustration. Plynn passed away some years ago. He was not only artistically talented, he was a nice guy.

• •

Acknowledgment

I have published about twenty books over the last thirty years. There is one person, above all, who is responsible for allowing those books to be written. She raised the kids (I played with them occasionally), did the laundry, cooked meals, cleaned and vacuumed, paid bills and taxes, celebrated the holidays, dealt with the home service providers, had the cars serviced, attended to our social responsibilities, regularly massaged my ego, and did all those thankless, unexciting tasks that allow a home to function while I played games, built ropes courses, traveled extensively, and then wrote books about having fun, choosing your challenge, and expressing yourself playfully. If you are a reader who has at some point felt a sense of gratitude for any of the information I've tried to gently and humorously bend to fit your needs, thank the woman (as I do) who so graciously arranged my life to allow that to happen, my wife of 40 years, Gloree Rohnke.

Introduction

Raison d'être

The purpose of this game, stunt, and initiative gallimaufry is to provide you with proven educational tools that do what they were designed to do—promote teamwork, elevate fun to its essential status, encourage the efficacy of sequenced failure, establish and solidify trust, and consistently revisit the classic troika of increased communication, cooperation, and self-awareness. The skill demonstrated in the use of a tool in construction or education is, of course, a function of the user's ability and experience. If you are new to the field, don't flinch; initiative problems and adventure games are user-friendly and are well-received by almost everyone.

The following chapters offer those educational tools that have proven over the years to be the most valuable; they are easy to use and people like them. Initiative problems, adventure games, and all activities of that get-to-know-you; get-to-know-yourself; have fun; be challenged; get scared; cooperate; share; fail or succeed genre have been collected and written about in a number of recent publications and less formal printings. There is no dearth of video or written material concerning experiential adventure methodology, in fact, the number of activities and theory available can often seem daunting, even overwhelming. Be aware, however, it's not the number of activities or debriefing scenarios memorized that's significant, rather when, where, and how to use a few chosen activities you are comfortable with, and recognize as being the correct educational tool for what you are trying to programmatically achieve.

The situation has always been that when a group needed a morale boost or a means of gaining behavioral insights, a well-sequenced game or initiative problem was a surefire and enjoyable way to accomplish that goal. The original *Silver Bullets* book numbers in the hundreds of thousands of copies sold over the last 25 years. That tells me there are heaps of people around the world using games and initiatives as fits their personal, geographic, and cultural needs—very satisfying. Here's hoping *Silver Bullets, Second Edition* finds a new generation of players looking for just the right game or trust activity to fulfill a one time rally or

a semester agenda, and further provides a satisfying dollop of nostalgia for the adventure veterans.

Lentz Learning Goals

In 1971, before Project Adventure became an Inc., the fledgling staff had a pretty good idea of what we were trying to accomplish, maybe not how necessarily, but we all had more or less the same vision. What we did need was a specific set of learning goals that could be applied to our ongoing, creative curriculum efforts. Robert Lentz, the founding director at Project Adventure, contributed the following four goals. I am duplicating them here exactly as they appeared in that first printing of *Silver*

Bullets (1984) and also appeared in the tens-of-thousands of copies sold and distributed worldwide over the next 25 years.

Goals

1. TO INCREASE THE PARTICIPANT'S SENSE OF PERSONAL CONFIDENCE. The aim of many activities is to allow people to view themselves as increasingly capable and competent. By attempting a graduated series of activities which involve physical or emotional risk, and succeeding (or sometimes failing) in a supportive group atmosphere, a person may begin to develop true self-esteem.

2. TO INCREASE MUTUAL SUPPORT WITHIN A GROUP. The assumption is that anyone who conscientiously tries should be respected. Success and failure are less important than making an effort. In many cases, the success or failure of a group depends on the effort of the members. A cooperative, supportive atmosphere tends to encourage participants.

3. TO DEVELOP AN INCREASED LEVEL OF AGILITY AND PHYSICAL COORDINATION. A number of exercises and games entail the use of balance and smoothly flowing movement. Balance and coordinated movement form the basis for many physical activites ranging from dancing to track and football. People who perceive themselves as physically awkward often see themselves as inadequate in other ways. Balance, coordination and agility can be improved by practice. Such improvement often generates a feeling of personal worth well beyond the tangible accomplishment.

4. TO DEVELOP AN INCREASED JOY IN ONE'S PHYSICAL SELF AND IN BEING WITH OTHERS. One of the criteria used in assessing various activites is that **it must have an element of fun in it.** Instructors are not solemnly engaged in building confidence, social cohesion and agility. Just as people approaching new situations may be anxious and even fearful, so should they experience joy, laughter, anticipation.

Reprinting these goals was not done just to fulfill a historical function, or fill a page. Take the time to read them. You have to be impressed by their comprehensive nature and how contemporary they seem after 35+ years of programmatic adventuring.

Organization of This Book

All the activities are included under the following chapter headings:

Adventure Games
FUNN & Stunts
Initiatives
Trust

Whether you can use a particular game, initiative problem or stunt might depend upon the space needed, materials at hand and the activity level planned for the group. To help you choose an appropriate activity I've incorporated a few symbols next to each title that will help identify what the activity's limitations are and what it has to offer.

 - an outside activity

 - an indoor activity

 - can be accomplished as well as either indoor/outdoor

 - activity level high (includes considerable movement or running)

 - activity level not so high (no perspiration or hard breathing)

 - needs props of some kind

 - no props necessary—people only

Before you start gaming and facilitating, here's a foreshortened adventure education formula that is the distillation of many years experience with educating and training people; age and location notwithstanding.

The essence of this formula (no panacea intended) deals with so many educational and psychological theories, opinions, jargon, and programmed confusers that I have probably oversimplified in hopes of demystifying a potentially complex approach. I have written it as I try to remember it.

1. NO TRUST—NO BEGINNING
2. NO FUN—NO RETURN (of students)
3. NO CHALLENGE—NO CONTINUATION

1. If your students don't trust you; your purpose; their peers; the approach; program time will be limited to hassles, bickering, reluctance, and a huge waste of time.

The activities in this book engender trust—you need it.

2. If you are so into the seriousness of educating that the essential fun inherent in learning has been squeezed out, then "by-the-numbers" is in. Rote learning is OK for multiplication tables, but there's certainly more joy in learning than $7 \times 9 = 63$ provides.

The activities in this book have fun in mind—it's essential.

3. If what you are doing is so geared to successful completion that failure is nonexistent, then boredom replaces challenge.

Understandable stress and commitment to challenge are woven throughout the activities in this book—you gotta have it.

Basic Disclaimer and Safety Reminder

"You can pick your challenge but you don't get to choose your consequence."* Just a wet blanket reminder that risk, no matter how reasonable, can be associated with things going wrong. No grumbling over there . . . remember, this is a disclaimer.

The reasonable risks presented in this anthology of games and initiatives that could result in emotional upset or physical harm can be minimized by operating within the parameter of a programmed approach, i.e., having a solid idea of what the results will be of whatever adventure task you are promoting. Huge suggestion—don't experiment with clients.

If I'm preachin' to the choir here I apologize, but you need to know or at least recognize, that adventure does not necessarily co-exist with physical risk and danger. Adventure is ". . . *an activity of uncertain outcome, characterized by risk and excitement.*" Is attending a dinner party adventurous? Look at the italicized definition above and apply it to a social engagement you attended where you knew practically no one. Was that adventurous? Was the evening predictable? Did you take a risk in attending? As you entered the building were you excited? The point is, just because something you do is adventurous doesn't necessarily mean it has to involve physical danger.

If you and others of your adventurous ilk (I've always wanted to use that word) are free-associating with possible adventure activity schemes for curriculum use, contemplate the possible consequences of your plan then put <u>your</u> safety and/or ego on the line before you ask students or clientele to try the activity. **"Calculated abandon"** is an OK approach as long as the calculations are well-thought-out and conscientiously tested. I prided myself as a ropes-course builder in that I would not hand over a zip wire, Pamper Pole, etc., to a client without having tested it for functionality (did it work?), and safety (imminently, my safety). This was during the early 70s before there were ANY ropes-course standards.

In keeping with these BE CAREFUL chidings, be advised that Karl Rohnke and Project Adventure, Inc., cannot, and do not, assume responsibility or liability for the use of information offered in this book, written or implied.

*Dr. Lee Gillis

Adventure Games

Introduction to Adventure Games Section

This new and re-scripted congerie of games and initiative activities is the result of hours of reading and determining what the original *Silver Bullets* text had yet to offer, and correspondingly, what to do with those aging pages whose time had come and gone.

As author of that original text, it was difficult to say goodbye to a game that had seen its zenith (or never reached it), but satisfying to know it would be replaced with a newer and more innovative bit of experiential **"edutainment."**

Seriously, who needs more games? There are tons of them available on web sites, CDs, and recently available books. Inspired authors* not only offer game set ups and rules, but also include where, when, and how (in various languages), finishing up with the proper questions to ask postexperience, included amidst a veritable flood of photos and illustrations . . . and in color! Personally, I've found that most of my program and presentation needs are easily fulfilled by using maybe 25–35 activities. "Knowing" in this context refers to sequencing, best choice of activity, variations, what to be aware of as facilitator (safety, venue, weather considerations), and what processing questions best reveal what the students have experienced and need to know.

When someone comes up to me at a workshop or conference and says, usually jokingly, "Karl, you need to write another game book; I've about run out of ideas," my response is to chide them for knocking back too many Starbucks caffeine specials. Then I suggest spending more time (attempts) and discussion with students on what they have obviously run through too quickly.

If your ongoing program could use a boost because of scheduling problems, personality conflicts, or activity repetition (boredom), try playing a couple of the games or initiatives herein. Challenging activities presented in a paradoxically lighthearted and purposeful manner, can provide the morale growth that facilitates group cohesion and enthusiasm for a program and the people that make up that program. De-emphasize win/lose competition and try to present the activities in such an attractive way that everyone will want to participate. OK, but how do I get things started "attractively"?

Play Pointers

- If you are going to play with the concept of play, you better be able to define it. Don't look it up, you will be disappointed (or should be) with the dictionary definition. Describe fun as a gut reaction to what fun feels like, where it comes from, and where to look for it. Whatever your description, if it's meaningful to you, it will serve as a better definition than the "joyful entertainment" pap available in *Webster*.

- Don't put yourself into the position of being a play proctor; involve yourself. You don't have to play every game you present, but be ready to personalize the play with your person. The more you involve yourself in play situations, the more you will be able to conceptualize what play is and isn't and how to programmatically use it. But don't feel that you have to encapsulate play either, otherwise you will be like the researcher dissecting a frog to find out what keeps it alive.

- Keep the rules to a minimum and be able to state the rules without hesitation.

- Be ready and willing to change the rules as fits the players and the situation. (ref. Calvin & Hobbes)

- Try not to run a good game into the ground through repetition; that's why some students don't like archery, basketball, or badminton, or anything presented too many weeks in a row.

- Keep players playing; avoid rules that permanently eliminate players.

- Establish teams that are fair. Don't use the disastrous sociogram technique for choosing up sides, i.e., asking two students to pick their own teams. Try using some of the comparison stunts from the activity Categories. See the books *The Bottomless Bag Revival*, page 143, or *QuickSilver*, page 85.

- Play games that allow as much of a 50/50 (male/female) split as possible.

---

*Inspired gaming authors (including) — Chip Candy, Jim Cain, Chris Cavert, Mark Collard, Michelle Cummings, Faith Evans, Laurie Frank, Dick Hammond, Tom Heck, John Hichwa, Adrian Kissler, Sam Sikes, Tom (Old Raccoon) Smith, Mike Spiller.

- Emphasize competition against self or time when competition seems natural. Trying to best a time established by your own team or attempting to smash a nebulous **WORLD RECORD** is great fun, with none of the negative ramifications of the second place syndrome. "You won a silver medal at the Olympic Games? Too bad, maybe you'll do better next time."

Alienation

I've had a bundle of fun over the years presenting and playing this game, now referred to as Alienation.

Objective

For an unknown Alien to "alienate" (eliminate) all the people involved in the game before they discover who he/she is.

Set Up

There are many ways to choose an Alien for the game. The easiest method I suppose is to walk among a group of eyes-closed players, eventually touching someone on the shoulder. (Don't touch heads, there's too many sects and ethnic groups that consider a head touch as rude and, in some cases, an insult. You never know anymore; play isn't as easy as it used to be.) The player touched is the chosen Alien.

There is another way to choose the Alien that allows a facilitator to play as well. It's called the T*humbo* technique. To wit: Everyone joins together in a circle-like cluster and puts one fist (right or left) into the center of the cluster with their thumb boldly sticking up. You announce (with everyone's eyes closed, <u>including yours</u>) that you are going to feel amongst the thumbs, then squeeze a chosen thumb once. That person who received the single squeeze (eyes still closed) will feel around all the still-extended thumbs, choose one, and squeeze it twice. The person with the double squeezed digit is the Alien. Slick, eh?

Rules

- All the players, Alien included, begin to mill around one another in the center of your play area.
- To alienate a player the Alien must deliver a wink at the chosen person during this random milling session. If the wink (not a blink) is delivered and identified, that receiving player is alienated and can no longer identify or have congress with any of the other not-yet-alienated players. Symbolic

of their new and isolated state, that player must (after one minute and less than two) enter a catatonic state prefaced by placing both hands over their face and loudly moaning an extended "Ohhh Noooo!" That person is out of the game and becomes a silent observer, (refer to catatonic above). The reason for waiting a minute before intoning your "Ohhh Noooo!" statement of having been alienated is to allow time for the Alien to move away from their winked-at victim.

Killer

Many years ago, when Alienation used to be called Killer, some players took their ersatz death sequence quite seriously, using this lighthearted opportunity to gain not only personal satisfaction for pulling off an extravagant demise scenario, but to also enjoy the well-accepted and anticipated, role-playing that went along with the theme of the game.

While pursuing the 24-hour version of Killer during an adventure based workshop in Georgia, the entire group, en route to a rock climbing venue, had stopped for lunch at a scenic pull out. Killer–the game–had already caused a half dozen "death" sequences that morning, so it wasn't as if another recreational casualty was not anticipated.

I heard the screams before I saw what was happening. The screams were high-pitched, piercing and unrelenting, becoming more intense and louder as I tried to find their source amidst much confusion and angst in the group. A young woman was bent over with both hands grasping at her abdominal area; her screams had changed to choking gasps for breath. What I saw still bothers me to this day. One of her hands was wrapped around the handle of a large kitchen knife that was apparently imbedded deeply into her mid-section; red gore seeping through her fingers plopped heavily onto the pavement. Then she looked up and smiled. . . . It was a Killer ruse and we had all been taken in.

The blade of the knife had been removed from the handle and the red gore was a combination of ketchup and red raspberry jam. Though her macabre histrionics were well-done and highly applauded, there were some, like me, who had been too emotionally drawn in to recommend a continuation of "deaths" at that level of reality. Even with additional rules added to tone down the angst, Killer was never the same lighthearted game after that day.

- As the group mills about looking at one another and someone thinks they know who the Alien is, he or she shouts "I accuse!" The accuser must be seconded by another player within ten seconds or the game continues. But, if someone says "I'll second that accusation," both players (the accuser and the second) wait until the facilitator counts to three. On THREE, both point directly at who they think is the Alien. If the accusing fingers indicate two different people, both of the pointers are immediately alienated. If both accusers point at the same person and that person admits to their nefarious role as Alien, the game is over.
- If the Alien was not identified by the accusers, the game continues until either the Alien is caught or all the players have been alienated, either feat worthy of applause and a rousing "Good Show!"

Variations

- Allow the Alien to alienate by shaking hands, at the same time pressing the victim's wrist with an extended index finger. It is obviously not necessary to alienate every time you shake a hand.
- If the idea of alienating everyone is just too hard to bear, try this "nice" variation. Everyone in the room must mill about, whispering something nice to each player encountered. The exception, of course, is the Alien who will whisper something pejorative, purely negative. For example: "Your blouse is outstanding." "I really like your hair cut." Then, from the Alien, "Your socks are uglier than argyle."
- If the games are dragging a bit and you would like to bring things to a quick and acceptable end, introduce the *plague variation*. Whenever a player is alienated he or she can, after waiting for the Alien to move on, take another player down with them by placing their hands on that player's shoulders, simultaneously moaning "Ohhh Noooo!" That infected player can then pass the alienation along by grabbing another slow moving player, etc. The initially alienated person cannot run around the room alienating one person after another—think chain reaction—nor can the initial person grasp the Alien. However, if an Alien is careless enough to get

caught in a plague sequence, that person's either doing some fast talking, or keeping a low profile hoping no one noticed their invulnerability.

- If your group is to be together for a couple of days, you might want to consider playing Alienation over a 24-hour period. The long game is played essentially the same way as the shorter version presented above, with a couple of differences. The alienation sign is displayed by making the OK symbol with finger and thumb, then juxtaposing that sign directly on your own body somewhere below the waist. If anyone makes visual contact with that sign, in that location, they are immediately alienated. The situations available for alienating are practically endless, particularly with 24 hours to plan your clandestine moves. Also, player responses to having been alienated, other than just a simple Ohhh Noooo! could be expanded and embellished, but that's up to you. Go for what's fun and acceptable with your group.

Review Questions

Although this game is presented to promote a high level of histrionic fun, what actually happens and how people respond to the dynamics of the game might be interesting to talk about.

- If you were chosen as the Alien, were you pleased?
- If you were the Alien, how did you respond to your role?
- Was trust a part of this game?
- What was the most difficult part of the game for you?
- Did you like any of the variations better than the rest?
- If you were to change any part of this game, what part would that be?

Am I on the *Right* Team?

Use one of the Category techniques (*QuickSilver*, page 85, or *The Bottomless Bag Revival*, page 143) to split your group in half. If you don't have access to either book just count off 1-2, 1-2 around the circle, or have everyone born in the months January through June get together in one group, July through December in another, then adjust. Don't let the players choose up sides, as the predictable results are always an emotional disaster for the people chosen last. Call the two groups Team A and Team B or something more creative, just so they have a recognizable name.

Ask everyone to distribute themselves randomly within the playing area (a gym, a field, some amorphous section of turf), and for members of Team A to extend their right hands and members of Team B to extend their left hands. "Distribute themselves randomly" means players get to go wherever they like within the play area (the play area does not include the bathrooms or the bleachers). Once they

choose a position they have to stay there, i.e., both feet remain in place until the action starts.

Choose one member of each team as either "right initiator," or "left initiator." Call that person any acceptable name as long as they recognize their right/left designation. The two initiators then jog to opposite ends of the playing area and stand ready, about ten feet from the nearest "distributed" person.

At the start (GO!), the right initiator looks for a player with an extended right hand, and grasps that person's hand. Then those two connected players look for another extended right hand and connect with that person and so on, until all the right-handed players are connected hand in hand. If the "right" team accomplishes this before the left-handed players complete their connection, the right team wins.

Rules and Considerations

- Yelling and shouting instructions to teammates after the START is allowed and expected.
- If anyone on the field (other than an initiator) moves their feet before their hand is grasped, five seconds is added to their team's final time.

- Physically interfering with the other team is not allowed.
- If anyone in the developing line breaks grip, ten seconds is added to their team's final time, i.e., every time a break occurs.
- For a second more cooperative attempt, suggest that a final team time (both groups operating together) will be established when both groups have completed their hand grip lines.
- Want the groups to be cooperative from the get-go? There's no formula here, do what you think is best for your group of students, or what they seem to gravitate toward. Remember, the activity represents the trip, your questions and resulting discussion are the destination.

• •

Ankle Biters

I have to keep reminding myself, the text of *Silver Bullets* is at least 25 years old, and that things change. On page 40 of the old book there are a couple of paragraphs outlining what I called, at the time, Sit Down Dodge Ball. Not a bad time-consumer in a pinch, but nothing special. Since that time, and with copious help from friends and working compatriots, Sit Down Dodge Ball has morphed into one of the most popular and simplistic games I've ever used in workshops, now called Ankle Biters.

Objective

To hit someone with a soft **throwable**, causing that hit person to choose one of two alternatives: to kneel on one leg after being hit, and from that position (1) attempt to get back into the game by picking up a "spent" throwable off the ground, or (2) try to tag someone's ankle as they run by, causing them to have to stop and present themselves as a TARGET. Last person standing—wins.

(If you have just read the Objective above and said to yourself, "No, I don't think that game's for me; too much like Bombardment." Wait! Give me a chance to explain further. People <u>really</u> like this game.)

Rules and Considerations

- There's a simple throw-and-hit game called Asteroids (*Bottomless Bag Again*, page 77) that serves as a prelim to Ankle Biters. People stand in an expanded circle holding two throwables.

Ready, Set, . . . Go! All the throwables are tossed into the center of the circle. The object is to grab a throwable off the ground and hit someone with it. The hit person sits down as the game continues for another 15 seconds or until only one person is left standing.

- Use the identical start for Asteroids to begin the action for Ankle Biters.
- This time when someone is hit they go down on one knee and are allowed to pivot off one foot from that position. If they want to get back into the game they must wait for a throwable to end up within their ability to pivot on one foot and still reach the ball, (honor system). If and when they do grab a ball they must stand up before throwing the ball, i.e., no throwing from a kneeling position.
- If the action has been fast and furious, resulting in a noticeable level of oxygen debt, a player might choose to catch a breather after being hit and stay in that kneeling position for awhile. Or if they want to vary the action a bit, they can attempt to tag someone's ankle as a still-viable player runs past. If the tag is honestly made and received, the tagger will immediately, loudly, and repeatedly begin yelling "TARGET!" as they identify the targeted person by holding onto that player's ankle. The tagged person must stop and tolerate the ignominy of being a target until hit with a ball—won't take long.
- The beauty of the game is that after having briefly visited the win/lose simplicity of Asteroids, there is the anticipation that Ankle Biters will basically play the same; it doesn't. Although the facilitator has announced that the winner of Ankle Biters will be the last person standing, it's not long into the game before everyone realizes there is no win/lose end to the game. The action will continue undiminished until a halt is eventually announced because of no time left or general exhaustion.

Players can literally choose whatever pace best suits them, from totally active to remaining contemplatively on one knee.

- Many games can be ruined by players that don't play fair. Ankle Biters does require adherence to some basic rules, but it's one of the only games I have ever found that seems to proctor itself. If there are some infractions, it doesn't seem to affect the action or excitement of the game. If the infractions become egregious, the person responsible is either ganged-up on (playfully) or ignored.

Caveat If you (I mean YOU), play Ankle Biters for ten minutes straight, don't plan on making any profound postgame facilitating comments to the group that extend beyond interjections or exclamations . . . this game is flat-out aerobic.

Adventure Games

Blindfold Soccer

Happen to be looking for a game that blends cooperation, trust, communication, and excitement? Here 'tis.

Objective

To score a goal, each team (two teams) attempts to kick a ball past the end line of a football field or soccer pitch. For you sports purists, who need to know what the end line is, it's the last marked line on a field or the last length of rope stretched out for this purpose. A kick of the ball over that line scores a goal.

Set Up and Procedure

- Divide the group into two equal teams; equal in this case means the same number on each team. Each team divides into pairs and one member of each pair commits to wearing a blindfold. Not being a fan of blindfolds, I would simply ask one member of the pair to keep their eyes shut. If they want (need) to sneak a peek occasionally, that's an example of **peek-by-choice,** go for it.
- Soccer rules serve as a guide toward establishing parameters of play, but skills such as heading the ball, passing, and trapping when blindfolded are impractical at best.
- Allow the newly established pairs some practice time toward getting their act together, i.e., let the sighted leader verbally guide his sightless partner around the field for a minute or so, then switch roles.
- To begin play, have both teams line up at opposite ends of the field. The referee (probably you) then throws or kicks two soccer-type balls onto the field in as neutral a manner as possible. A compassionate facilitator would suggest using half field as the venue for play.
- Slightly deflating both balls before play reduces the distance a ball travels if kicked solidly, making getting hit by a well-kicked ball less risky, i.e., less painful.

Rules

- Only the sightless member of a pair can make physical contact with a ball. The sighted member can only provide verbal directions and physical protection for their partner.

- Members of a pair are allowed and encouraged to verbally communicate.
- Members of the pairs, or groups of pairs, are not allowed to purposefully touch one another. Normal game contact is OK as long as the contact is not of a directional type, i.e., pushing a sightless player toward the ball.
- There are no goalies. The words goalie and redundant are synonymous in this case, but if someone wants to be goalie . . . be a goalie.
- If a ball is kicked out of bounds, a referee will kick the ball back into play.
- Do not allow, and constantly warn against, high kicks. Encourage a side-of-the-foot, putting-action type of kick. Eliminating high kicks (high foot) is essential to safe play. If players continue to kick with a high-foot-follow-through, stop play; otherwise someone *will* get hurt.
- Heavy boots? No! Open-toed sandals? No. Running shoes? Yes.

Considerations

- A sighted player is not only there to give directions but also to act as a spotter for his partner, or any other sightless player who seems imminently at risk. If a sightless player is obviously at risk, the "no touch" rule is waived.

- There are two balls in play, which means either ball can score a goal. If the group is particularly large, use three balls as this tends to keep the players separated.
- After one sightless group has stumbled and laughed their way around the field for a few minutes (or after a goal is scored—not likely), ask the pairs to trade roles. Give the new pair a chance to try out their command/reaction functions before starting again.
- Before the game begins, teach the **bumpers up** position so that blindfolded players have protection for the upper ventral part of their bodies. Keep reminding the sightless players to maintain bumpers up, particularly when near other players.

Debrief Questions

- Which role did you like best and why?
- Did you feel any particular emotion while functioning in either a sighted or sightless role?
- Did you sneak a peak?
- Were you more interested in scoring a goal, or just experiencing the game?
- What did you feel was the big difference between the two roles?

Body English

This is so simple I hesitate to offer a write up, so I'll keep it short.

A group tries to spell out the words to a well known proverb or catch phrase by using their configured bodies as letters, or if it's a small group, perhaps just one meaningful word. Another group of equal number tries to decipher what the first group is trying to say, with groups switching roles from time to time so that everyone gets the chance to be either contorted or perceptive. Body

English encourages discussion, decision making, cooperation, and performing beyond the norm. Succinct enough?

Boop

*"You will know when those **play** moments happen. You can't anticipate **play**, you can't find it, you can't even create **play**; it just happens."*
Steve Butler

Perusing Caveat   If you are just leafing through the pages here, kind of looking for an activity that doesn't require numerous props, is easy to present, and people will like; you just stumbled on one of the best. I have successfully presented *Booop* well over one hundred times to large and small groups varying from elementary to corporate. Why such good results? People like BALLOONS, particularly big, colorful ones.

Since I'm going to be writing about games and initiatives that utilize balloons as props, and, considering myself as somewhat of a cognoscente concerning balloon play, let me suggest you bolster your budget and buy balloons by the gross (144). A gross of 12" diameter multi-colored balloons, as of this writing, will cost you about 11 bucks and change. Notice I suggested 12" balloons; don't even think about the 8"-10" variety that just don't exhibit the same play potential. Party stores seem to be the best (least expensive) place for purchasing these useful inflatables; in contrast, supermarkets seem to charge the most.

One small thing I should mention; party stores push their helium filled Mylar balloons because of the high profit margin. Don't be drawn in by their initial good looks and promised longevity. The unmentioned truth is that helium filled balloons don't stick around long enough for satisfying play unless highly string-controlled; one hit and poof, they're gone, never to return, unless you're traveling out of state or playing in a gym.

To begin, and as a demo, blow up one of the balloons and tie off the neck. (I'm sure this may be hard for you to believe but there are some people who have NEVER tied off a balloon. Don't make fun

or criticize, these benighted folks need your help.) As you blow, inflate to a diameter that satisfies, but will also allow some solid hits without bursting. There's nothing worse than an underinflated balloon. Well, maybe a few things . . . like weak coffee!

Finally, Boop—the game. Ask a small established group (3–4) to join hands in a circle (triangle or square, it doesn't matter), then try to keep their tied-off balloon off the floor by hitting it with their joined hands <u>only</u>. During this practice time, try to encourage an occasional hard lateral hit so they get the feel for rapid movement as a "team."

Here's the challenge. Indicate to the small groups that you will be calling out different body parts with which they are allowed to strike the balloon (remember, their hands are joined). If a balloon inadvertently (or advertently for that matter) hits the floor, that contact is considered a penalty. Penalties in this case can be either added up for later comparison, or exist simply as a means of quality control for the team. If a balloon does end up on the floor, the casual plan is to get it back into play as quickly as possible. The penalty does not have to be announced . . . mostly because no one would care.

Caveat   Boop is an indoor activity. Anything more than a zephyr will cause the balloons to become flukey and unruly, i.e., no fun. Stay inside and save yourself the hassle of changing venues.

Think of yourself as kind of a square-dance caller as you shout out the various anatomical areas allowed for striking the balloon. Here's a possible sequence you might want to try, recognizing I vary the sequence every time I lead this activity. Change portions of anatomy every 15–20 seconds.

- Hands only
- Index finger only
- Alternate hand and elbow
- Elbows only
- Alternate elbows and ankles
- Feet only
- Alternate heel and head
- Noses only
- Nose to shoulder
- Pelvis to chest

Call a halt to the *Booping*. By this time the penalties are stacking up and all thoughts of consequence have dissipated. When the excited talk and laughter has calmed somewhat, suggest that each team finish off with the following challenge; try to keep their

balloon off the floor without physically touching the balloon. Expect some quizzical looks and comments of "impossible," until someone thinks of a team blow, i.e., jointly puffing the balloon up toward the ceiling. This final challenge ends up with a lot of dizziness, carbon dioxide overload, laughter, and sometimes a team that gets their breath propulsion act so in sync that their balloon could be mistaken for a helium ringer.

Does this activity meet the standards for the golden debrief triumvirate (communication, cooperation, and trust)? Oh Boy . . .!

For you trivia buffs, the name B*oop* comes from the onomatopoetic gentle sound of a body part striking a balloon. Also, some people (usually south of the Mason/Dixon line) spell B*oop* with a third O, as in B*ooop*—your choice, of course.

Braaaaaaack-Whfffff

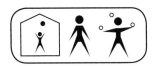

You gotta love the name and appreciate the obvious difficulty of getting the pronunciation correct. If you have ever wanted to flaunt the word and sounds of onomatopoeia, verbally attempting *Braaaaaaack-Whfffff* could be the sine qua non of using and abusing lip, cheek, and lung.

Anyway . . . the game! Each player gets one limp 12" balloon of variously available colors. Ask everyone to stand inside the jump circle at the center of the basketball court. No court? Fabricate a temporary circle using colored gym tape. No gym? Circle up a rope on the grass outside where the gym isn't. (If there's more than a zephyr currently caressing your billowing balloon blowing alliterative cheeks, turn the page and try another activity because any wind at all is going to cause chaos with the lofting latex.)

Considering that we are in a dead-air-space gym, ask everyone to blow up their balloon to just short of popping. Having said that, one or more eager inflators will inevitably blow up their balloon just past popping, so have a few extra limp ones available. Don't tie off the balloon, just hold tightly onto the neck and get together with other fully-inflated folks who have the same color balloon as you. If you and 3–4 others, are shuffling about pinching plump, taut, red balloons, you have become inextricably part of the RED team—congratulations.

If RED decides to be the first team to begin, one of the players steps into the jump circle, holds up his/her red balloon for all to see, then releases it, allowing the Braaaaaaack-Whfffffing to manifest itself by jetting about willy-nilly until the contracting latex falls limply to the floor, hopefully some distance from the release point. The second member of the RED team walks to that exact "dead" balloon location and, with their right foot just touching the deflated balloon, releases their own balloon. This process continues sequentially until all members of the RED team have released their individual balloons.

Using a 50' tape measure, the facilitator measures the distance from the circumference of the jump

circle to the nearest edge of the last balloon released. This distance represents the combined results of each RED team player's highly skilled participation, i.e., their team total.

Each team, represented by a different balloon color, repeats the procedure above so that in the end there are measured distances to quantify and qualify the performance disparities between competing teams, and specifically to allow awarding of 1st, 2nd, and 3rd place plastic (but really nice looking) trophies.

Performance Tip   Try launching your balloon like a football; the forward arm motion doesn't seem to add any distance but it makes you feel like you are doing something for the team.

Final Word   After playing *Braaaaaaack-Whfffff* a couple of times it becomes obvious there is absolutely no skill involved in the game, so the angst of losing gently deflates along with the balloons. Fun once again trumps serious competition . . . not bad, Mr./Ms. Facilitator.

Bump

Playing Bump requires a certain level of maturity, so take it as a pre-emptive caveat that this game has "touchy" co-ed implications. Be restrictive as to chosen anatomical catching positions if you feel that your group is too immature to handle brief but occasionally suggestive juxtaposing of bodies. Now that I have your interest, here are a few rules and guidelines.

Objective

Working in teams of three, the object is to throw, catch, and transport a knotted towel, or Frisbee, or rubber chicken approximately 50 feet to an empty wastebasket and deposit the carried item into that container without letting the item touch the floor.

Procedure

Divide into groups of three with one member of the troika acting as thrower. Standing about 10–15 feet away from the two catchers, the thrower gently lofts a rubber chicken toward his/her closely aligned teammates. The two catchers must bodily trap the ersatz chicken between one another without use of hands, arms, or shoulders, thus the name *Bump*. If the caught and tenuously held chicken is dropped on the way to the container the participants must run back and redo the throw-and-catch scenario.

After a successful deposit, the three teammates return smartly to the throwing area, chicken in hand. The throw and body catch is once again attempted, this time with one of the former catchers becoming a thrower. Play continues until the chicken has been successfully deposited into the wastebasket three times, i.e., each player gets the opportunity to be the thrower.

The first group accomplishing three valid drops wins the championship amidst great acclaim and shouts of "Huzzah!" Second and third place get some decent support, and everyone gets a ribbon for having participated.

Catch 10

I admittedly have a soft spot in my heart for this game, having created it with friends on the beaches of Southern California in the 60s. We* played Catch 10 as if each contest were about to be filmed by the Wide World of Sports and, considering our age and fitness level at the time, I suspect we played it well. The original game was played with a football, then segued to a Frisbee because of the flight variety that a Frisbee offered and because it was the 60s!

Objective

To cause your opponent to add a point to his/her score total (low score wins) by causing them to miss a thrown Frisbee. A missed Frisbee results in the accumulation of a point; ten points loses.

Set Up

- The play venue (there's no boundaries) can be any field area that doesn't have obstacles to run into or trip over. Turf, as for most outdoor games and sports, provides the best playing surface, unless a sand beach is handy, and that is absolutely the unsurpassed barefoot surface for all jump-around, feel good, land-on-your-head games.

Rules

- When a player accumulates ten points they are out of the game. The remainder of the players continue until only one remains, *el campion del mundo*, or at least that stretch of the beach.
- The throws are made in keeping with a pregame determined sequence (Pete-to-Liz-to-Rod-to-Jane, etc.) and continue that way unless a player,

PLYNN

*We—The originators of this game: Tony (snow cone) Conkle, Adrian Kissler, and John Harry Herbert

after having just missed a thrown Frisbee, shouts "Challenge." Active play stops briefly, as the player who just added a point to his total, gets to make a controlled throw at the person who made him/her miss. This challenge throw must be made from a measured distance of ten yards. In the event of either a miss or a catch as the result of this challenge throw, the Frisbee then continues in that reverse sequence, i.e., opposite to the way it was going.

- Missing the Frisbee during the flow of the game does not mean a "Challenge" must be called. Taking that ten yard throw is entirely up to the person who just missed a throw and can be used as a form of game strategy.
- Compassionate rules are in effect throughout. For example, when a throw is made, the potential catcher must make a 100% effort to snare the Frisbee, even if that maximum effort results in a miss and addition of a point to their total.
- If the disc flies beyond a 100% effort, a point is added to the thrower's total.
- If the catcher obviously "dogs it" or "short-arms" an attempt, he/she has a point added to his/her total, in addition to whatever disparaging comments from the players result from their lapse of effort.

- Catches must be made with one hand only. If the thrown Frisbee touches any part of the player's body, other than his/her hand, it is considered a miss.
- Multiple touches with either hand while attempting to catch the Frisbee are allowed.

Considerations

- To keep the game interesting, beyond just throwing and catching, throwers should use their tossing skills to test a catcher's judgment as to where a powerfully thrown Frisbee will come down.
- Running toward the person who will be receiving your throw is allowed, and is actually a good offensive move, but the pursuing player must be at least ten yards away (at a full run) when the throw is finally made.
- Trying to keep the sun at your back, although not particularly empathetic, is another bit of gamesmanship that works . . . and is allowed.
- Try to make the game as much of a running/catching game as possible by lofting high throws well beyond where the catcher waits, or by running to place yourself, as a potential catcher, nearer to the person you will be throwing to.

Think up strategies, make up rules, modify rules, breathe hard, sweat, love life!

Circle the Circle

Circle the Circle is one of those game names that is not only descriptive but feels good to say.

Objective

To see how quickly and efficiently a hand-in-hand circled group can pass two hula hoops in opposite directions around the circle without breaking grip. This is a timed event, and as such, the watch stops when <u>both</u> hoops are back where they started.

Procedure

Place two regulation hula hoops (the kind they sell at Wal-Mart) between two people in the circle so that the hoops rest together on their grasped hands. When the hoops meet on the far side of the circle one hoop must fit through the other. You might be wondering how two hoops of the same diameter can fit through one another . . . don't be concerned, they do.

It's interesting and revealing to see what the group's response is when asked, "Which hoop won?" It takes some thought and perhaps a discussion, mayhap even a brief debrief, when the realization is made that the entire group was working as a team "You mean . . . we didn't really win?"

If you want more action for a larger group, have pairs of hoops located at the cardinal points of the circle, i.e., NSEW. If you are doing this for time make sure the hoops are color coded. With this many

hoops in play I think the action itself precludes use of a stopwatch.

If you are playing the game Quick Line Up (QuickSilver, page182), and want to add some action and excitement to what is already a frantic game, indicate that after a team has located themselves in relationship to where you are standing, they must all pass through a carried hoop before yelling "Quick Line Up!" A passage from QuickSilver—

"Provide each of the groups with a hula hoop. As the group moves from one position to another, players must pass the hoop over their bodies before reaching their destination—providing yet another dandy way to lose, considering there is no way to win; gotta love it."

Variation   See Hoop Relay, page 29.

Colossal Pairs Tag—Marco/Polo

This way-expanded variation of the classic game Pairs Tag (*The Bottomless Bag Revival*, page 2) can be played with 500+ people, and more if you have enough room. How about 500 pumped-up middle school students in the lunch room on a rainy day in March? Seriously . . . get serious!

The Lead In

Ask everyone, via your neat-o lavaliere mike* arrangement, to touch (tag) the person nearest to them without any intent of returning or avoiding the touch; just a plain, ordinary, appropriate tag to the shoulder . . . make it a social thing. Briefly mention what an inappropriate tag might look like, i.e., a jab toward the eyes, a punch/slap, or a surreptitious nether-grope. They need to know, but don't make a big deal out of it.

Now ask everyone to attempt a tag of anyone, at the same time trying to avoid an incoming tag. No running, just casual walking and fluid avoidance; this is not the Olympics. Let this melee of gracefully moving bodies and wide smiles happen for at least 30 seconds. The younger, more immature the student, the more apt they are to relate being tagged as somehow losing, as walking changes rapidly to running. Control the speed of the players; stop the game if necessary . . . speed in this context too often equates with injury.

(**Project Adventure's** well known safety/accident questionnaire and follow-up study indicates that gym or turf games that involve bodies moving rapidly in random fashion display the most potential for injury as compared, for example, to ropes course oriented activities. Sooo, you might want to mention this interesting factoid via your electronically enhanced voice, considering the very large number of people that are about to move their bodies randomly.)

After you have called an eventual halt to the immediately chaotic mass of people seeking and avoiding one another (above), ask them for a word that best describes what they were just doing. Congratulate and recognize that person who eventually volunteers the word PLAY, because that is exactly what they were doing . . . playing,† and unfortunately it doesn't happen very often for adults. (Or for kids for that matter, considering all the electronic gizmos designed to obviate the need for active play.)

Now . . . THE GAME. Ask everyone to actively seek a playing partner, and none of this standing around waiting to be chosen stuff; grab a partner. Didn't find one immediately? Raise your hand, and those people with raised hands seek out one another until there is no one left. Facilitators, help this happen, i.e., facilitate. Ask partners to share first names, an important thing to know considering what is about to happen.

Back to the basics of TAG. One of a pair needs to be IT; decide quickly . . . person with the smallest shoe size, the oldest, the tallest, etc. The not-IT person is allowed a ten second head start to distance themselves from their IT partner. (Audibly count out the ten seconds.) Please note the very restrictive boundaries§ for this game and the huge number of people playing. The small play area reduces the temptation to run, and also ups the fun quotient considerably.

Object of THE GAME

Don't be the last one of your personal pair to be tagged (IT) when the facilitator yells STOP! It's a strange and wonderful game that allows 500 people to duck, dance, and flow around one another while interacting with only one other person.

You will find with this many people playing, that it is very easy, as tagee, to lose yourself in the crowd, so, every 5–7 seconds into the game the tagee (Is this a real word?), must yell their own name very loudly, *unless* they notice the tagger is visually honed and radar locked onto their geographical position. Name shouting is an honor system thing, but a full throated name-yell adds considerably to the joy and chaos of the game, particularly if the tagee responds by shouting their name . . . thus the Marco/Polo connection. (I really dislike the pool game, Marco/Polo!)

---

*lavaliere mike—Don't even think of working with a group numbering over 75 without some kind of audio voice enhancement.
†playing—Doing something for the intrinsic joy of just doing: no reason, no competition, no scores, just joyful participation.
§boundaries—Try not setting visual boundaries. Indicate the play-action is right here, or right around here. It's like coloring outside the lines . . . don't worry about it. If you notice students disappearing over the horizon . . . worry about it.

Rules and Considerations

- Don't let the game go on for more than a couple of minutes. Most people will be up for another round if they still have some O_2 left.
- If you are tagged during the game, do a 360° spin before chasing the person who just tagged you. Essentially you are playing this game with just one other person as 498 other people swirl and dance around you.
- If you <u>really</u> feel uncomfortable without using boundary markers, make sure you don't blow a whistle every time someone steps over a boundary line.
- If you identify some people who don't want to test their antiperspirant (**Challenge by Choice**), ask them to stand motionless within the action area

and role play a mid-stream rock, as the tide of people swirl, bump, and hide amidst and among those "rocks."

- Honestly, for this large group activity to work you need a majority of players who want to play. An immature younger group, or an uptight older group, may have too many hormones or too little sense of *joie de vivre* to allow the game to happen.

I think the concept of **FUNN** and Colossal Pairs Tag go well together, but if you need to justify this tidal wave of motion, lean heavily on the concept of establishing trust, i.e., trusting your partner and the group to keep each other emotionally and physically safe. If this isn't happening, call a brief debrief break and get some conversation going about why it's not happening.

Count Coup

I just looked up *Count Coup* on the Internet and Wikipedia told me what I mostly knew 25 years ago, *Counting Coup* was something Great Plains Indians did to prove or establish their bravery, i.e., to touch an enemy with your hand, or coup stick, and get away unscathed. The number of coups collected by a brave was recorded on his coup stick or by the number of feathers in his bonnet. Seems like a great way to fight a war, particularly if both sides were only concerned with touching one another; sounds like a tag game actually.

Once again I am blown away at how easy and quick it is to find esoteric information on the Net. (Come on guys, gimmie a little slack here, I was born waaaay before TV made it into American homes. I'm still impressed by things some people take for granted, like digital watches. Where <u>do</u> those numbers come from?)

Just this morning I needed to know how to remove an

imbedded tick. CW has indicated for years that you were supposed to cover the tick with petroleum jelly to suffocate the bugger or coax it out by holding the lit end of a cigarette near its swelling belly, both wrong, which surprised me. The point is, there aren't many things you can't find on the Internet.

Count Coup, the game, involves making physical contact with someone who has agreed previously to play the game with you, or a few others. Just touching someone and saying "Count Coup" isn't going to stimulate much interest, and may revert to the old

BOY-O-BOY, DID WE EVER COUNT COUP!

Plains Indian consequence of getting whacked before you can get away. But, if you are in agreement with someone that "the game is on," and a coup might be forthcoming at any time, then the ability to unselfconsciously keep a distance, or remain "cool" at close quarters (shaken . . . not stirred), becomes essential and engrossing, particularly if both in-the-know players are among a group of people who have no idea what's going on. This, then, becomes the real game; knowing that a blatant, head-long attack (a la The Pink Panther) would surely result in a coup, but also recognizing that such a shallow victory would be gauche to the extreme, completely unacceptable. Ah, the satisfaction from lulling your opponent into a state of belief that your interest and intent are far removed from *counting coup*, then quietly, with delicious intent, making subtle body contact and uttering, **sotto voce,**

the words "count coup" at the instant he/she registers the profound state of "being had." That's COUP with panache; that transcends gaming; that's . . . sneaky.

Counting Coup someone in an elevator, on a stage while making a presentation, on the way to the loo, in a lighted pool underwater—all well-received coup techniques. However, if you're going to play, recognize the difference between the banality of a simple touch-and-talk game and the sweet significance of stinging without being stung. Good luck SB, wherever you happen to be.

"In every real man a
child is hidden that wants to play."
Nietzsche

Fire in the Hole* (FiTH)

There's been a bunch-a-balloons busted over the years as the result of being the object of play in this off-the-wall activity, variously recognized as "a game for all seasons and no reasons." But before I introduce what used to be the best game going (now perceived by some as a sketchy non-PC activity), allow me a couple of paragraphs to fill you in on some historical vignettes of "the way it yousta be."

As part of Project Adventure's dynamically changing curriculum in the 1970s ("What do you want to try today?"), we were using a ton of balloons for various games and activities. After a typical class session utilizing balloons (Boop, for example) there were usually a dozen or so inflated balloons drifting about, and unless your storage proclivities are out of sync with the world, we needed a fun and functional way to get rid of those latex air-storage-receptacles. So, most of the time we used the ole stomp and/or sit, generic explosion technique for reducing our inflated inventory, effective but not very creative.

After class one day, while the sittin' and stompin' was still going on, a balloon lifted off the floor and was inadvertently popped between two moving bodies. Both players recoiled from the WHUMP! sound and feel, then laughed, both at one another and the fleeting body bumping that caused the balloon to break. We (staff) tried to duplicate the spontaneous exploding scenario and couldn't get it to consistently happen, so we began placing the balloons where it was determined we had the best chance of causing an "explosion." It didn't take us long to perfect what has become the classic **vis-a-vis** positioning (with hug) that explosively scores on 99% of serious popping attempts. (See photo).

The PC Conundrum   I don't want to get into the developed ills of society and schools, but things we used to do or say without concern or fear of social consequence are now often perceived as politically incorrect. I'm sure you could list any number of things you used to comfortably live with that have become politically incorrect today; unfortunately Fire in the Hole seems headed in that conformist direction. We have included this activity in the Silver Anniversary Edition, not to flaunt conservative decision makers,

*Fire in the Hole—Historically, these words were shouted out as a warning just before sticks of dynamite were electrically charged to explode. The classic visual was someone about to press down with both hands on a double handled, horizontal lever attached to the top of a box; a staple image in grade B cowboy, and World War II, flicks.

but rather to benignly encourage folks who have been joyfully playing Fire in the Hole for years, and would like to know there is still support out there for continuing the "game."

Fire in The Hole—The Technique

Announce to a gaming group that you need some help getting rid of the balloons they just finished using while playing Boop or Balloon Frantic (Located in *Bottomless Bag Revival*, pages 65–66). Emphasizing the futility of storing air-filled balloons, ask your players to watch the following demonstration and volunteer their continuing efforts to help out.

Choose an inadvertent volunteer, that bright and breezy person you think will be the most accepting of the zany sharing about to happen. Standing directly in front of your volunteer, indicate in a confident voice that you are an expert with compressed-air explosives, and that you would like the group to observe how two willing and brave participants can actually withstand a contained explosion (air burst) that takes place between the two of them.

Without hesitating and continuing your confident patter: "The most important part is knowing how and where to place the charge." Position a fully inflated balloon directly between the two of you at about belt level . . . buckles help break the balloon. "Then place the electrical leads (both of your arms) around the charge (hug each other)." The moment of truth is a squeeze away. Shout "*Fire in the Hole*" together, simultaneously squeezing and pulling toward one another with gusto. Most of the time you will be rewarded with a loud BOOM sound and cushioned WHUMP feeling. Back away smartly, congratulating one another for a job well done.

Point out all the inflated balloons drifting about on the floor and encourage the slack jawed, beginning-to-squirm group to have a go with their own FITH sequence. If there is a general reluctance to get things started, quickly demonstrate with your former partner (still in smiling semi-shock) something called <u>Running</u> Fire in the Hole. In this case you and your collaborator back away from one another about ten feet. Then, holding a balloon at about abdomen level, move swiftly toward one another, rounding off your midsections for the impending contact. The explosion experienced is fully as impressive as that derived using the squeeze technique. By this time, you should be able to get a few folks involved and as soon as the BOOMS start, the chaos begins.

Caveat   Choose someone for this demo that approximates your weight. Rarely, the twixt-body balloon does not break and acts as a rebound device causing both people to fly apart with some velocity. If one of the rebounders is a lightweight, guess who's going to rebound the farthest and fastest? If you see a big and small person about to run toward one another, quickly position yourself as a spotter behind the smaller of the two.

If you observe a Fire in the Hole pair pulling and squeezing with determination and no BOOM forthcoming, walk over and add whatever double-arm squeeze you can muster. If a cooperating pair just can't seem to make it happen, even with squeezing help from the group, unobtrusively reach in amongst the frantically squeezing corporal mass, tightly grasp the balloon with your hand, and twist . . . BOOM! That's actually a professional FITH secret, so don't tell anyone.

Frantic

The game Frantic, and its variations, just seem to get better as years go by. As I said (wrote) some thirty years ago, "Here's a unique game that requires little skill, tons of cooperation, includes practically any number of players, and it's 100% active"; still a hard combination to beat.

Objective

For a group (large or small) to keep an equal number of assigned tennis balls (one ball–one person) rolling on a gymnasium floor (any smooth unencumbered surface) until six penalties have been VERY LOUDLY indicated by a referee; this is a timed event.

Before we get to the rules, the vocabulary used in this game, which is key to contemporary tradition, needs to be considered. If words and procedures used in a game are studiously different from what participants are familiar with, there's less chance for a player to pre-determine their wanting, or not wanting, to play. Students (players) not only want to be challenged and have fun, they want to be intrigued, in this case by something different, something not including jumping jacks, push ups, or repetitive drills. What I'm suggesting is, use the vocabulary outlined below, trying not to corrupt the game and the opportunity for cooperation by falling back into a whistle-blowing win-lose scenario. Here are a few words and concepts that help to make the game different.

- **Rabid Nugget**—A tennis ball in motion; doesn't matter how fast or slow, just in motion.
- *Hectic*—A stationary tennis ball, i.e., not moving.
- *Berserk*—A referee's full throated scream, designating a penalty. One scream = One Berserk. If you must use a noisemaker, don't use a coach's whistle.
- *Frenzy*—An elapsed time period measuring six (6) *Berserks*, i.e., six penalties.
- *Logic*—A tennis ball that becomes unintentionally lodged on, or behind something.
- *Illogic*—A tennis ball that is purposefully lodged on, or behind something.
- *Paranoia*—Player's personal suspicion that the refs are *Berserking* unfairly.

Rules and Use of Terminology

- If 30 players are on the gym floor, 30 *Rabid Nuggets* are thrown, rolled, or kicked simultaneously onto the gym floor by one of the refs. Impelling the *Rabid Nuggets* in motion initiates the game and starts the timing.
- There are three refs for championship matches (all matches are at the championship level), one

at each end of the court and one off to the side at mid court. It is the responsibility of the two refs on the floor to spot *Hectics* and to generate an hysterical *Berserk* (scream), so all will recognize a penalty has been assigned. The group has five seconds to get the *Hectic* moving again or another full throated *Berserk* is issued. The *Berserking* ref must point condemningly at the *Hectic* until either he/she issues another scream (*Berserk*), or the *Hectic* is put back into motion.

- Every 15 seconds after the start, the side-line ref tosses an additional *Rabid Nugget* into play, continuing these frenzied 15-second additions until the final *Berserk* has been recorded.
- The team (everyone is on the same team!) is allowed six *Berserks*, at which juncture the side-line ref, who is also responsible for timing this melee, jumps up and down waving his/her arms, yelling **STOP!** . . . STOP!! . . . STOP!!!
- The team intent has been to keep the *Rabid Nuggets* moving as long as possible before six *Berserks* were recorded. This time span is called a *Frenzy*. After a recorded *Frenzy*, ask the group to talk about and develop a strategy to keep the *Rabid Nuggets* moving for a longer span of time, i.e.,

increasing the duration of the *Frenzy*. Looking for an opportunity to discuss the usefulness of the **Experiential Learning Cycle (Spiral)?** Perchance the facilitating iron might be hot.

Rule Refinements for Frantic Freaks

- A *Rabid Nugget* must be moved via foot action only, no hands, elbows, knees, etc. A ball may not be held underfoot and simply moved back and forth. This rule was included to counter the basically sneaky player who is always looking for a way around the rules in the guise of displaying initiative or creativity. Don't get me wrong, creative ideas are always welcome as long as their implementation doesn't create an initiative **travesty.**
- If a *Rabid Nugget* becomes a *Logic* or *Illogic*, the *Berserking* ref must toss the *Nugget* back into

motion. An *Illogic* receives an immediate *Berserk*. There is no penalty for a *Logic*.
- If you can't or won't scream, try not to use a whistle to identify *Berserks*. Whistles smack of basketball drills, sit ups, and shuttle runs, i.e., not great memories for non-athletes. Try a bicycle squeeze horn . . . loud, raucous, and unfamiliar.
- If you know an avid tennis player or two, ask them if you can have their used "nuggets." Even better, ask for used tennis balls at a local indoor tennis facility. (Real tennis players use up an inordinate number of balls.) Tell them you are a teacher and will be using them for curriculum development.
- Official optic yellow USLTA tennis balls are not essential for satisfying play, but if you end up with more *Rabid Nuggets* than you know what to do with, Frantic provides a functional "what-to-do-with" activity, as does Beau Coups Balls, page 115.
- A more challenging and daring version of Frantic involves using bowling balls in place of tennis balls. Karl, are you serious? Sometimes . . .

Balloon Frantic**More than a Variation

Substitute balloons for tennis balls and voila, Balloon Frantic! This lofty game is best played in a gymnasium with a high ceiling, or outdoors on a windless day (good luck!).

Ask each student to blow up a balloon to duplicate the one you have already inflated (about 12" in diameter) and tie it off. If people need help with that, ask other players to lend a hand or lip; some people seem to have a knack for blowing up and tying off balloons. Try not to use so called "penny balloons" as they are too small when expanded, and after being hit, drop to the floor too rapidly. Inflate and tie off at least 8–10 extra balloons to serve as throw-ins for the 15-second rule (as in Frantic with tennis balls, see above), or as replacements for the inevitable broken balloon (boomers).

The basic rules for both games are practically identical (hit the balloons with your hand, no kicking) except for the start. Ask each player to throw their balloon into the air rather than having the ref start things with a kick. Be sure to have a digital camera or camcorder available to record this game because the panoply of technicolor action is poster material.

Concerns and Tips

- Some gym floors seem to cause balloons to break, I don't know why (dirt? grit? splinters?), whatever, be prepared with extra balloons.
- When you buy balloons, purchase them by the gross to save money. As of this writing a gross of 12" balloons costs eleven bucks and change.
- Some people are honestly freaked out by exploding balloons. Before the balloons are launched, announce that some balloons will probably break during the game. Suggest that those who are troubled, cover their ears or leave the room temporarily. This is a valid way to build trust with your students, as they will

*Balloon Frantic—credit Steve Butler with the idea of substituting balloons for tennis balls. Steve was my co-author on the book *QuickSilver*.

notice and appreciate your concern about their feelings and fears.

- Buy as many different colors as possible. I wasn't kidding about this activity being a fantastic photo-op.
- Balloon Frantic is a high profile game and one I'd suggest including in your lesson plan if parents are going to be around, or if an administrator is evaluating your class. Just make sure to have a cogent answer when someone asks why you are using Balloon Frantic as a school (or corporate) activity. Communication, cooperation, and trust within a matrix of fun . . . you know the drill.

- Make sure you allow the students to try this activity more than once, this _is_ experiential education after all.
- Just to give you something to go by, if a group can keep the balloons off the floor for two and a half minutes before collecting six B*erserks*, they are operating at an elite level. Try this game as a participant at some point, you will be impressed by how long two minutes can seem.

Full House

Full House is another throw-and-hit game of the mini-bombardment genre, and as such will appeal more to some groups than others. This isn't a long write-up, so take a look and see if this Capture The Flag/Bombardment-type game has appeal.

Objective

Two equally numbered teams attempt to exchange geographical locations, the first team to do so wins this throw-and-hit confrontation.

The name, *Full House*, originated from the first time we tried playing this freewheeling game in an old house, as we tried to switch starting locations, while dashing through the rooms and hallways of the house, while throwing marshmallows at one another. Here's a few rules to help clarify this nebulous, marshmallow introduction.

Set Up

- Two equally numbered teams separate and go to opposite ends of a house, gym, field, etc.
- Each team member is given three marshmallows of a particular team color. (Marshmallows are sold in different pastel colors, but they are easily, and more distinctly colored by using food coloring or Easter egg dye, if you have some left over.)
- The object of winning is achieved by moving all members of a team to the opposite side of the house, actually where the other team started. "Winning" means that team members are offered the choice of eating their weapons, but only if their individual immune systems are off the charts, and the "weapons" have been thoroughly torched, or, if the attendant facilitator is so kind as to offer out-of-the bag NEW weapons to gobble.
- The more covert object of play is to squeeze the most possible enjoyment from running around throwing things at each other. I suppose you can adjust your thoughts and vocabulary to fit whatever curriculum need is expressed or desired, but I see this game as pure inner child

fun-fodder—run aimlessly around throwing marshmallows at one another, while yelling and laughing . . . be a kid.

Rules?

- As the players attempt to pass (sneak) by each other, they can "freeze" (cryogenically suspend) opposing team members by hitting them with a thrown marshmallow of the proper team color, i.e., if a blue player is hit with a blue marshmallow, no freezing takes place.
- Players may only collect and throw marshmallows of their team color.
- A frozen player must remain immobile for 30 seconds after being hit. (If you don't have a watch, count 30 seconds, then add 10 more . . . because you're counting too fast.)
- Head shots don't count and are designated as no-throws . . . they didn't happen.
- Designate SAFE starting areas with a circled length of rope that will easily encompass all team members of one side. No one can be hit inside either SAFE area.
- Use blindfolds as headbands to differentiate team affiliation; that's blindfolds as headbands, not vice versa.

Concerns and Considerations

- If you are concerned about eye safety (certainly a worry if the players are rocket-armed teens), provide safety goggles.
- Upstairs/downstairs provides exciting variety.
- When the game is over, discard the used weapons. Marshmallows out-of-the-bag are quite soft, but over time dry out and become distinctly hard. Rule of play: "If hard, discard."
- Do not use a friend's house for this game with the hope that nothing will be disturbed.
- The game plays almost as well in a gym, with mats and gymnastic equipment spread around as hiding areas.

Hands Down

Magicians count on the fact that people generally see what they want to see or only what seems most obvious. From the standpoint of trying to solve an initiative problem, such tunnel vision often results in frustration and limited success. More pragmatically, in a day-to-day context, such attention to only the evident or recognizable, allows a shyster to shade the truth, or subvert reality, to take financial advantage of an individual who sees only what the perpetrator wants them to see. I have a drawer full of illegal money making schemes received via the Internet that I have collected to remind myself that, "If it looks too good to be true, it probably is."

Objective

To point out that immediately observable facts are not necessarily the combination needed towards achieving a solution.

Set Up

Obtain five lengths (about 6") of any type of matching material (e.g., pencils, dowels, sticks, pens). Kneel on the floor, grass, etc., placing the five pencils on the flat area in front of you so that a pattern is formed—any pattern will do. For example:

Ask the surrounding group to indicate what number from one to ten this arrangement of pencils demonstrates. Then incrementally set up two or three different patterns, with a given numerical answer for each example, so that the group gets to see and guess what "number" you are symbolically displaying each time. Set the pattern, provide some time for them to figure out the number, then tell them what number is being displayed. Don't be in a

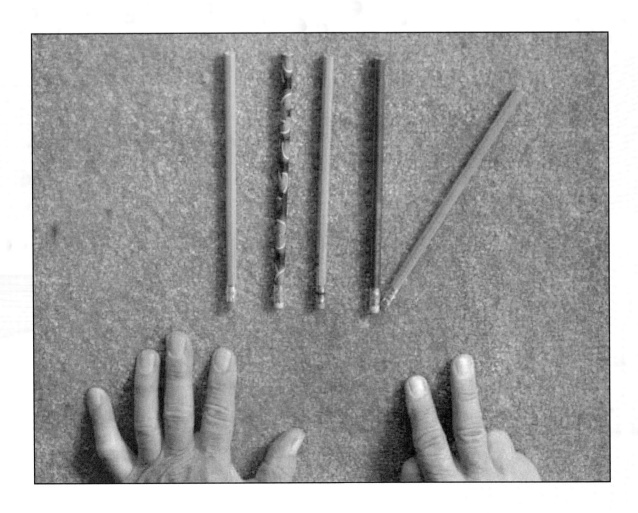

hurry to reveal what you are doing; play the group, make them uncomfortable, let them viscerally feel what you want them to acknowledge (refer to *Two points to ponder* #2, to the right).

As you work the *Hands Down* ploy, players knowing there is an answer and recognizing that some members of their group already know the answer, is incrementally agonizing to those still in the dark, particularly if the digital play has gone on for some time.

The Gimmick revealed . . . before you get frustrated and leave! Set down whatever fanciful pattern of pencils your imagination conjures up, concurrently placing your hands, palms down, on the floor near the pencils with the number of your fingers blatantly exposed, indicating the number you have in mind. You mean the pencils have nothing to do with the number? Too true.

The pencils do not imply or suggest anything; the intricate pencil patterns you have so carefully set are purely window dressing. Change the pattern of pencils while arranging a different set of fingers exposed, and you change the number being exhibited. (Number 7 is being blatantly displayed in the photo.)

Eventually someone will figure out what you are doing, usually someone standing behind you. Use that in-the-know person to maintain the group's interest by asking him/her to offer the number of each succeeding pattern, but not giving away the "secret." If no one catches on after a few more patterns have been shown, place your hands closer to the pencils and slightly wiggle your fingers. This will be hilarious to those who know what's going on. Throw the pencils into a pile onto the floor and slap your hands, all fingers extended, for a dramatic #10. There will still be people who continue to see only what they want to see. Review both *Two points to ponder* and initiate a discussion, AFTER you eventually give away the answer. Remember, this is not summer camp. Your goal is not to antagonize the group, rather to make a sentient point or two. You can't (shouldn't) say, "Come back next summer and I'll give you the answer."

Two Points to Ponder

1. Society allows (promotes) social cliques to form; small groups that perceive themselves as in-the-know. These basically antisocial groups maintain a sense of elitist satisfaction based on their knowing something important that other supposedly less significant groups are not privy to. Whether these cliques have any valid claim to special status is neither here nor there, the fact that they and others believe they do is sadly significant. It's no fun being left out, to feel you are not being included in a social setting. Participating in Hands Down allows a brief personal introduction to both sides of this nonfunctional social scene, i.e., being in *the know* or out of *the know*, and emotionally believing it matters.

2. A key concept in trying to solve an initiative problem is being able to "think out of the box." If everyone in the group consistently sees things the same way and thinks in lock-step with one another, the solution to a sticky problem will probably continue to elude the team. Being able to see beyond the obvious is often necessary to solve the impossible.

Hands Down is one of perhaps a dozen other verbal or performance oriented what's-the-answer type of knotty enigmas. (Whoops Johnny is another popular ploy. See the book by this author, *Funn 'n Games*, page 22). Unfortunately there are some minimally experienced presenters who see these conundrums as entertainment, (mostly for themselves). Use the activity to make a point, not to make fun of any individual who finds themselves out of the know. And if you use two puzzlers of this genre in a row, ask yourself why.

Hoop Relay a.k.a. Is That You Fifi?

Hoop Relay represents a game unto itself but strongly resembles the action of Circle the Circle, but if you don't care, I don't either.

Objective

For a line of people, bent over and holding hands front to back (with one arm passing through their own legs (see illustration), to pass a series of hoops over their bodies so that each person has the opportunity to run from the back of the line to the front. When everyone has made that switch, the watch stops.

Procedure

This timed relay requires a starter. The starter, grasping 5–10 hoops, stands in front of a bent-over-hand-holding line, (the number of hoops should equal the number of people in the line.) On a signal, the starter (also a participant), begins the action by gently resting a hoop on the neck of the first person in line. As soon as that hoop has passed over and beyond the first person, the starter places a second hoop over the first person's head. This continues until the starter has one hoop left and situates him/herself as first person in line with grasped hands and hoop-over-head in place.

When the first hoop reaches the last person in line, that person grabs the hoop as soon as they have passed through it, then runs to the front of the line, duplicating what the starter just did above as first person in line. Continue with dispatch until your original front line person returns to that starting position. Done!

What's the difference between this and Circle the Circle? Other than linking-up in a line rather than a circle, not much. Are people generally reluctant to participate in Hoop Relay? Check out the illustrated smiles, and btw . . . Is that you Fifi?

PLYNN

I've Got the Beat

OK, one more puzzler, but don't you dare use all three of these (Hands Down; Passing Crossed . . .; I've Got the Beat) at one setting or I'll come and cancel your FUNN certification.

Utilizing any object, or even your own finger, establish a simple beat by striking that object on a table, window, the floor, etc. There should be no more than 8-10 movements to the beat. After you have performed the sequence a few times announce proudly that, "I've got the beat!" Offer your striking object to anyone who also thinks they have the beat. If your beat sequence is simple enough you will have a couple of volunteers who think they can duplicate your actions and sound, but they will want to hear it again, at least one more time. Strike the beat again and perform with confidence.

As in all these do-as-I-do problems we know the key has nothing to do with the obvious, the beat, but is revealed as a pre- or post-movement or sound. In this case *clearing your throat* before starting is the indicator of a successful beat. Predictably, the people who think they know how to duplicate your beat are concentrating on exactly your physical motions. If, after a few tries, no one has joined the club, so to speak, make the *throat clearing* more obvious. It is amazing how zerod in some people (like me!) can become to extraneous actions they think are the essential movements. As obvious as you think your actions are in trying to expose the key, there will still be some myopic individuals who say, "Do it one more time slowly." I can commiserate, having been that short-sighted person more times than I'd like to admit. Other than the fact that this type of activity makes some pertinent and useful points about the way people act and react in problem-solving scenarios, I don't like fooling people, and don't like being fooled myself, a commiserating trust concern perhaps. Something worth talking about after the fact?

Medley Relay

Objective

This is a performance relay where the group competes against their own best effort as a team, with each member of the relay team fulfilling his/her best effort toward increasing the team's total distance from a starting line. Attempts are carefully marked and measured, with every person trying each event for a total team distance.

The events to choose from, and not limited to, are the following. All of these events are measured from an initial starting line—rope or tape. Measure distances as if measuring a track & field event.

Caveat Personally try each of your created event ideas to make sure they can be accomplished safely.

Medley Relay Events

- Standing long jump
- Standing backward jump (to count, the participant must remain on their feet)
- Cartwheel (take-off foot must be behind the take-off line). Measure from where the second foot makes contact with the ground.
- Jump and turn 360° forward from a stand; use spotters. Players must remain on their feet after the jump. If the turn is less than 360°, the effort is forfeit.
- Dive and shoulder roll (measure first contact with the mat after the dive). No roll, no score. Use a gym or wrestling mat for this event. To keep this diving effort safer, require starting the dive from a squat position.
- One legged hop; right and left legs
- Handstand walk in 15 seconds (measure where final hand contact is made)

For additional events, add whatever type of forward movement that seems to make sense, or more appropriately, that which is best received by the group. Perhaps an event based on placing a team member as far past the start line as possible without using kinetic means, i.e., throwing or propulsion. Medley Relay becomes more enjoyable through repetition, and as the events become more oriented toward what the students have suggested.

All the above individual events should be practiced at "half speed" before a participant commits themselves to a maximum effort, particularly the dive and roll, and 360° turn.

Moonball

Approaching the various subtitles in *Silver Bullets* with the anticipation of deleting, adding to, and rewriting, I turned to page 31 (What's with those guys in short shorts, and no shirts? Must be the 70s!), and noticed that under the rubric *Moonball*, there's more space taken up with the photo than text material; four short paragraphs (barely half a page), but with ample descriptions of a game that has become one of the most popular and well-used game/initiative of the past 30 years. I'm disinclined to change anything in that write up, not because the prose is scintillating, or particularly clever, but because the 1984 write up is sooo *Silver Bullets* . . . here's the game, the rules, a bit of tongue-in-cheek, something about the object of play, a caveat, and then, have-a-go.

I've learned a few things about this game in the last 25 years that I'd like to pass along, and will, but first, here's the original *Moonball* description, succinct and to-the-point.

"*Moonball* is an excellent one-prop-game that develops cooperation and fast reactions. Play becomes intensely competitive, as a group competes against its last best effort.

Scatter your group (any number, but use 2 or more balls as the group size demands) on a basketball court or a field. Use a well inflated beach ball as the object of play. The group's objective is to hit the ball aloft as many times as possible before the ball strikes the ground.

Rules

A player cannot hit the ball twice in succession.

Count one point for each hit.

The tension and expectation builds as each "world record" is approached. Moonball is popular with all ages because it's simple to understand, requires little skill, and involves (like it or not) everyone.

Do not use a volleyball, basketball, etc., for the game. A beach ball is a non-intimidating, fun-related object of play and its flight characteristics fit in well with the low key emphasis [of Moonballing.]"

Historical Aside You need to know, the only reason this game is called Moonball is because the original beach ball we used for batting around was essentially a smallish, inflated, vinyl globe of the world. At about this time, **The New Games Foundation** was using a really large, inflated (bladder), canvas-covered globe of the world for various games, calling it, appropriately enough, an Earth Ball. Not wanting to copy their lead or step on global toes we named our small inflated beach balls, *Moonballs* . . . which seemed to make sense at the time. Also, it seemed that saying *Moonball* required less tongue action than mouthing Earth Ball. A small point perhaps until you realize after articulating both game names, that *Moonball* is more fun to say, particularly when it's italicized. You just tried it right? See what I mean? You need to be aware of these things.

Sequential Moonball   To score one point, everyone in the group must hit the ball in sequence before the ball hits the ground. To score a second point, another sequence must be completed. A miss sends the group back to the start, i.e., the count begins again at one.

Macro Moonball   The group must attempt to hit the ball eight consecutive times without the ball hitting the ground (floor). For a ball strike to count, the hitting person must deliver a maximum effort; a controlled hit (determined by the facilitator) does not count. If you are playing in a gym, only floor contact with the ball is reason to begin again, i.e., contact with walls, backboards, alarm bells, championship pennants, and ceiling are all OK.

Two Ball Moonball   Same game as the original above, but with two balls being hit concurrently. Counting the hits is possible if the facilitator steps back away from the action so he/she can peripherally see the movement of both balls. If either ball hits the floor, the count begins again from zero. Set a goal of approximately 37 hits.

Machine Gun Moonball   How many ball strikes can be recorded in 60 seconds? Each hit must be distinct, not just a series of uncountable pitty-pats. No one person can hit the ball twice in succession. The facilitator needs to be creative in his/her counting during a Machine Gun attempt, with the awareness that ending the game in laughter is more significant than setting a new record.

Speed Moonball   How fast can the ball travel from person to person, i.e., every person in the group touches the ball in sequence? Levy a five-second penalty for every ground touch of the ball.

Islands Moonball   Each established dyad within the group is provided with a large hula hoop. When the hoop is placed on the ground, each of the two players must keep one of their feet inside the hoop at all times. Then, in concert with other paired hoopsters, they must decide where they want to place their hoop to give their team the best chance to establish a high score. Once a hoop is placed on the ground it may not be moved. The game is played in the classic fashion, as above, with the proviso that the score reverts to zero if either the ball hits the ground, or a player steps out of the hoop with <u>both</u> feet.

A word about the object of play itself, the *Moonball*. For years we used and abused beach balls as *Moonballs*. On the positive side, they were comparatively inexpensive, lightweight, brightly colored, and were not used for any known competitive sport (no NCAA affiliation).

Contraindications of using a beach ball: oral inflation was sloppy, time consuming, and they punctured easily. A few years ago I started using a play object called a *Gertie Ball.** They are expensive, but . . . they inflate orally with only about six full breaths (as compared to at least twenty for the beach ball), their texture is "interesting," their bounce energetic, and they last much longer than a beach ball. There is one serious drawback for unorganized players, like me. Each ball comes with a loose plastic plug that has to be manually inserted to maintain inflation; lose the plug, bye-bye ball; even so I'd currently go with the *Gertie*.

*Gertie Ball—Google *Gertie Ball* to find out all you could ever want to know about this "huggable, catchable, kickable . . ." action/reaction ball.

Night Exercises

Consider the next few pages as a nocturnal bonus; night exercises that seem to be well-accepted by young and old alike. If you have people spending the night away from home at a camp or conference setting, with evening hours warm enough and bugs few enough, give these feel-comfortable-with-the-dark activities a try.

• •

Commandant

Remember playing this game when you were a kid, when the play venue was a suburban street, and not a thought was given to the possible social and environmental dangers of running around in the semi-dark? I can't remember any broken bones or stitches resulting from the game back then (which didn't mean there weren't a few bumps and bruises), and the specter of child molestation was a non-item.

I also remember that our parents had nothing to do with the games we entertained ourselves with, and certainly didn't burden us with caveats concerning our post-prandial shenanigans, except the nightly admonition to head for home after the street lamps came on. So when did all that don't-get-hurt stuff begin? Maybe gradually over the years as population densities increased, and trust levels diminished; whatever the reason, it sure did reduce the fun factor.

Objective

For one person (The Commandant) to keep all the rest of the players from making it back to home base in the dark, without being spotted and identified.

Set Up

• You need one powerful flashlight and a portable home base (automobile). The portable base isn't necessary, but it allows some flexibility in choosing a game site.
• The field area chosen for play should be free of large rocks, guy wires, fence posts, and whatever else could ding (put holes and dents in), your body.

Rules and Considerations

• The Commandant stands at home base and counts slowly to 50 while the rest of the players scatter throughout the dark play area. The Commandant flashes their light off and on at the end of the 50 count to signal the start of the game.
• If a player can make it back to home base, after touching two required objects within the field of play, they shout "Home Free!" announcing their successful return. The two required-touch objects must be in the Commandant's field of view and at opposite ends of the field. The objects could be a tree, boulder, house, auto, etc.

- At the end of the Commandant's counting, players may be located no closer than ten yards away from either of the required-touch objects.
- The Commandant may roam wherever he/she likes, recognizing that staying near home negates many captures, while roaming far from home base encourages players to initiate an exciting dash for home.
- A catch is made if the Commandant hits someone with the flash and calls out their name.
- A caught player casually walks to home base and shares adventures-in-the-field with the people already collected there.
- After about 15 minutes of play, a five-minute "game over" warning is announced with one long, shrill blast from a whistle.
- After the warning whistle, as people make a desperate dash for home, just hitting a running player with the flash counts as a catch.
- The first person who gets home FREE is the next Commandant, if the group chooses to play again.

I have never had a group that did not want to play again if the weather was decent and the bugs weren't bad.

- If you want the original game to continue without having to deal with a restart, insert the rule that if anyone can return to base without being caught, they can yell the time honored "All-e, all-e, in-free" release call, liberating all the caught players. I love this rule, associated with fond memories of belting out that release call as I made it back to home base without getting hit by the Commandant's flash.
- Although there is a catch/no catch competitive aspect to this game, I have found that players involved in the excitement of "returning home" are much more interested in the action than the result.

Your Decision
Can this game be played with reasonable safety within parameters of the player's maturity level, the physical geography available, whatever Murphy-like laws beset us 24/7, amidst fears of not being the plaintiff in a tort (wrongful act) legal situation?

Izzat You?

Of the three nocturnal games offered here, Izzat You? has to be my favorite. I have been confounded by skilled hiders so many times you would think I would learn to be a better seeker, but . . . nocturnally bewildered I remain, and willfully so; I like being fooled.

Objective
To walk along a defined trail or walkway at night, with no flashlights, and try to find people who had previously hidden themselves a maximum of 20 feet from the trail.

Set Up
- Divide your group in half and ask which half would like to be hiders, with the understanding that the other half (seekers) will flip/flop and be hiders later on.
- Explain to everyone how motionless objects (people) in the dark, can take on other forms that appear to be rocks, stumps, clumps of grass, etc.
- Walk out with the hiders so you can place them comfortably, and in such a semi-exposed hidden location they are convinced the other half (seekers) will find them immediately.
- If someone is reluctant to hide alone, let a buddy hide with them.
- The seekers wait patiently in a building (with lights off, letting their eyes adapt to the dark), until the facilitator returns and announces that all's ready.

Guidelines for Seeking
- The object of the game is to find as many of the hiders as possible with point scores kept for each team.
- The seekers are taken to the trailhead and told that from this point on there may be hidden bodies along the trail.
- *Seekers may not leave the trail.*

- Flashlights cannot be carried by seekers.
- When someone thinks they have spotted a hider, that person calls others on the team over to take a look. If the consensus indicates someone is hiding where everyone is pointing, the attending instructor shines his/her light directly at the indicated spot for three seconds. If a hider is revealed, the seekers get a point. If there is no one there, the hiders get a point.
- If the seekers completely pass a hider on the trail, the instructor calls the group back, reveals the hider with his/her flashlight, and awards the hiding team a point.
- Revealed hiders then join the seekers on the trail to silently cheer on their team.

The trail crawl continues until the last hider is either found or eventually revealed. Points are added up to establish a nocturnal champion for that round, then the teams reverse roles, and the game is played again.

There is something uniquely exciting about being hidden only a few feet away from many probing eyes and remaining unseen. As such, offering camo face paint adds to the excitement and the capacity for remaining unseen.

In an outdoor education setting, this exercise provides a natural segue to a discussion about the adaptations made by nocturnal animals in support of life in a reduced light environment: bats, owls, cats. How about the human eye? Remember what it's like to try and find a seat in a crowded, dark movie theater when you first enter? There's more than one teachable moment available here in the dark.

Whooo?

A nighttime acclimatization activity allowing a player to travel and/or hide alone in the dark without having to locate themselves far from other players or home-base, this activity is designed for use at an outdoor education camp or rural conference setting.

Objective

For seekers to find five hidden players in the dark and receive from them a slip of paper numbered sequentially. The seekers attempt to collect all five numbers. The objective is not to "win," rather to comfortably find the hiders.

Set Up

- Ask five people to be hiders (ersatz owls).
- Each hider takes about 12 identically numbered slips of paper and heads out to find a hiding spot. Each hider should have a flashlight to help them find a comfortable hiding nook. When their light is turned off, that's a signal to the facilitator indicating they are individually ready; all dark, let's go!

- During this hiding time, the seekers should all remain indoors, allowing the hiders to do their thing, at the same time destroying the seeker's night vision—part of the evening's science lesson.
- Each hider has the option of making a night animal's sound, or whatever unique nocturnal swishing, clattering, hum, or thud they can come up with. This gives the hiders something to do and certainly adds to the fun of finding.
- When a seeker actually makes contact with a Whooo-hider, the hider silently hands over a numbered slip of paper. When a seeker has collected all five numbers they get to retire from the chase and watch what's going on, and perhaps try to confuse things with their own owl interpretation. Houuuu – Houuuu

There's no rules associated with Whooo?, and therefore no winners or losers. The game helps younger players get used to the dark, while offering an engrossing nocturnal activity that seems to appeal to all ages.

Paper Golf

"Life is play time or the fun is gone."
Thomas G. McAllister

Playing golf <u>on</u> a piece of paper? Must be a fanatical substitute for the real thing pursued by frustrated golfers. Could be, as dedicated golfers are known for their quirkiness, but if you are in the position of teaching the peripherals of golf (vocabulary, etiquette, rules), Paper Golf is a clever, intriguing, and ultimately useful game. Useful? Sure, as it becomes obvious that this paper game of golf uses the same vocabulary, rules, and etiquette as followed in regulation golf, and as such, provides an enjoyable method of learning the basics of the game without suffering the frustrations of, "keeping your head down," "maintaining a straight left arm," or "controlling the back swing." And, you don't have to deal with an outrageous green fee, or the supercilious attitudes of scratch golfers.

To Play

- Golfer #1 places the point of his/her pencil (pen) on the paper (see illustration) anywhere between the two markers designating the tee area. The player eyeballs the distance from tee to green, recognizing the added stroke obstacles that will increase the score, and plans a first stroke (drive) that will place the ball (tip of the pencil) in a safe area of the fairway.
- After the player has planned her drive, she must close her eyes and keep them closed for five seconds before moving the pencil tip. Only one continuous move, straight or curving, may be executed. When the pencil tip stops, the ball stops. If the pencil tip ends up in a bunker or hazard area, strokes are added to the score.
- The player must then plan the next stroke with her eyes open and execute the stroke with her eyes closed, as before. To finish the hole, the pencil tip must end up in the circle constituting the hole.
- After Golfer #1 had taken his first stroke, Golfer #2 would have stepped up and delivered his first stroke, followed by #3 and #4, before Golfer #1 took his second stroke. Golf is a game of tradition and politeness, the reality of which can be transferred to the paper game.
- Consider—the larger the sheet of paper, the longer the drives and approach shots. Long sheets of butcher paper would make for an exciting game. I'd suggest felt-tipped pens as "clubs" for such a championship course.
- Use a different colored pen or pencil (or felt-tipped pen) for each player.
- As you develop each hole on separate pieces of paper, use your imagination to vary the obstacles (sand traps/water hazards) and distance (yardage), and thus the par value for each hole. Remember the old putting adage, "Never up, never in," and as you approach a par five hole you might want to, "let out a little shaft!"

I discovered recently that the word GOLF spelled backward pretty much defines my game.

Paper Links Golf Club
Hole #18
Par 3

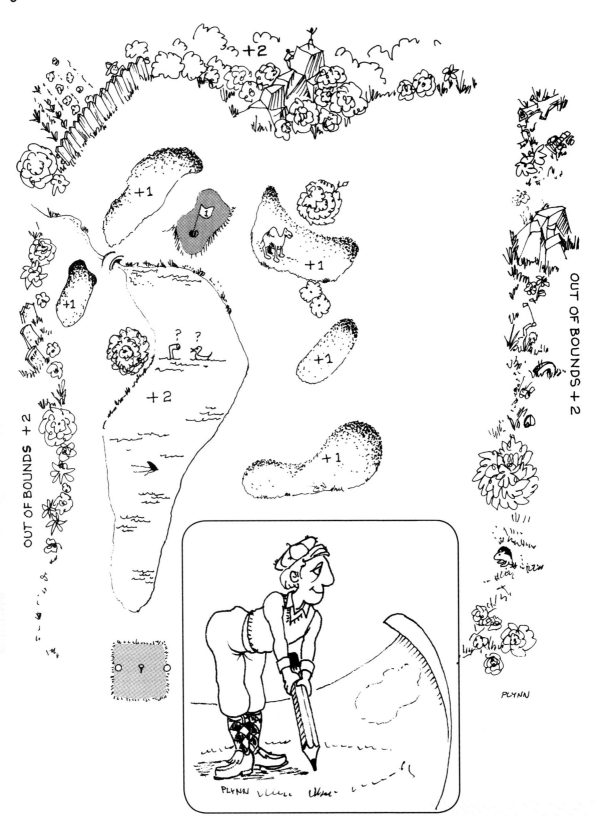

OUT OF BOUNDS + 2

OUT OF BOUNDS + 2

+2

+1

+1

+1

+1

+2

+1

PLYNN

PLYNN

Passing Crossed or Uncrossed

This around-the-campfire game is historically played with a pair of scissors, but can be as effectively played with two sticks, two pencils, etc.

A leader initiates the activity by passing two pencils to either the right or left around a circle of people. Once chosen, maintain the sequence in that direction. As the pass is made, the leader says one of two things: "I am passing these pencils to you crossed," or "I am passing these pencils to you uncrossed." The performance object is for each person to individually receive the pencils and then pass them on crossed or uncrossed. The crux of the passing and receiving is for the group to figure out why, if a person passes two obviously crossed pencils they say, "I am passing these pencils to you uncrossed." Upon hearing this contradictory statement the players look to the leader for confirmation that the person passing the pencils is wrong. When the leader responds, "Correct, and well done," there is a period of disbelief, then, remembering the recently learned lessons from Hands Down, the search for *Why* begins. Why are obviously uncrossed pencils being passed verbally crossed? As we know in all of these what's-the-key problems, the obvious probably has nothing to do with the less-than-obvious answer.

The key in this case is the leg position of the person doing the passing, and also the leg position of the receiver, i.e., crossed or uncrossed. For example, the person who knows the secret and is receiving the pencils, says, "I am receiving these pencils crossed." (Are the passer's legs crossed or uncrossed?) "And I am passing them along uncrossed." (Are the receiver's legs crossed or uncrossed?) Are the pencils significant?

Other clues in games of this type could be body or limb positions. If the group becomes adept at spotting clues, try using "eraser clues," i.e., body movements or positions that indicate the opposite or an extension of a previously used clue. For example, if you extend two fingers in the game Hands Down and say the answer is four, what's the key? Double the number of fingers extended? Correct. Too easy? Remember, "Truth is obvious after its discovery."

"I see," said the visually impaired carpenter, as he picked up his hammer and saw.

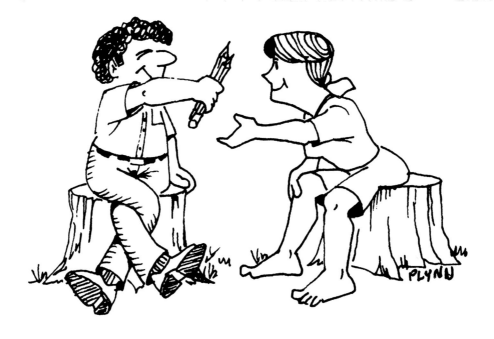

Pick & Choose

Pick & Choose is an initiative game that allows everyone to participate to the maximum of what they think they can do. You will need lots of used tennis balls; "lots" in this case would number about 150. Actually you can use any throwable item in place of tennis balls, for example, Nerf or fleece balls, wadded up pieces of paper, stuffed toys. But . . . tennis balls do afford a certain flair that wadded up paper balls just don't provide.

Objective

For a group, numbering about 10–35 players, to throw as many tennis balls as possible in two minutes into three creatively placed receptacles (wastebaskets, plastic milk cartons) set out on a gym floor.

Rules and Procedure

- Each receptacle has a different point value. The closest = one point, the second = three points, and the farthest = seven points. Make up the distances and positioning of the receptacles prior to the students arriving. Try a few shots yourself to determine the **Goldilocks** performance line between frustration and challenge, i.e., not too close and not too far.
- Prior to the start, the group must decide who's going to throw and who's going to retrieve. Once this decision is made a player must maintain their role for that particular two minute time span.
- Allow practice throws before the start to apportion the players a greater sense of what role they should choose.
- The throwers must remain behind a throwing line (tape or rope). First step over the line gets a warning, each additional step past the line subtracts a ball from the closest receptacle, i.e., one point.
- The retrievers may roam about anywhere on the court, being aware that their function is only to retrieve missed balls and get them back to the throwers as efficiently as possible.
- Retrievers may not help or guide balls into a receptacle.
- Balls that bounce in, then bounce out, do not score any points.

Considerations

- If you have friends that play a lot of tennis, particularly at a tennis club, ask them to check and see what the club does with discarded balls. It's amazing how quickly tennis balls are used and discarded by elite players.
- Throwers and retrievers are all on the same team. The group is competing against itself in trying to score as high a point total as possible, either by

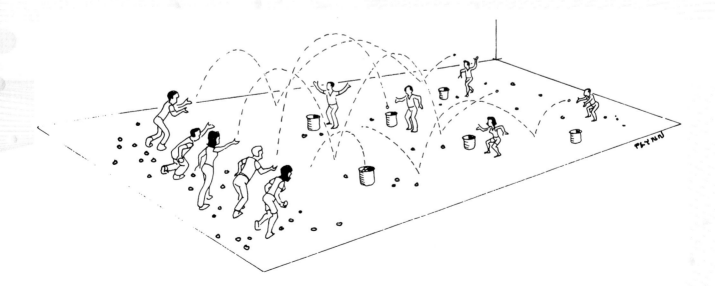

shuffling thrower and retriever positions between attempts, or making a decision about which receptacles should be targeted by the majority of throwers.

- This is a decision-making game and as such should be played more than once so that players can attempt to change positions and tactics. Allow enough time between attempts so that people with ideas can make themselves heard.
- Resist the temptation to make suggestions; let the action flow.
- A tennis ball purposefully thrown with velocity will hurt and can cause corporal damage.
- Demonstrate what a lofted throw looks like before dumping out the balls.

Debrief Questions

- If a good shooter is recognized, should that person be encouraged to continue shooting rather than taking a turn as a retriever?
- If someone continues shooting when it's obvious they don't have the "touch," should they be asked to "give it up"?
- What's more important, a good shooter or an excellent retriever? Or is there something else just as important?

Quick Touch a.k.a. Cutey (QT)

Impulse used to be the name of the game. People would hold hands in a circle and see how fast they could pass a squeeze from person to person. Quick Touch uses the same concept but encourages a greater level of creativity and speed.

Objective

To pass a touch sequentially from person to person in a group, and to accomplish that start-to-finish-sequence as fast as possible; obviously a timed event.

Set Up and Procedure

Announce the challenge to your group, state the objective clearly (as above), and let them have at it. Be there to support their efforts and answer questions. Be sure to clarify the difference between a squeeze and a touch. You may also have to explain what sequential means.

What You Will Probably See

- Almost all groups begin by standing in a circle and passing a touch to the person standing next to them by tapping that person on their shoulder. After 2–3 attempts it becomes clear that touching in a circle allows a time to be recorded but is essentially a creative dead end.
- Someone will usually/eventually ask if standing in a circle is required. Your response: "Stand anywhere you like." So, is passing the touch down a line of people faster than touching in a circle?
- "What if we all put our hands out in a line, real close together, and then . . ."; timed results near two (2) seconds for a group of 30 participants are commonplace and impressively quick.

Facilitation Tip

Don't limit a group's creativity by what you have previously seen or experienced, and for sure don't prompt or kibitz; let it happen. Also, when the group is obviously and genuinely satisfied with their time, accept that result, don't compare with previous efforts by other groups.

This activity is one of my favorites because it speaks to so many of the things we try to achieve by using initiative situations: leadership, thinking outside the box, effective communication, cooperative learning, and promoting the veracity of functional failure.

Quail Shooter's Delight a.k.a. Phones & Faxes

Most failure is by degrees, and if you know that failure is imminent and shared, it sure makes trying and the fear of failure less of a trauma.

Objective

For you, and a couple of partners standing in the middle of a large circle of people, to grab and hold onto as many soft objects as possible that are being simultaneously lofted directly over your heads by the people in the circle surrounding you.

Procedure

Ask two to three people to stand back-to-back in the center of a people circle. How many people in the circle? Many . . . say 15–50, the more the better actually. Each person in the circle should have at least two soft throwables in hand, (Nerf or fleece balls, soft Frisbees, bath toys, sponges, rubber chickens). On the count of three (or two if you are in a hurry), have all the circled players loft <u>all</u> the throwables simultaneously, so that they reach an apogee of say 12–15 feet and come down like rain on top of the three frantically grasping folks in circle-center.

The catchers attempt to hold onto as many descending objects as possible. First bounce catches off the floor are not allowed, and do I have to even mention picking an object off the ground? The catching results of team **troika** are predictably poor, but unanticipated; the catchers thought they were going to perform better . . . much better, and the people who haven't tried yet wonder why the people in the middle are having such a hard time. With the potential number of throwables to be caught numbering near 75, the number actually caught (kept off the floor) is usually 0–2; that's right, zero to two. How can that be with the anticipation of catching so many more?

Multi-tasking, does it work? Is multi-tasking an efficient way to operate at home or in the office? Apparently not according to various recent studies, with this game slamming the door on any hands-on doubters. As you move through teams of three you would think that people observing the action would learn something, but the bright eyed I-can-do-this look is there every time, dimming only after the throwables come crashing to the floor. Don't get me wrong, this game is not perceived as a downer, people like it and usually can't wait to come up with another way to fail with gusto.

It's probably a good idea to set the standards for allowable catches right away, unless you want to promote creativity. If you allow the following ploys, the number of objects caught will increase:

- lying down next to one another (depends upon the accuracy of the throwers)
- pressing against one another back-to-back, allowing the angled bodies to act as a funnel
- using clothing

But typically, techniques and attempts abound with pretty much the same results—much grasping and minimum grabbing.

Historical Factoid The original game name was based on the sport of quail hunting. If a shooter kicked-up a covey of quail and blasted away with his/her shotgun pointed in the general direction of the frantically fleeing covey, all the birds would generally escape. If the shooter concentrated on, and aimed at one bird, that bird was usually "bagged." The change of game name occurred because some folks, opposed to hunting, were offended by the name and hunting scenario, thus the alternative name *Phones & Faxes*, i.e., attempting and failing to juggle more than one thing at a time in the office. Just part of the growing PC thing I guess, but Hey, I'll call it whatever you want as long as you play the game.

Adventure Games

Rasta Balls

Old socks weighted with sand, rocks, or flour have been used for generations as objects to be centrifugally launched toward a variety of targets, some more parentally acceptable than others. The New Games Foundation popularized this spontaneous centrifugal fun by replacing the rocks with a Nerf ball and calling the whirling device a something-or-other, a whimsical name I can't recall. Did the old spinning sock have a name when you were a kid? I can't seem to ever remember calling it anything but a "rock sock," a sobriquet that mothers and homeowners near my adolescent turf learned to be wary of. But the old Nerf sock, although certainly safe, just didn't have the pizzazz, or centripetal momentum, to hit the excitement switch.

Since then I've tried putting a tennis ball into the end of a woman's knee-high stocking, and was pleased with the distance and height achieved as the result of a spinning throw and release. The stretch of the stocking is key, allowing a rebound, sling-shot effect not available in a regular man's tube sock. I even tried slicing the tennis ball and inserting a few marbles to add some weight (inertia). This worked (more distance), but catching the ball end of the sock became problematic (pain), which then led to the experience-directed attempt of catching the sock by its tail. Considering that a well-spun-and-released pantyhose sock can reach an apogee of close to 100 feet, catching the plummeting device by the tail before hitting the ground presented a grand challenge.

As time went by, knee-highs fell from favor mostly because of cost, compounded by how rapidly a nylon stocking would develop runs and begin to disintegrate in the toe area where the ball consistently made contact with the ground, parking lot, etc. On the rare occasion when a tennis ball came rocketing out of a rapidly rotating, torn and tattered stocking (Whoops . . . sorry!), the <u>horizontally</u> launched missile caused much ducking, associated with anatomical words not usually encountered in a cooperative environment.

Notwithstanding the occasional scattering of disgruntled throwers, knee-highs are still a good choice if you check the sock tip regularly. *Shopping tip*—buy in bulk, and try to purchase colored knee-highs. You will find that red, blue, and green tinted knee-high stockings are more accepted by young players as compared to the flesh colored brands. *Longevity tip*—spray-paint the toe area (with ball inserted) to practically eliminate runs in the fabric.

Moving on from knee-highs, we needed something that would fly well (aerial satisfaction), was inexpensive, would last a decent amount of time, would not become easily lodged in trees, and could be easily handcrafted by the students; enter the *Rasta Ball*. The Rasta Ball (RB) was simply a tennis ball that had been sliced with a knife, into which cut the knotted end of a 1/4" × 3' rope had been inserted.

Use a sharp knife, with a sharp point, and a <u>locking blade</u> to make the inch and a half slice. For safety and blood conservation, you should take on the role of designated slicer. The inserted knot is a simple overhand, and the chosen rope is three-strand twisted polypropylene. After the knot is inserted into the slice (squeeze the ball like a change purse to open the slit), use some type of construction adhesive, in one of those gun-like applicators, to squirt a dab or two of gooey glue into the slit and onto the knot.

If you want an RB that travels far and fast (depending upon the thrower's expertise, of course), unravel only about two inches of the tail and wrap plastic tape around the rope at that level to prevent further unraveling. If you want an easily caught ball that will not go far when thrown, completely unravel the tail right to the surface of the ball. (An unraveled Rasta Ball tail looks very much like a <u>Rasta</u>farian's long hair, get it?) A group of half a dozen students, working with you, production style, can make about 20–30 Rasta Balls in half an hour, allowing some extra time for the glue to dry. Essentially, the more Rasta-effect with the rope (frayed strands), the slower the ball will travel because of air resistance.

Bring a batch of RBs out onto a field area so all can see, then spin and casually launch a ball straight up, saying at the same time, "Anyone can do this." Try to catch the descending ball by the tail, saying, as the ball streaks past your hand, "Not everybody can do that." Distribute the balls (before the students attack and grab them), suggesting that everyone have-a-go at spinning, throwing, and attempting to catch. If there are any trees or flat school roofs around,

count on losing a couple of balls, as tree limbs and gym roofs are known Rasta Ball eaters. Don't allow students to climb trees to retrieve a captured ball; there's plenty more where that one came from, and where's that tree climber's belay?

Stand back and watch the play, the joy of movement, the thrill of adventure, and the panoply of high arced throws everywhere—watch your head! If you have enough Rasta Balls available, I'm sure the students could entertain themselves for longer than you're assigned to be there, but, since you are supposed to be suggesting and doing things, try this . . .

Split the group in half (If you were born in the months January through June, you're over there; July through December, come over here.), then give ALL the Rasta Balls to one of the groups, so that there is at least one RB per person, maybe two. Separate the two sides on the field so that there is about a medium length throw between groups. Explain that the group with the Rasta Balls are going to start spinning the balls, and on three, i.e., 1-2-3, release all of them toward the other group simultaneously. The receiving group will try to catch as many RB's as they can and hold the caught ones over their heads for a team count; you do the counting. (You need to be not only the ref but the impresario—keep things moving.) The catching team now becomes the throwing team and reciprocates the spinning throw. This throw and catch sequence is repeated for three innings and the final scores are tallied, or not tallied, S'up to you. This game is called Three Inning Rasta Ball, or whatever the participants want to call it.

Rules (if you need some)

- Each player can throw more than one RB at a time.
- All RB's are released at the same time.
- All legal catches must be caught by the tail.

- More than one catch per person is allowed.
- If the ball end hits the ground, even though you have a firm grasp on the tail, it is not counted as a catch.

In the guise of good sportsmanship, balls must be conscientiously thrown with the intent that the arcing ball will land somewhere near the other group.

Rasta Ball Horseshoes

This is a simple, but consistently fun RB game.

Objective

For competing players to reciprocate spin-throwing RB's at two strategically placed hula hoops in order to score points.

Set Up and Procedure

Use two hula hoops, or used bicycle tires, as targets and place them approximately 25 yards apart. Score as follows:
- 10 pts.—The RB rests <u>completely</u> with the hoop/tire.
- 5 pts.—Ball is entirely within the hoop but the rope is touching the hoop.
- 2 pts.—Ball is within 12" of the hoop; not the tail, the ball!
- 1 pt.—Ball is within 24" of the hoop.
- Also 1 pt.—Ball hits within the hoop and bounces out.

- More than 48" from the hoop—subtract 1 point.
- Have a measuring tape available.

Rasta Ball Golf

There's the idea, all you need to do is follow the rules of golf. RB Golf is a grand way to learn the rules and vocabulary of regular golf without having to buy clubs, take lessons, wear the proper clothing, keep your head down, and pay a green fee. This one teeny game more than pays for this book . . . you owe me change!

Rasta Ball Stunts

- Gather your whole RB'ing group together and announce that the following challenge is truly Challenge by Choice. (Sometimes I invoke CbC just because I know it adds to the drama and suspense of what's coming up.) Ask everyone to stand close together, but not so close that you will be hit by a spinning RB. With everyone standing there spinning their RB's, indicate that on the count of three, i.e., on 3, everyone is going to launch their RB straight up, then look directly at someone in the group (NOT UP), and wait for the inevitable (gravity wins) result. This zany attempt at getting cranially clocked by a tennis ball is called appropriately *Nutsy*. No one hit? Well, you can always try again.

· ·

Sacky Hack

For sure, one of the most frustrating and infectiously popular and portable pastimes to come out of California is the symbolically cultist bean bag called a Hacky Sac. (I'm not sure of the spelling, or where the word *hacky* came from, but . . . no matter; if you're interested there's always the Internet.) Essentially, the commercial Hacky Sac is a small (about the size of a shriveled kiwi fruit), stitched

up leather bag (sometimes knitted bag) that's filled with cherry pits. Cherry pits? There must be *something* exotic in there to justify the price tag.

The game idea is to strike this small sac with some portion of your lower anatomy (no hands, head, etc.) so that the sac travels to another person without making contact with the ground. This provides the other players the chance of personally experiencing either missing or misdirecting the sac. ("Never say you're sorry!"—Official Hacky Sac rule, that seems pretty cool actually.) I have to admit that trying to keep the sac aloft for the maximum number of kicks possible is a just-one-more-try affliction that is not only individually insidious but wildly contagious.

You might assume from my irreverent tongue-in-cheek comments about various players' abilities that use of a Hacky Sac is an elitist activity. Not so! Everyone has the same opportunity to appear inept and descended of maladroit. Skill level obviously increases with practice, but not everyone has eleven hours a day to kick around a pit sac, so here's a suggestion or two for those of you who are employed.

I have invented the *Sacky Hack* for us hackers who want instant gratification from our physical endeavors. Simply do the following. Blow up a balloon, with about an ounce of water inside, tie it off and kick away. The sloshing water provides erratic flight characteristics (the challenge), but the size of the inflated balloon provides a better than average chance of making contact (the satisfaction). If even this slowed down version gives you trouble, fill the balloon with helium and after the first kick it will float beyond your ability to make second contact, relieving you of further responsibility to keep saying you're sorry; also conveniently providing you with the opportunity to seek other diversions that require less practice time . . . like hang gliding.

Sacky Hack—(finally)

Provide your players with 2 3-inch diameter Nerf balls or fleece balls and ask them to split up into small groups of about 4–6 players. Start playing the real game of Hacky Sac, which is to keep the sac in the air by kicking, but this time hitting the ball with your open hand is allowed to keep the ball in play. Be aware, you only get points for a kick, not for a hand strike. (Strict rules require being allowed only three consecutive hand strikes before you have to kick the sac.) This handy rule makes sense for ego-driven but basically unskilled players, like me. See how many kicks your team can collect but don't tell the other teams; your superior score might have them looking for a helium balloon.

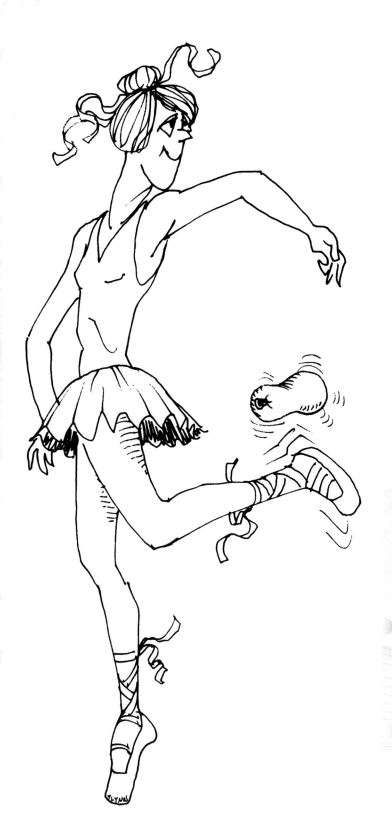

Adventure Games

Samurai

Samurai is a role-playing game that seems to capture people's imagination, allowing and encouraging total **histrionic** participation. I have also noticed that observers appear just as fascinated by the action and sound effects of the game as are the players.

I'm pretty sure the game Samurai originated via the fecund imagination of the folks at The New Games Foundation. Their original version is contained in one of their publications, *More New Games*, now unfortunately out of print. But stick with me here and I'll offer you the basics, plus a dandy variation.

(By-the-by, before we get into the intricacies of Samurai, if the name of this game (or any game) is unwieldy or perhaps culturally inappropriate, change it. And that's true of any game, activity, or initiative in this book, or any book I've authored. Also, if you don't like the rules, change them too; if Calvin & Hobbes can do it, so can you.)

Objective

A designated samurai-type person locates him/her self in the center of an extended people-circle. The Samurai then tries to eliminate everyone by symbolically slashing his/her ersatz sword in a wide arc around the circle. The circled people, responding to the sword's arc, either duck, jump, or suffer elimination from the game.

Set Up

- Ask your group to form a circle around a person standing in the center, maintaining about four feet between people in the arc. The person in the center is a designated Samurai, wielding an ersatz sword of mighty symbolic power.
- Armed with any easily manipulated sword-like weapon (Boffer, broom handle, rolled-up newspaper), the person in the center attempts to eliminate everyone in the circle with either noticeably high or low slashes of their sword. The overt slashes are token strokes only, although

delivered with maximum effort and ferocious shouts. Actual contact must be studiously avoided or the players in the circle will either lose trust and disperse, or lose trust and retaliate.

- If the Samurai person slashes high, each person <u>within the arc of the stroke</u> must duck or lose his/her head and be eliminated, (falling to the ground where that person can comfortably sit and watch the ensuing action). If the sweep of the sword is low, a hop must be made to avoid serious trauma to the legs (total truncation), and subsequent removal from the game, as above. You may have to step in from time to time to clarify what high and low slashes mean, as the occasional epinephrine fueled Samurai gets excited and delivers all strokes at about sternum height.
- All of this martial manipulation is accompanied by the inscrutable, very oriental, shouts of the Samurai, and groans of the various truncated players—a cacophony of oral action and reaction. I did mention histrionics, right?
- The last person in the circle to remain standing takes on the role of ascending Samurai, and, accepting the symbolic sword, steps into circle-center to begin the next round.
- After the basic game has been played a couple of times, try the following kamikaze variation.

Sovereign Samurai

To play this variation you must use either a Boffer or some other type of innocuous sword-like implement. Do not use broom handles, etc., as actual physical contact with the sword is made in this game.

- As the original game begins (as above), place a second identical sword on the ground near the center of the circle.
- As the Samurai begins his/her circular sanguinary forays, anyone in the circle can try to grab the second sword (Boffer) without being hit (actually whacked) by the Samurai's handheld sword.
- If a player gets whacked by the Samurai while attempting to retrieve the second sword, that person is eliminated, and the second sword is returned again to circle-center.
- If the "sword" has a wooden handle make sure the players know not to grab the sword by the tip and swing the handle.
- If a grab is made successfully, without that heroic player receiving a smack from the Samurai, the

two adversaries (Samurai and Sovereign Samurai) have at one another in a duel to the finish.

Rules for the Duel

- No slashing strokes allowed, only thrusts to the torso, a la fencing. Did you think we would be so déclassé as to allow vulgar slashing?
- A win is achieved by touching the tip of your sword to the torso of your opponent; any contact to the head and appendages is considered non de rigueur, and does not count as touché.

- Once again, for those totally immersed in the martial aspects of this game—DO NOT use a rigid "pretend" sword for this duel.
- If the Samurai loses the duel, everyone who had been eliminated, up to that point, is all immediately reinstated as once-again viable players, and the game continues. If the Sovereign Samurai wins the duel, the sword of the vanquished player is returned to circle-center, and the game continues.

Adventure Games

Sardines a.k.a. Seek & Hide

> "I was never good at hide and seek because I'd always make enough noise so my friends would be sure to find me. I don't have anyone to play those games with me anymore, but now and then I make enough noise just in case someone is still looking and hasn't found me yet."
> Brian Andreas

Objective

To turn the old, old game Hide & Seek around, and play the antithetical, equally old, game of Seek & Hide.

I was introduced to this hide-and-go-seek game by the participants in an adventure workshop some thirty years ago. So maybe you're thinking, "Wow, what an old game,,", considering that most of today's adventure curriculum activities have been developed within the last couple of decades. Although there has been a fairly recent influx of recorded ideas and publications, many of the currently used adventure-based games are becoming generational, and multi-generational, as in the case of Sardines.

I've made it a habit over the years to peruse old game books, and by old I mean with at least a 50-year copyright date, and occasionally (when I am lucky enough to find one), a century-old game tome. Many of the interesting "old games," I've discovered have old rules, but often contain the germ of an idea or notion that could be developed into a modern winner. Years after having played my first Sardines game, I found the basic rules for that game under exactly the same name, in a book entitled *Games of the Victorian Era* . . . definitely before Elvis.

Traditionally, in a hide-and-seek game, the person designated as IT counts to 100 with their eyes closed while everyone else dashes around furtively trying to find a hiding place; ". . . 97, 98, 99, 100! Anybody around my base is IT!" However, in this creative

variation of the classic hide-and-find, the IT hides and everyone else tries to find that concealed person and <u>joins them in their hiding place,</u> thus the name *Sardines*, as in tightly packed *Sardines*. If you are still somewhat confused by this wonderfully creative reversal of the role of IT, be aware, as the seeking folks wander about poking into closets and behind doors, that when IT is finally found the seeker(s) must join that person by sharing the hiding place, i.e., juxtapose those bodies.

This is not a game to build trust as you must be fairly sneaky to join the found IT without being seen by the other still-in-the-dark seekers. For example: "Sue, you go down the hall and I'll go this way," knowing full well that *this way* is to join the well-concealed IT, while Sue seeks the wild goose.

Sardines

A memorable Sardine game of yore, during which time I was the hider (IT person), allowed me to pick an out-of-sight hiding location in an obscure dark room. I was absolutely invisible in that Stygian corner and no one had found me 20 minutes into the game.

I was sitting motionless in the corner trying to control my breathing, knees tucked to my chest, when a tenacious seeker entered the room for the third time, announcing to the dark with conviction, that she knew I had to be in this room. I could see her body outlined against a dimly back-lit window as she slowly groped her way toward my crouched and cramped position, hands outstretched, reaching for the "sardine" she ESP'd was near. As her hand neared, I leaned my head back as far as possible so I was looking almost directly at the ceiling. Her hunting instinct sensed prey was near as probing fingers jutted toward my tenuous position. Then abruptly, and totally, a trembling digit entered one of my well-positioned nostrils. End of story. End of game.

School Locker Name Game

Remember the printed instructions that came with your school locker combination lock? "Take at least two full turns clockwise. Stop at the first number in the combination sequence. Turn counterclockwise to such-and-such a number, then turn back . . ." Didn't have a school locker? Well, take my word for it, there was a lot of turn this-ways, and that-ways before the opening tumblers fell. This following name game might not follow the combination sequence exactly but that's where the idea came from.

Line up your group in a circle and place in their hands a tied-in-a-circle length of rope* that allows at least 18" between participants (distance is not critical, nor is the knot used). Ask them to pass the rope clockwise from hand to hand until the knot has made a 360° trip (full circle), then suggest a counterclockwise trip back to the beginning, this time a bit faster.

Announce that all this circular rope passing was to serve as a warm up toward participating in a name game. (If you were going to sequence this game, and you are, would you use it toward the beginning of a group experience together, or as a culminating exercise? At the beginning? Correct-a-mundo; you must be a fas-CIL-a-tatter of great renown.)

Pass the rope one way or the other, from person to person, until the knot is in the hands of a player with an alphabetical first name closest to pure A, say Aaron for example. Then the knot (and rope) is passed clockwise to the next person in sequence alphabetically, say Andrea. Then the knot and rope is passed counterclockwise to Bob, then clockwise to Cindy, etc. Andrea, Bob, Cindy . . . you did notice that alphabetical sequence and reversal of rope at each name change? Just checking.

The group must find each sequential alphabetical goal (person), so anticipate a lot of who-are-you conversation and name sharing. As the circling knot reaches it's alphabetical goal, that person announces their name with some emphasis, i.e., let that name be heard. If Don has just definitively announced his name, after receiving the clockwise rotating knot, and Edwina is directly to his left, the rope must make almost a full 360° counterclockwise rotation to reach her; it's just the luck of the draw, or alternating rotation in this case.

After the group has rotated and re-rotated until everyone's name has been announced and reached, ask each participant to find another place in the circle and re-grasp the rope, i.e., change positions. Then suggest playing the same game, except this time to see how quickly the group can complete the name rotations; a timed event. Passing the rope is

*length of rope—Use "soft" rope, i.e., rope that will be easy on the hands. Three-eighths to three-quarter inch diameter Multiline or Dacron rope would be a good choice. Avoid sisal, polypropylene, or manila rope. These types of rope develop short, sharp, frayed sections of yarn that can penetrate the skin of the palm, a troublesome, painful, and avoidable consequence.

basically a fun thing to do, but if your group numbers 20 or more, this, like any other repetitive task, can get tedious. Two attempts are reasonably all you can expect from a larger group. (Make sure you ask the group to change positions *before* you announce timing this attempt otherwise, an adept player will suggest, and rightly so, lining up in the circle alphabetically.)

Will this identity game cement all those disparate monikers and allow immediate, unerring first name recall for the remainder of the time the group will be together? Well . . . no, but it will provide a dandy head start and allow some kinetic fun to be had at the same time; a pleasant and useful combination.

Stumblers

The old *Silver Bullet's* recounting of The Mine Field initiative is simplicity itself. To wit, *"Roll out beau coups tennis balls onto a gym floor, then try to cross the floor blindfolded, with a partner offering verbal-only directions, and without making physical contact with a ball."*

A quarter century ago we had access to heaps of tennis balls because one of Project Adventure's trainers also worked at a tennis club. (It is absolutely astounding how many fresh-out-of-the-can tennis balls it takes to keep a tennis buff happy.) So the immediate thought was to utilize that optic-yellow abundance with as many activities as possible involving lots of balls, thus the balls-only Mine Field application in the original edition of *Silver Bullets*. Since that time The Mine Field obstacles have changed and multiplied considerably and the name of the activity has been changed (see above). But, before we get into what has or hasn't changed, for those readers who are not familiar with this classic initiative situation, let's review the set up and rules.

If you plan to use the initiative Stumblers with numerous groups, I'd suggest setting up more or less permanent boundary markers on a gym floor using 3/4" blue painter's tape; tape that's easily applied and removed with no gummy leftovers. There are no NCAA approved dimensions for Stumblers, but it's generally a rectangle measuring approximately 15' × 30'. (I noticed in the original write up there were <u>no</u> suggested measurements for Stumblers; what wasn't I thinking?) If you are planning to situate outside on a grassy area use a section of retired climbing rope

(or any available cordage) to outline the Stumblers area. Use standard tent stakes to set and hold the four corners of the rope rectangle. Be sure to push the stakes well into the soil so they are flush with the surface of the grass to reduce the chance of tripping. Use a rubber mallet to whack the stakes in if the soil texture is uncooperative.

Here's the fun part. Dump out your bag of curriculum "toys" on the ground and ask participants to distribute the playful contents evenly within the confines of the rectangle, i.e., let them create their own Stumblers venue using as many different bizarre objects as possible. The visual results are often creative and, I hesitate to suggest, occasionally aesthetic. Be available to make humorous but insightful comments about using too many "mines," or perhaps not enough, i.e., establishing and ensuring the challenge. Examples of toys used: fleece balls, hula hoops, rubber chickens, rubber deck-tennis rings, tennis balls, stuffies . . .

If you want to make Stumblers particularly challenging, try the following:

- Place about a dozen set mouse traps (the classic wooden Victor-type) throughout the available

area. A stepped on trap will certainly *snap*, but without peril to the blindfolded participant if shoes are worn. Insist on shoes being worn; DO NOT allow wearing flip flops, sandals, or going bare foot. DO NOT experiment with rat traps!

- Distribute a few small plastic bowls within the area and fill them with water.

Caveat   Avoid spilling water on a wooden gym floor to maintain a congenial association with the custodian. Use foam "peanuts" (packing material) in the bowls to keep everybody happy.

Take a Bight

This is a knot testing game, i.e., an activity to gauge the effectiveness of your riveting knot tying instructional sessions. If your players are introduced to this activity before they have a working knowledge of a few on-the-bight knots and knot systems, the game will not be well-received, and neither will you.

Split the larger group into smaller working groups of six. Each of the smaller groups is assigned a single 12 foot section of rope; retired 9 mm rope is a good choice. The challenge for the group is to tie whatever knot-on-a-**bight*** the instructor calls out, and to demonstrate that well-tied series of twists and turns to the instructor for his/her evaluation. See right for a list of bighted knots.

Rules and Considerations

- The group has 90 seconds to tie each announced knot.
- Each separate knot (six of them) must be manipulated by a different member of the group, however, anyone in the group may offer verbal aid.
- After the time limit is up, no further changes are allowed. Place the completed knot on the ground.

Keeping score or competing with other groups is probably counterproductive in this context, so downplay the rivalry aspect and encourage sharing between groups. There's nothing like **teacher** approved cheating (variously referred to as *cooperation*) to dull the counterproductive edge of win/ lose competition.

For your further cordage edification (which has little or nothing to do with the functional aspect of this activity) the word *bight*, as applied to knot tying, came from a sailor's geographical definition of a bight, "a bend in the coast forming an open bay." The topographic visual of a curved open bay as compared to the curve in a slack rope was too coincidental to ignore, thus, tacking a vessel within the bight (the bay) resulted in calling that curved bend in a rope, a *bight*. Also extending your nascent knowledge of this fascinating subject . . . a loop in the rope is not considered a bight, primarily because it isn't. The ends of the rope must remain uncrossed to receive the *bight* designation.

Bighted knots for benighted learners

- Bowline-on-a-bight
- Figure Eight Loop
- Butterfly Knot
- Stevedore Knot
- Sheepshank
- Double Figure Eight Loop a.k.a. Figure Eight-on-a-bight
- Extra credit: Man-O-War Sheepshank or Jury Mast Knot

*Bight—That portion of the rope that occurs between the working end and the standing part, i.e., both ends. A knot-on-a-bight can be tied without using either end of the rope.

bight

bite

Can all these middle-of-the-rope knots be used on a ropes course? Yes, but . . . how many times have I avoided a Sheepshank as part of a belay or haul system? Applicability in this case is not so significant when you consider what the six knots above are being used for: establishing a sense of team and sharing, as well as providing the advertised knot review.

Texas Big Foot

I suppose you could call this *New Jersey Big Foot*, or any state you happen to call home, but TX has the rep for being big and bold, just like the game. I don't use *Texas Big Foot* with just any group; they need to show me via smiles, giggling, open body language, and a bent for the bizarre that they can handle an activity that has no functional value . . . well, maybe some.

Texas Big Foot doesn't require much explanation and provides a humorous low-key activity that is more apt to fail than not. If personal expectations aren't paramount, and image isn't on self-destruct, it's kinda fun to fail, particularly when supported by a bunch of co-failers.

Objective

Make a big circle (you included) so that everyone is standing hip to hip with arms around shoulders; a friendly-type circle. From this starting position take three purposeful and consecutive giant steps, trying concurrently to maintain the integrity of the circle . . . not personal integrity, you know what I mean.

Optional Rules and Sometime Considerations

- In a commanding voice, tinged with anticipation and a touch of angst, initiate the first step by saying, "Take the first step!" All of a sudden the next two steps seem a lot more problematic. Have the folks look around to appreciate their predicament.
- Launch step #2 and don't bother commenting, as the disintegrating circle speaks for itself.

- If the participants are still listening to you, suggest trying to take another step which, if attempted, usually results in considerable laughter as the "circle" becomes a clot of contorted people, having given up all semblance of "successful" completion.

Admittedly a lightweight activity, but a decent tone setter toward sharing laughter and heavy duty acceptable touching. Follow up with Tickle-a-Pickle.

Tickle-a-Pickle

I doubt I would have included this "quickie" activity if it wasn't such a natural follow up to Texas Big Foot.

As the group collapses at the end of the Texas Big Foot third step, ask everyone (now hanging on and balanced against one another) to pack closely together, even closer than they are now, and pretend they are pickles in a small jar. (Dill or Sweet, your choice). There is only one thing to do in a sealed jar situation like that: here you initiate a quick tickle move on someone, saying loudly at the same time, **"Tickle-a-Pickle!"**

Tickling attempts sweep through the group as finger forays and attempts at escape run rampant.

Caveat I probably don't have to say this, BUT . . . Tickle-a-Pickle is a fun, one-time activity for a group that is ready for this type of interaction. If you think close-encounter tickling might not be well-received, be preemptive and go with that gut reaction—don't use it. Your role should not always involve after-the-fact facilitation.

Toss-a-Name Game

If you have trouble remembering names in a just-met group situation and you dislike those *Hello-My-Name-Is* stick-on-tags as much as I do, this game provides an action packed sequence that makes forgetting harder than remembering. Wishful thinking hyperbole from a venerable (sounds better than *hoary*) facilitator? Well, maybe just a little . . .

Break into groups of about 10–12 people and arrange yourself in an informal circle, (no holding hands or dress-right-dress necessary). A leader (that would be you) introduces the game by announcing his/her first name then gently tosses a tennis ball* to the person on his/her right or left. As tosses continue in the chosen direction, each person says his/her first name and continues lobbing the ball in sequence around the circle until the ball makes it back to the leader. Any consequence for drops? Nope, just retrieve the ball and continue.

This names-in-a-circle preliminary exercise is simply to allow everyone to hear everyone's first name, so make sure that all names are clearly stated, with perhaps a touch of verbal volume.

The leader then calls out someone's name in the arc (pressure's on mate; you do have to remember at least one name), and lofts the ball to him/her, then that person calls out another individual's name, and lofts the ball . . . Emphasize saying the person's name clearly and loudly enough so it can be heard. Also, take the time to explain what the word *loft* means so that rocket-armed ex-jocks won't be so inclined to show off their stuff.

After the ball has been lofted from person to person for a couple of minutes, or more usefully until you begin to get a feel for a few names in the circle, start up another ball. This obviously increases the frequency of names being called, establishing perhaps an uneasy feeling that the game is moving beyond their control. Let it happen, let the players recognize they are fallible participants in a real game, not simply the initiator of an eye/hand electric impulse being manipulated on a motherboard. I'm chagrined to bring it to your attention, but this might be the first person-to-person *real* game some of these participants have <u>ever</u> played.

As the game progresses, and you would like to throw the ball to someone who's name you don't know, just establish eye contact and say with conviction, "What's your name?" then toss the ball. What a concept; asking someone's name! I've heard it said that the sweetest sound in the world is the sound of your own name, and now someone is asking to hear that sound? Very cool!

Toward the end of the game add a third or fourth ball to the name-calling melee, as diminishing returns and laughter solidly indicate that play has trumped attainment. Is that OK? I mean, didn't we play this game to learn names? Yes, but . . . these games (facilitation tools actually) are meant to initiate thought, emotion, and enjoyment, including as much personal interaction as you can facilitate. Did you learn a few names? That's good; use them and optimistically pick up a few more as time goes by. Did you enjoy the activity, maybe laugh, share some conversation, form a few opinions? That's better; laughter, talk, forming opinions, that's the stuff of life . . . then learn a few names. Names are always there, facilitating moments aren't.

To continue: If there are other small groups playing the same game, stop occasionally and ask about 1/3 of each small group to exchange places, and begin the ball tossing action again as above. After a couple of exchanges, announce that anyone can change groups whenever he/she wants to, ensuring that each player is empowered to make the game fit their needs, and eventually hear each person's name.

Variations on the Toss-a-Name-Game Theme

1. As part of the established lobbing and naming, begin slowly expanding the diameter of the circle (walk slowly backward) while concurrently tossing and calling names. As the arc of the circle expands and the space between people increases, it becomes obvious that more volume is necessary

---

* tennis ball—tennis balls are easy to come by, but their use for tossing-type games is questionable. As part of the developing trust package amongst participants it's important to use words, actions, and props that don't hurt, emotionally or physically. Being blind-sided by an innocuous tennis ball may cause pain, but more significantly, even mild discomfort results in a diminishing of trust. A wadded-up piece of scrap paper might not have the panache of a Nerf or fleece ball, but the price is right and getting hit by a paper wad doesn't cause harm; it also makes you look institutionally frugal, and ecologically creative.

to be heard due to the increased distance and expanding dissonance of name shouting. Be aware however, that although names are being shouted with intention, and rotator cuffs are being primed for discomfort tomorrow, there is probably minimum name learning taking place as screams, hollers, bellows, and wild throws rachet up the fun quotient.

Now, slowly begin moving closer (balls and names continue) until the group is so contracted (whispered names and ludicrous lobs) that the game dissolves into laughter. For this expanding/ contracting variation, have at least one ball per three people; lottsa balls, lottsa fun—and don't use tennis balls.

2. After the names begin to flow, and as a means of reinforcement, ask the ball catcher to say "Thank you" to the thrower, including the thrower's name. Rote + Repetition = Remembering.

3. As a finale, bring the whole group together (balls aside) and ask if there is anyone who can name everyone. In a group of 25 you should get 2–3 confident volunteers (Pick Me!, Pick Me!), and the person you choose will probably be 100% correct in their naming prowess. How do they do that? It's an impressive and predictable feat; some people just got the gift!

4. Then announce, "Let's end this activity with a Shirley Temple cocktail party." Assume and demonstrate the proper social positioning and air

of cocky self-assurance (check out the flick *Wedding Crashers*; one arm bent, holding an imaginary beverage, the other appendage poised and ready to shake any available hand), and commence mingling. At this point you step to the nearest person (if you remember their name), make eye contact, and say, in an overtly confidential voice, one octave lower than normal, "Glad you could make it Doug" (or whomever), while purposefully shaking his hand. Move quickly to the next person, and so on. Include a superficial hug occasionally, but be careful not to spill your drink. Invite the group to join your conviviality, explaining that it's their party. Come on down! This name sharing encounter usually continues for a couple of minutes, gradually and predictably expanding into spontaneous individual conversations. Nice going—you have facilitated.

Name Game for Dummies (like me!)

A draw back for me of playing Toss-a-Name Game is the ongoing requirement that you actually have to remember people's names, a skill of which I am genetically bereft. You would think after leading hundreds of adventure curriculum training sessions, including an equal number of name games, that my ability and proclivity for recollecting names would have somewhat improved, but I can forget a name faster than a computer can crash; *creative* and *concrete sequential* just don't complement one another I guess. So I made up a name game (for me) that I'm hoping will jive with our joint malady, i.e., forgetting at the speed of light. If you are one of those idiot savant name wizards, turn off your inherent recall superiority for a few minutes and have some fun with the rest of us.

The name of this game is called **Who!**, a name game that does not require remembering names. I'm not kidding, check it out.

Ask the participants to line up in a circle, with some distance established between players; extended finger-tip-to-finger-tip is about right. Indicate that you (*you* are part of the circle) are going to start the action by pointing directly at someone else in the circle (include eye contact, extended arm and hand, purposeful body positioning, etc.), at the same time announcing in a loud voice, Who!

as you walk toward that indicated person. They are required, in response, to state their name with conviction, i.e., also loudly, and begin walking toward someone else in the circle, at the same time pointing at that chosen person, announcing *Who!* You, the initiator, take the place in the circle of the first person pointed to, and the *Who-ing* cycle continues. The beauty of this name game is that you don't have to know or remember anyone's name!

Pointing and name announcing continues until at least half the people in the circle have been heard from. Then, unannounced, start a second sequence by again stepping into the circle, pointing to someone, and saying *Who!* (Here's a chance to include someone who has not yet been *Who-ed!*) As the names become more recognizable, step into the circle a few additional times until there are half a dozen players concurrently crossing the circle *Who-ing!* one another. This confusing owl-like hullabaloo won't last long, but it's a fun finish to a functional game.

Want more? Ask the pointing person to announce their name also, and to shake hands (or share a High 5) with the designated person as they pass one another within the circle.

The anti-angst delight of this name-game is that a player can relax and not have to worry about recalling a name, although rote-remembering happens like it or not.

References

New Games Foundation. *More New Games.* Main Street Books, 1981.

Rohnke, Karl. *The Bottomless Bag Revival,* 2nd ed. Kendall Hunt Publishing Company, 2004.

Rohnke, Karl. *Quicksilver: Adventure Games, Initiative Problems, Trust Activities and a Guide to Effective Leadership.* Kendall Hunt Publishing Company, 1995.

Games of the Victorian Era.

Initiatives

A-Frame

When I was doing ropes course inspections I always spent time in an organization's adventure programming storage area, checking out their gear, and there IT was, the unmistakable, often crudely fabricated, A-Frame. All the requisite props were there that identify a "proper" adventure site (trolleys, all aboard platform, hoops, bag-'o-balls, crabs, ropes, etc.), but the A-Frame, being what it is, tends to stick out and announce, "Here I am, let's have a go." Here's a six person initiative problem that requires a unique combination of creative thinking, balance, cooperation, and concentration.

Objective

To move the A-Frame apparatus, and one person "aboard," from point A to point B (about 30 feet) using only the props available.

Props

- The A-Frame itself
- 5–20-foot small diameter ropes (suggested—½" Multiline rope, or retired ⅜" **Kernmantle** rope)

Rules

- The A-Frame must maintain at least one point of contact with the ground at all times, and never more than two points of contact, i.e., it may not be dragged.
- Only one person can make body contact with the A-Frame apparatus and he/she must avoid all contact with the ground.
- Ropes may not touch the ground at any time during the passage.
- None of the five assistants (rope managers) may approach closer than five feet to the A-Frame during the actual passage. Use brightly colored tape to mark that five-foot restrictive distance on each rope.
- Any digressions from the above rules necessitate starting over.

- If someone breaks a rule? Make up a forfeit that fits the situation.

A Solution for You—Not to Be Offered to the Students

- Tie one end of each length of rope to the apex of the A-Frame. Use your favorite never-slip knot. My knot of choice in this case is the constrictor knot. As in most noncritical applications **Lottsa Knots** also works perfectly well . . . if your steel-trap memory has slipped a notch or two.
- Stand the A-Frame vertically (two points of contact at the base), and ask one of the six participants to stand on the crossbar while the frame is being supported.
- Have the five assistants move from propping up the frame manually to supporting it by individually providing tension on the five ropes. Now you're ready to move.
- As the "rider" sways from side to side, he/she alternates a concurrent thrust forward with each rocking motion as the assistants support each movement with their five taut ropes.

Considerations

- There is little chance of the frame and riders falling over if the rope holders remain alert; however, inadvertently stepping off the frame is commonplace.
- The long side sections of 2 × 3 lumber should measure about 8'.
- The cross section of the **A** itself (2 × 4), should be long enough to keep the rider fairly close to the ground: 12"–14" high.
- Use ⅜" × 3½" galvanized carriage bolts for the three lumber attachment points. Don't forget to use washers on the bolts.
- Rout or chamfer all edges of the wood to preclude sharp edges and splinters. Paint? S'up to you.
- Wolmanized or pressure-treated lumber is not necessary.
- Do not attempt to use this activity on a gym floor or any other smooth surface. This initiative was designed to be used on grass, unless . . . you provide rubber "booties" for the frame. Booties or no, custodians are not going to be pleased with <u>your</u> frame slamming onto <u>their</u> basketball floor . . . and it will.

A-Frame

All Aboard

I first experienced this classic, let's-get-close, initiative while I was an instructor (Watch Officer) at Hurricane Island Outward Bound in 1967. I remembered it as about a 2' × 2' platform nailed to the top of four vertical 4" × 4" boards that had been sunk and secured in the ground. The platform itself was 18" off the ground. The first few platforms I built for Project Adventure a few years later were of that permanent/high type; if it was good enough for Outward Bound, it was good enough for me . . . until someone asked me why it had to be so high. And then someone else asked if I could make a portable

one. So I removed the "legs" placed the 2' × 2' platform directly on the ground and named it the All Aboard.

Objective

To balance your entire group on top of the available 2' × 2' surface area of the platform, and to remain balanced (off the ground) for five seconds after the last person's foot leaves the ground.

Rules

- No props allowed—just people. This precludes clothing used as "rope."
- There is no particular time limit.
- Stacking people—Lincoln-log style—is dangerous, painful, and not allowed.
- Piggybacking is OK, if adequate spotting is available.

Initiatives

Considerations

- A committed group can get 12–15 average-sized people balanced on the platform for five seconds. The most I have seen was a dedicated 19. Getting 20 on top would be impressive but not necessarily significant; it's how well the group works together . . . not the size, height, or number of the stack.
- This popular exercise lends itself to useful discussion about team effort, group and individual commitment, leadership, compassion, and group problem-solving dynamics.
- For variety, and to fit your group size needs, provide a 3' × 3' platform for a group of 18 to 20+. You can also use this 3 × 3 platform for the swinging initiative, Prouty's Landing, page 88.

Construction

- Cut two 2' sections of 4" × 4" lumber and place them parallel to one another on the ground two feet apart (measure to the outside edges).
- Cut three 2" × 8" × 2' boards and rasp or rout the edges. Finish with sandpaper if the edges still seem rough. Considering the somewhat less than 8" width of the board, there will be a narrow space between the three boards after being secured (see below) to the 4 × 4's.
- Using 4" screws, secure the 2' boards on top of the 4 × 4's. Pre-drill the boards to prevent splitting. Make sure the screw heads are completely flush with the board to prevent injury.

Historical Aside   In the 1984 edition of *Silver Bullets* I started off this particular write-up by saying, "The 1980's answer to the 1950's stunt of how many people can fit into a telephone booth." I think I said that because in the 60s, while working as a trail-teacher at an Outdoor Education Center in California, I used to challenge my 6th-grade students to see how many could fit inside my 1956 VW. In my mind's eye, I can still see and sense the excitement that resulted from that simple exercise in teamwork. "Look out for that shift knob!"

Initiatives

The Almost Infinite Circle

I have to admit, when first suckered into the **impossiprobability** of this activity, I was convinced that it was presented just to see how we (a pair) would handle frustration. After five minutes of close quarter maneuvering and fruitless juxtaposing, I was persuaded by my partner, and our doomed manipulations, that we had been tricked. I have to admit to being easily deceived, but even so, being tied together as two circles—two infinite circles—then being asked to separate seemed so daunting, so . . . hopeless.

Objective

To separate two loosely tied-together people from a seemingly impossible, but engagingly simple, crossing of ropes.

Set Up and Procedure

- Tie each end of a 10-foot long rope (cotton laundry line) comfortably around the wrists of one participant. The knot you use is irrelevant and how tightly (painfully) the wrist loops are drawn has nothing to do with the solution. Uncomfortably tight ropes should be avoided.
- Before applying the identical wrist-tie set up to the second person, pass one end of the not-yet-tied rope through the circle formed by the first person's arms and rope, then tie the ends to both wrists of the second partner. See illustration.
- Set a time limit for separating from one another.
- Answer as many non-solution questions as the pair might ask, continually emphasizing that there is a solution, because logic, sooner or later, dictates that a sharp knife is the only solution.

Rules

The two intertwined people attempt to separate from one another without:

1. Cutting the ropes.

2. Untying or loosening the knots.
3. Slipping the knotted portion over their hands.

The ONLY solution:

- Take a bight in the center of your partner's rope.
- Pass this bight under either of your wrist loops so that the bight portion is being pushed toward your palms/fingers.
- Pull the bight up and through the wrist loop, then open the bight to a size that will accommodate passing over your hand.
- Pass the bight over your hand and pull it intact down and through the wrist loop.
- You're FREE! No? Then you better release your *bite* on the rope, check the Glossary in this book as to the definition of a *bight*, and try again.

Variation

This exercise can also be attempted by a single person; not as much fun, but . . . Tie the two ropes to that person's wrists and ankles, with the "magic" circle-in-a-circle arrangement included, of course. This variation often results in copious conversation with self.

The Amazon

*"Work consists of whatever a body is obliged to do. **Play** consists of whatever a body is not obliged to do."*
Mark Twain as Tom Sawyer

I have to admit I've given this activity short shrift over the years, and it doesn't deserve the neglect. I suspect my disregard has more to do with it being a prop-heavy, site specific initiative, because whenever I have chosen to use it, people have responded well to the action/fantasy aspect, with the debrief always lively and useful.

I noticed in the old write-up there were precious few comments about dimensions, etc., because Bob Nilson's illustration did that so well, at the same time accurately depicting the necessary leveraged, cantilevered, geometrical solution. So there you have The Amazon initiative, including a few words from me so I feel necessary, and Bob's excellent illustration.

Objective

Using the provided props, a group must attempt to retrieve a container placed some distance from a simulated riverbank. Make up some outrageous, blatantly unnecessary but enticing reason for retrieving the can.

Set Up and Considerations

- The participants may use only the provided props and themselves.
- Using the cartoon dimensions, set up and try this event before presenting it to the students. You will obviously need a few staff to assist.
- If a participant touches the ground (water) between the riverbank and the #10 tin can, he/she must return to the bank and try again.

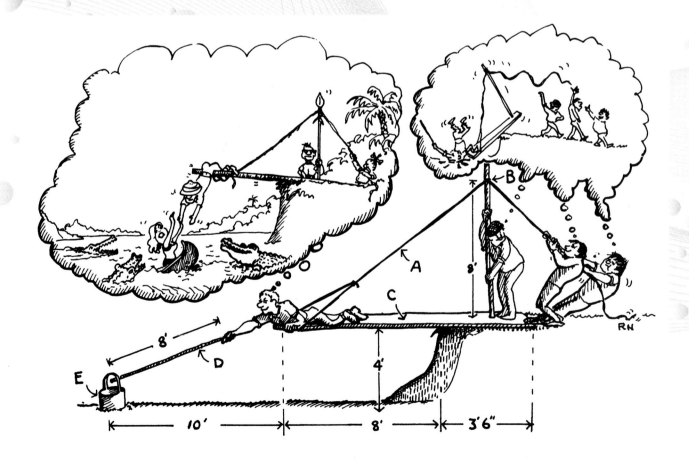

- I've had the most luck presenting this initiative on a make-it or don't-make-it basis rather than trying to accomplish the container retrieval for time.

Props

- Multiline rope—$^5/_8$" × 25'
- 1.5" × 8' pole to support the cantilever
- 2" × 8" × 12' board. Rout the edges of the board before use.

- Reaching pole—Fairly straight, small diameter, tree sapling measuring about 8 feet
- #10 tin can with wire bail (handle); a make-it-yourself prop
- After going to all the trouble of retrieving the can, make sure there is something in the can worthy of being retrieved. Perhaps something that tastes good and is not particularly good for you.

• •

Be the Rope

You need a length of rope; a 30-foot section of ½" Multiline, or an equal length of retired 11 mm climbing rope, or adapt, depending upon the size of your group and what's available. Don't use inexpensive rope (sisal, manila, polypropylene) displaying sticker-like yarn splinters, because it is apt to cause pesky palm punctures.

Here's the set up. Using a 30-foot section of rope tossed on the floor, ask 8–10 people to pick up the rope, then evenly distribute themselves along its length.

Objective

To tie as many overhand knots as possible in the held rope.

Rules and Considerations

- Allow 120 seconds for this challenge and encourage multiple attempts.
- Each person must maintain his/her position on the rope.
- Each person must keep one hand on the rope at all times.
- No time is made available for discussion. Time is started as soon as the participants are "on" the rope and you have announced the challenge.

- After a first attempt, allow ample time for discussion and practice before a second attempt is made. Is the group up for a third and maybe fourth attempt? Go for it; take advantage of their enthusiasm for this challenge. Minimum enthusiasm? Don't force it; and review your sequence of activities. No previous knot tying practice? Hmmmmm . . .
- An additional challenge—ask for figure eight knots to be tied, or alternate overhand and figure eight knots along the rope. And for your high-performing group, suggest attempting a single bowline.

Variation

Ask the distributed group on the rope to tie as many knots on-the-bight as possible (no duplicates) during the next 120 second time span. Allow two minutes of discussion time before the attempt, but no practice. Consider—overhand loop, figure eight loop, bowline-on-a-bight, butterfly, and many others.

Either of the above challenges makes sense for a group who has had previous training in knot systems. Presenting a knot initiative to a group without prior knot tying instruction would only cause frustration and disinterest.

The above rules and names for either challenge are offered only for your consideration; always feel free to vary and tweak an activity. Be aware, every game and initiative in this book is available for change, tweaking, and deletion as fits where you're coming from, the group's attitude, venue, and perhaps the humidity.

Bridge It

"It seems paradoxical that although most people love having fun and enjoy humor, they are often resistant to their use. Perhaps the greatest resistance by people to the use of humor is the ingrained sense that work is work and **play is play.** Our puritan ethic subscribes to the idea that work should be hard, serious, important, direct and efficient. Humor and fun suggest a lack of focus, a misuse of time, and a lack of attention to what is really important and to be rewarded. Not only is humor related to silliness, wasting time and laziness, but it is often seen as a measure of immaturity."
Napier/Gershenfield

After reading what I wrote about Bridge It in *Silver Bullets*, I'll admit to a degree of loquacious rambling. So, if you would like to be rambled upon, check out page 127 in that quarter-century-old book, otherwise here's my latest attempt at being more succinct.

Objective

Two groups, using identical props, attempt to build a symbolic bridge toward one another without being able to see what the other group is doing. The objective of this task is to not only have the two half bridges meet at the same location, but have each half bridge appear as identical as possible.

Props

After perusing the extensive list below you will realize that many of the items can be replaced or substituted for. Consider, one of the goals is to have the two halves of the bridge meet, but the other, as-significant goal, is to have both halves of the bridge look alike.

You will need the following props × 2; i.e., one set for each group:
    4—styrofoam cups
    8—wine corks
    8—small-diameter, 8" long dowels
    1—roll of ½" masking tape
    1—small box of LEGOs, Tinker Toys, or the like
    1—paper and pen (pencil)
    1—set of terminology

The following items to be used by both groups:
    2—folding card tables
    1—large opaque sheet, blanket, or bedcover
    1—folding chair for each participant (optional)
    1—folding chair for each representative (mandatory)
    2—rooms (The ideal set up allows both teams to exit the bridge construction area without being able to see what's happening on the other side of the sheet.)

Set Up

- Place the card tables next to one another, then hang the sheet vertically over the separation point of the tables. Divide the chairs equally on each side of the sheet.
- The terminology papers should read something like this:
  Side A—The word TOP means *BOTTOM*, SIDE means *UNDER*, to LAUGH means *ON TOP OF,* and SQUEEZING YOUR NOSE means *I AGREE.*
  Side B—The word TAPE means *WIDE,* STICKING OUT YOUR TONGUE means *HOW MANY,* CRISSCROSS means *PARALLEL,* and FOLDING YOUR ARMS WHILE FROWNING means *YES.*
  After trying this initiative, change or expand the terminology as fits your needs or sense of creativity and humor. Beware: Too much terminology is contraindicated.
- Divide the props equally on each side of the vertical sheet.

Procedure

- Fabricate a story about two countries separated by a body of water that want to establish a trade and cultural relationship. The river separating the two countries seems constantly plagued by dense fog (the sheet). Because of a Hatfield-and-McCoy-type of feud that began generations ago, the dialects of their common language are practically indecipherable to one another. In order to establish dialogue between groups, three 5-minute meetings have been arranged at a common meeting site (another room).

- Only one designated member from each group may talk at each of the three meetings. These two individuals sit facing one another directly, separate from the other people in the room.
- No comments from the group are allowed during this time—only shared laughter.
- The timing, planning, and building sessions should proceed like this: At a signal to begin, the two groups are shown their respective building areas (tables) and props, and are then allowed seven minutes to discuss the announced task of building the bridge (above), and to begin construction if they choose to. After the initial seven minutes have gone by, follow this three-meeting schedule:

1st—five-minute vis-a-vis meeting of the two chosen group reps. A new representative should be selected each time. This 5 minute meeting is immediately followed by a seven-minute team discussion and building segment back at the "bridge" site.

2nd—The second representative meeting at the meeting area, followed immediately by a five-minute discussion and building time at the "bridge" site.

3rd—Final five-minute representative meeting, followed by a final eight-minute race to get the work accomplished.

Be strict as far as the timing and dead lines are concerned. Then comes the unveiling, followed by groans of dismay and/or exclamations of delight . . . and laughter, always laughter. Also, remind the reps to use only the supplied terminology if they need to use one of the assigned words or concepts.

Be sure to set aside a sufficient amount of time, after the initial emotion of seeing the bridge, to allow discussion of what went on during the various time segments associated with building the bridge: comparisons of approach, leadership emerging, choosing the reps, utilization of time.

Bucket 'o Balls

Set Up

- Hang a plastic milk crate (or the like) at a height of about 15 feet. The most efficient way to achieve the "hang" is to toss a length of approximately ¼" diameter cord over a limb or beam at say 20 feet. Then tie on the crate using a suspension system from each corner of the crate. (If you can't remember a proper knot, tie lots of whatever you do remember.) Haul the crate up to about 15 feet and tie off the cord you're holding with the same amorphous bulky knot arrangement. Put a piece of marker tape on the cord so that the crate hangs at a consistent height each time it's pulled up.

- Provide each participant with one tennis ball.
- Make sure there are no obstacles on the ground to run into or trip over, considering everyone will be looking up most of the time.

Objective

To toss all the tennis balls into the crate in the least amount of time.

Rules and Considerations

- The balls must be tossed individually, i.e., the balls cannot be wrapped together.
- Time stops when the last ball is successfully tossed into the crate.
- The crate must hang square, i.e., not tilted to one side.
- People pyramids are allowed with proper spotting, however the crate may not be touched.
- No props are permitted.

Bucket-'o-Balls

I don't remember where I saw or experienced my first cardboard tube, but I knew immediately that it was an adventure prop worth pursuing. After asking around, I discovered that these macrotubes were manufactured by The International Paper Company and used as cores for large paper rolls, bigger-than-you paper rolls . . . much bigger; this was no toilet paper tube. The cardboard tube itself measured about three feet long with a diameter of 14 inches. The thickness of the tube's wall was ½", sturdy enough to laterally support a 250+ pound person . . . an impressive piece of cardboard.

I called the local International Paper Company in Framingham, Massachusetts (International Companies have to be local somewhere!), and asked how we could obtain surplus cores, and how much. The laconic desk jockey at the other end of the line indicated, with absolutely no interest why I wanted the cores, that the cores were disposed of twice a week and if we wanted some to "Come and pick out what you want." I asked how many we could have, he said, "Bring a truck." I always wanted to drive a "rig," but a pick-up was the best I could manage. As it turned out, we could squeeze and stack about 26 cores into the pick-up truck's bed without losing any on the return trip down Route 128.

During the core's hey-day as an initiative prop, someone (might have been me) suggested seeing how high the cores could be individually stacked before the column collapsed. The highest stack I personally observed was 13 cores, about 17 vertical feet worth. Tales of a 15-core stack were legend. Can you imagine a surreal stack of cardboard cores that high, just sitting there without someone wanting to knock it down? It was irresistible. Someone suggested blowing the stack over (funny but fruitless). Another idea was knocking over the stack by hitting it with tennis balls; an adjunct to the activity Tattoo. But the actual idea for an initiative task came from a workshop participant. "Let's see how long it would take to throw all these tennis balls up and into the core's column." What a great idea . . . and it was.

When all available balls had been cooperatively tossed into the stack, and a time for that attempt recorded, the column of cores was carefully lifted about 4–5 inches off the floor by the group and the contained balls were quickly swept out. Great idea! Any problems? A few . . .

Each cardboard cylinder weighed just under 10 pounds, resulting in a 16-foot stack weighing in at about 150 pounds. That total weight certainly contributed to the difficulty of adding another core, or completing the lift and sweep procedure. The safety concern wasn't with the bottom cores, rather those 3 or 4 out-of-plumb cores at the top of the stack, and the momentum their 9+ individual pounds generated by the time a tumbling cylinder struck the gym floor, or something more pliable, if you get my drift. Visual spotters, standing some distance from the stack were given the responsibility of shouting a warning if the cores began to topple, but a warning, no matter how loud or quickly offered, is still an iffy safety policy. This initiative, though greatly enjoyed and programmatically useful, was doomed by risk factors that were more than just perceived. A safety solution? See Bucket-'o-Balls, this book, page 67.

Reviewing Topics

- Should there be a quick identification of the best throwers, then use them exclusively as shooters with all other participants acting as feeders?
- Is fun and enjoyment more important than achievement? And in what context?
- Is there a way for both team and individuals to feel satisfied with an attempt?
- Who is setting the criteria for success? What is success?

Allow as many attempts as the group would like to make, considering that ultimately it's their sense of satisfaction, resulting from their efforts, that is important.

The Clock

Because of Project Adventure's early successes in the 1970s, the company found themselves in the enviable position of spending allocated National Diffusion Network grant money to "spread the word" about what we were doing and what we had already accomplished. As a result, the PA staff spent quite a bit of time and energy at a variety of schools, leading demonstration classes in adventure education.

On a Spring day in May, Mary Smith (founding staff member) and I were jointly teaching a class at a middle school in Danvers, Massachusetts. Functioning within our customary "What are we going to do today?" quasi-panic mode of operation, the two of us had come up with a bizarre variation of the old childhood game Ring Around the Rosie.* We didn't have a firm objective or solid set of rules established before class, but considering our standard MO and confidence so thick you could cut it with a butter knife, we presented what we did have, convinced that if things didn't work out we would, in the best Calvin & Hobbes tradition, change whatever needed changing to keep the fun quotient high. The following write up is not exactly what we played that day, but the fun 'n games was apparently good enough to get feedback from the players (our absolutely best critics) that led to modifications, embellishments, and changes that resulted in this dynamic and "child-like" initiative, The Clock.

*Ring Around the Rosie—A macabre fairytale usually associated with The Bubonic Plague. It was thought that *Ring Around the Rosie* was a tale, sung by children, that outlined the sequence of death by the plague. Snopes refutes that for any number of reasons. (See *Snopes, Bubonic Plague* on the Internet.) But, to continue this historical flaunting of tradition: "Ring around the rosie" symbolized red roseola marks on the skin of the victim; an initial sign of the plague. "Pocket full of posies"—Fragrant flowers were stuck in the pockets of plague victims to identify their cause of death. "Ashes, ashes"—Actually, Achoo!, Achoo!, as sneezing was another symptom of the plague. "All fall down!"—Everyone is dead. Cheery little ditty, even if of questionable authenticity.

Objective

For a circled group, holding hands, to rotate 360° in one direction, then reverse and rotate 360° back to where they started, and to do this as rapidly as possible.

Rules

- Considering the circle as a CLOCK, place four markers (Frisbees, rubber rings) on the turf inside the circle at 12, 3, 6, and 9 o'clock. The group must rotate around these markers.
- The circled group must start from a seated position (both glutes down) on the turf (floor), holding hands. The stopwatch is started from this seated position.
- Time is not stopped at the end of the double rotation, until everyone is seated in their original START position, still holding hands.
- If hand contact is lost at any time during the double rotation, the CLOCK stops and that attempt is forfeited.
- Before the first attempt, set the number of attempts allowed. Three or four tries should allow enough accumulation of experience to allow a useful

debrief session. Three or four tries (particularly 3 and 4) will also result in an impressive consumption of oxygen and increase in muscular lactic acid; let compassion be your guide.

Considerations

- It's important that you call out START and STOP and identify breaks in hand contact, but equally as important to be a cheerleader for their attempts. Literally cheer-on the circling joggers as they spin around the circle.
- What constitutes a fast time? Let the group establish their own world record, then do their best to break that record.
- If you want to give the group a time to shoot for, count the number of participants, subtract five and use that number for the number of seconds allowed for the double rotation.

Debrief Questions

- Why did the group have so much trouble maintaining contact?
- Was it important to have fast runners in the group?
- Would the team have achieved a better time by eliminating slow runners?
- Was the time important at all? What was important?
- What was this initiative task all about?

Corky

Objective

The object is to propel a single wine cork as efficiently as possible the length of the venue being used (large room, gym, field house), using only the rubber bands provided as means of propulsion. "First cork that hits the far wall wins." If you want the activity phase to last longer, ask the teams to move up *and* down the court.

Set Up

- Tape a starting line on the floor at one end of the gym, or better yet, ditch the tape and use the basketball lines on the court.
- Each team of three is provided with three identical #33 (3— 1/2" × 1/8") rubber bands and one cork. I usually present this activity after some other rubber band challenge (Two-Lip Traverse, for example), so that each participant already has a trusty, warmed-up rubber band.
- Each cork has been pre-marked with a number, letter, or symbol for identification. The team cork is then placed on the floor behind the START line and may not be touched again until the GO! signal is initiated.

- Teams are given three minutes to plan how to best move their cork. During this planning time the corks may not be touched, but teams can manipulate the rubber bands in any way (cut, wrap, connect, discard) that seems useful toward achieving their goal.

- After the GO! signal, the corks may be picked up and forwarded only by propulsive use of the rubber bands.

See the photo depicting what I believe is the best technique for distance... but then I've been wrong before; be ready for the unexpected.

Rules

- The cork may not be thrown, kicked, blown, carried, or propelled in any way other than by the inherent action/reaction of the rubber bands.
- After the start, members of the team may situate themselves on the gym floor as best suits their team's purpose.
- If a rubber band breaks, <u>one</u> substitute band will be provided.
- Try to use corks made of the same substance. (I know it must be shocking to oenophiles within the group, but many wine corks are now manufactured of a synthetic not-even-cork-like material. Gad!)

Variations

- At the end of the three-minute planning time ask the groups of three to join together with another group of three, then provide two additional minutes to share information among the now six players and come up with one cooperative plan.

As facilitator, do not announce that the groups of three will eventually become groups of six; let it occur as something they have to deal with. Discuss the positive and/or negative effects about the joining or redistributing of groups with the resultant sharing (or not sharing) of ideas.

- Set up as above, but change the challenge by stating that each troika will get only one shot and that the best distance will determine the winner. After an additional two-minute planning time, arrange all teams at one end of the "shooting range" and distribute the corks. Suggest the cork shots be taken in sequence, allowing ample time for comments and laughter. If more than one team hits the far wall of the room or gym, have a "cork off" to determine the ultimate cork champ for the day. Highest hit on the wall wins . . . something.
- Provide each troika with two corks and allow two shots. The corks can either be fired independently or together, i.e., corks held together by one of the rubber bands.
- It may interest you to know (particularly if you have money riding on the result) that a rubber band stretched and held at full stretch for a few seconds will lose a large percentage of its propulsive potential. A band pulled and released almost immediately from full stretch will provide much more of a kinetic "kick."

Count Off

I forget who first told me about this surprisingly effective initiative, but I do remember being astonished that it was so well-received; it just didn't seem to have what I thought was the predictable content necessary to capture and hold a group's imagination and interest. So much for my on-again/off-again gaming instincts. This no prop, no talking, easily presented initiative has a lot to say about how a group communicates and also how they handle frustration.

Objective

For a group to count out loud from 1 to 20 without having two people say the same number simultaneously.

Set Up

- For best results the group (10–30) needs to be re-arranged. (Without this re-arrangement, a group almost inevitably ends up in a circle, anathema to the challenge.) Ask everyone to put their "Bumpers Up," close their eyes, and mill around for about 20 seconds. Explain that you will be there to make sure no one "mills away." Do not announce the purpose of the initiative, closing their eyes, or the milling . . . yet.

At the end of the milling-about ask everyone to stop, open their eyes, but not to change the orientation of their body or their position, i.e., don't move. As you are offering instructions, keep moving around the clustered group so that members of the group are not tempted to change their orientation to hear you.

Rules

- State the objective as above, also indicating that unlimited attempts can be made.
- Indicate that no one is allowed to talk or give signals that indicate they are about to offer a number, such as a nod of the head, stomping their foot, grunting, etc. Be there as referee to make sure this rule is followed.
- If a minimum of two people say the same number simultaneously, counting starts over again. The need to return to one (1) does not have to be announced by the facilitator as the blunders become self-evident.

In the many times I have presented this no prop initiative, it is predictable that the group will come close, if not succeed, on their first attempt. Subsequent bids don't even come close, which I suspect has to do with being more relaxed and "unconscious" during the first attempt. If they do reach 20 on the first try, suggest they have-another-go to preclude being just lucky. I've never experienced a group reaching 20 twice in a row without a plan.

How can a group solve a problem without being able to communicate in a predictable way? How can members of a group let each other know what needs to be done without the predictable fall-back means of communicating: talking, uttering, or making sounds and body movements? Give the group an opportunity, after completing their attempts, to talk about what they did, or didn't do, toward reaching their goal. This might also be a good time to ask the group why they thought you had them mill around with their eyes closed before the challenge was stated.

Possible Solution

If the group (usually one or two people at first) begins to see (hear) a pattern and respond to that pattern in subsequent attempts, progress toward the goal can be recognized and acted upon. For example if, as a player, I say (1), and two people then say (2), starting over is indicated. If I once again say (1) and someone successfully says (2), then someone may even sneak in a (3) before two people mess up on (4), and we're back once again to the start. IF these four people eventually, through repetition, begin to recognize a developing pattern and insist on interjecting "their" number quickly and loudly, it

begins to dawn on the other players that they have to keep quiet, as the developed sequence is stated, then try to interject their own trial and error number until 20 is reached. If attempts are unlimited, there is no consequence to failure, and therefore incremental failures (trial and error) become less of a **pejorative** and more of a positive learning experience; a silently based experiential learning cycle in this case. Yeah team!

The Diminishing Load/The Monster

The Diminishing Load and The Monster initiative problems are much alike; both are non-prop initiatives that are easy to present, require an unequivocal physical effort, and must be evaluated carefully by the facilitator to preclude injury.

The Diminishing Load

Objective

To move a group across an open area (field or gym) as quickly and/or as efficiently as possible. This initiative can be attempted for either speed or lowest number of trips.

Rules

- To successfully cross the field or gym, a person must be carried.
- Keep the distance to be crossed challenging but reasonable considering your group's age and fitness level.
- If the carried person touches the ground en route, both people must return to the start.
- The carrier must return to the start and be carried.
- The only person allowed to walk or run across the open area is the last person, after having carried someone across.

- Remember, this problem can be done either for speed (stopwatch), or to see how few trips can be made (efficiency).

Caveat

Some participants (usually young, fit males) will often heroically attempt to carry more than their joints and ligaments can handle, particularly if encouraged by the remainder of the group. A piggyback carry with one, perhaps two, reasonably sized riders isn't much to worry about, but watch out for the Superman syndrome, i.e., piling on.

The Monster a.k.a. The Four Pointer

The question becomes, if both these initiatives are risky (possible piling-on injury), why use either one? Injury occurs when bad decisions are made, like in any **perceived risk** situation. Be there to make sure the right decisions are considered. On the positive side, both of these initiatives require a bounteous amount of **unselfconscious touching**, and the communication/cooperation dyad is in-your-face unavoidable.

Objective

To move a group of seven people across an outlined 20' span of gym floor or grassy turf using only a maximum of four simultaneous points of human contact with the floor/grass.

Rules and Considerations

- "Human contact" (as above) may be a foot, hand, knee, etc. How about someone's back? Is there only one point of contact as the person's back rests on the floor? Probably not, check it out. How about gluteus contact? Two glutes, two points of contact.
- The four points of human contact can be repeated over and over, but there can be no more than four contact points at one time.
- No props allowed, just people.

- All seven people must be in constant physical contact with one another.
- Depending upon the size of your group, The Monster can be set up with different numbers of participants by varying the points of contact with the floor (ex., three points of contact for five people).
- If a particular Monster looks precarious, provide appropriate spotting.

Remember, considering all these fabricated initiative-type problems, *physical success* is measured by getting the whole group through the task, not just the most capable members. *Conceptual success* is measured by how the group responds and feels about the effort made together as a team.

Everybody Up

At one time the simplistic initiative Everybody Up seemed to be everybody's favorite and probably still is with many: no props; simple presentation; lots of ideas for discussion; bunches of touches; heaps of sharing; a decent amount of laughter with one another, rather than directed at someone in particular; what's not to like?

Objective

Start off with two people sitting, facing one another, and attempt to pull each other into a standing position. Two people increases to four, then six, eight, and eventually the whole group–all standing together somewhat simultaneously from a sitting position.

Set Up and Rules

- Ask two people of approximately the same size to sit on the floor (turf) facing one another so that the soles of their footwear are opposed to one another, heels on the ground.

- Knees are well bent and hands tightly clasped with your partner.
- From this stylized seated posture ask the partners to push and pull against one another (counterforce—feet pushing, hands pulling) so that both players rise to a standing position simultaneously.
- If the pair is successful, ask them to seek out another pair who have also performed the duo stand effectively, then (after sharing first names and go-for-it comments), try to perform the standing maneuver as a quad.
- Continue adding people until either the group all make the stand successfully, or don't, and initially they probably won't.
- Criteria for a successful stand: (1) Constant hand and foot contact throughout so that a hypothetical electrical current could run through the expanding group. (2) All derrieres off the ground at about the same time. (3) All finish in a standing (staggering) position.

Considerations

An expanding group will soon find that the seemingly logical, and up-to-this-point usually successful, circular configuration of bodies cannot be enlarged beyond 8–10; the laws of levers and quantum physics* just won't let it happen. A change of thinking, or initiative, must be attempted to come up with a solution that allows large numbers of people (10 or more) to complete the task. Probably the

*quantum physics—I just said that to make it sound good. Hey, maybe it's true!

easiest technique as the group gets larger, is for them to remember what worked at the beginning and try to replicate that success. If one-on-one positioning seemed to work initially, flatten the circle until everyone returns to a vis-a-vis stance, i.e., face to face with another participant. This is humorously referred to as the "flat balloon technique." If an adrenalin pumped, enormously smiling group jogs over to you after having stumbled and jerked to a tenuous standing position and breathlessly asks, "Did we make it?",

need I suggest what your response should be? Are they emotionally high? Is it obvious they feel good about their effort and one another? Did they make it?

Variation

An alternate way to present this initiative is to ask the participants to sit back-to-back and try to stand as a pair, a quad, etc. Do not allow interlocked arms for safety reasons.

Initiatives

Group Juggling to Warp Speed

This ball-tossing initiative is one of the best, and may easily become your favorite "go-to" facilitating tool.

Objective

While standing in a circle, to establish a person-to-person throwing pattern among the participants, then add additional throwables, until there are as many throwables being kept aloft as there are people in the circle. Having accomplished this, or having made a decent attempt, segue to a speed challenge, determining how fast your team can pass a ball from person to person (completing the original sequence) without dropping the ball.

Group Juggling

Set Up

- Ask your larger group to break up into smaller teams of 8–12 individuals, and for that team to stand in a 12'–15' diameter circle.
- Have available enough soft throwables (Nerf balls, bean bags, stress balls) to equal the number of people in the group. Tennis balls are marginally OK if you make sure the group realizes that a smack in the head with even a lightly tossed tennis ball lowers the trust factor you have tried so hard to establish.
- Be a participant, i.e., you as part of the throwing circle. Put all the throwables at your feet.

Procedure

- Ask everyone to extend their arms, elbows bent and palms up. This tentative position is an unspoken indication that you have not yet received a ball. After you have caught and passed a ball to someone else, lower your arms.
- To begin, toss (loft) one of the balls to anyone in the circle except to the person directly to

your right or left. Explain what *loft* means from a throwing standpoint. It seems there's always some troglodyte who thinks it's hilarious to fire a ball at someone who is not suspecting a hard throw.

- Ask everyone to remember whom they threw to, and whom they received from. Keep the ball going until everyone has received and tossed a ball. You started the process, you should also be the final receiver. Ask the group to toss through this identical sequence again, and then one more time to cement the sequence.
- Indicate that if a ball is dropped to just pick it up and continue; don't stop.
- After the group seems confident with the established toss and throw sequence, start the sequence again, but this time add another ball. Every time you begin an additional sequence add another ball until, ideally, there will be one ball per person being "juggled" by the group. This will take some practice; don't be in a hurry.
- Suggest keeping the balls going, i.e., don't have the sequence end with you.

Variations

- Introduce a raw egg into the throwing sequence without announcing its inclusion. Have at least a couple eggs available; heh, heh. . . .
- Try reversing the sequence after 3–4 balls are aloft.

Consideration

There are a number of programmatic goals being sought here so don't let the group needlessly stress out on keeping the balls aloft. Balls are going to be dropped, and the group is going to have deal with that; talk about it.

Warp Speed

- Use the same throw and catch sequence as above, but this time use only one throwable and emphasize speed, i.e., how long it takes for the throwable to be touched <u>in sequence</u> by the whole team. Using a stopwatch, time these

thinking out of the box, suggests making a straight line with the sequenced throwers standing next to one another. All will look to you for an administrative yea or nay. Remind them that this is an *initiative* problem, and ask if standing in a straight line is representative of someone's *initiative*. They need to know that administrative decisions are not arbitrary but based on maintaining a realistic challenge.

- Allow attempts to continue until the team is satisfied with their final time and attempt. If you have seen faster times, it is not necessary to compare them with another group. If asked, tell them that their very excellent attempt was the best you have seen all day, and might even be a world's record.

attempts, suggesting that the team try to reach "warp speed," a nebulous but recognizable state characterized by spontaneous laughter, cheering, and/or applauding.

- The group will usually maintain their circle arrangement for a few attempts, until someone,

Consideration

Did they reach *Warp Speed*? Did they laugh, applaud, and cheer their own efforts? When was the last time you got to applaud (actually applaud) something you did? There needs to be more of this.

Hog Call

I think we named this loud and raucous game back in the 70s, but the game itself, even if we did tweak the rules a bit, looks and sounds an awful lot like

Barnyard. (You make the noise of an assigned animal to find your partner, who is also making an identical noise and looking for you—don't be a giraffe!) Hog Call is a useful game to play with a new group, allowing people to get to know one another better in a trust-oriented, and ice-breaking format.

Objective

To find your partner, after having been separated by some distance, with eyes closed, and repeatedly

Initiatives

yelling one half of an agreed upon . . . (1) pair of words (PEANUT/BUTTER), (2) split phrase (YOU CAN/DO IT), or (3) free-form verse (YOU ARE THE SUN/SHINE OF MY LIFE.)

Set Up and Rules

- Do a line up of some sort that keeps best friends from standing next to one another (ex., line up by birthday (day, month, and year), or your street number, or first name, alphabetically). Fold the line in half so that everyone is facing someone; paired off. If you end up with a single person, assign him/her to a pair to create a triplet.
- Have that pair choose two words that rhyme or go together somehow: Bing-Bang; Hip-Hop; Peanut-Butter; Hot-Cold; Wrigley-Field; Slip-Slop; Shrek-Fiona. The pair must then decide which word or sound belongs to whom.
- Choose one of the participant's words or sounds (yes, you!) and shout it as loudly as you can to demonstrate what type of volume is expected. Experience shows that if you want someone, or a group, to perform an action that is potentially embarrassing, or somehow difficult, you better be prepared to try it yourself. Remember, you don't have to look good, just "try good."
- Separate partners after they have had a chance to practice shouting out their partner's word or phrase, and take the two groups to opposite ends of an open, uncluttered space—sport's field, gymnasium, Wal-Mart parking lot.
- Explain to all that they will be trying to reconnect with their partner, with their eyes closed, by shouting . . . guess what? If you are operating in a gym, make sure you have enough spotters to protect the sightless screamers. Also take time to demonstrate the bumpers up position so that each person feels they have some responsibility for their own safety.
- As the two groups face one another at opposite ends of the field, and before everyone closes their eyes, the quick thinkers will visually connect with their partners and stand opposite one another at a distance. To obviate that advantage, after everyone has closed their eyes, have both groups mill around (bumpers up) for about 15 seconds.

(Have I played this game a few times, or what?)
- Ready, GO! Will everyone be yelling at the same time as the two groups slowly move toward one another? Does all that shouting help? Is this funny?
- When paired members finally find one another, amidst a cacophony of shouted sounds and barely intelligible shrieks, ask the seekers and finders to open their eyes and share with one another information that is appropriate for that group. If they are a just-met group, their names and where they are from make good topics for sharing. If they know one another, ask them to share what they were thinking/feeling (not groping) during the shout-and-seek part of the game.

After a few minutes of pairs' sharing, take the group to a comfortable spot out of the sun and away from distractions (mosquitoes, sun-in-the-eyes, lawnmowers, and the like) and, sitting in a circle, ask anyone to begin the sharing by introducing their partner by their real name and also their shouted name. During this intro, if either partner has something to say (usually funny) about what happened during the Hog Call segment, be open to that; support the sharing. When the second person of the pair is done, he/she chooses another member of a pair, and the introductions and comments continue.

As facilitator, interject observations when appropriate to emphasize a significant point, to keep the comments flowing, or perhaps to support a nervous participant, but otherwise sit back and enjoy the remarks and repartee.

Variation

If you are in an area where shouting would not be appropriate (particularly everyone shouting at the same time), try the Whispered Hog Call. It's simple, just substitute a whisper for a shout as pairs try to reunite. How do you feel about being a Hog Whisperer?

Knots a.k.a. Tangle

I can remember being shown this hands-on activity many years ago and thinking to myself, "This is really simple and effective, how come I didn't think of it?" which I've either said or thought to myself many times since, about a lot of other simple, effective initiative-type problems. The lesson for me was that effective games and initiatives do not have to be complex or prop heavy. Over the years "thinking simple" has served me well . . . most of the time.

Objective

After having formed a "clot" of humans (10–16 bods) by grasping the hands of two separate people, for the well-entwined group to then attempt to undo their "knotted" positioning and end up in an open, hand-in-hand circle.

Set Up

- Each person holds out their right hand and grasps the right hand of someone else, as if they were shaking hands. Then each of those people extend their left hand and grasps the left hand of someone else. Now each person is holding the hands of two different people. If you ended up grasping your own hands, well . . . what can I say.
- With hands tightly grasped, arms entwined, and bodies closely juxtaposed it's time to begin.
- The Gordian cluster (whose positioning transcends any description of "group" I've encountered except for the game Twister) eager to solve the problem (see Objective above), begins the twists, turns, manipulations, distortions, and contortions so inherent to this initiative.

Rules

- The hand-to-hand contact between people cannot be broken in order to facilitate an unwinding movement, in fact, cannot be broken for any reason. Sweaty palms may pivot upon one another, but skin contact must be maintained.

Considerations

- As a result of the initial hand grasping, and depending upon the number of participants, two or even three distinct people-circles (like the old intertwined Ballantine beer circles) might eventually result. Also, in the final circle(s), you may find people alternating as to which direction they are facing, and that's OK; be lenient, this tightly wound initiative already has enough difficulty built in.
- If the group has been struggling with the "knot" for longer than your planned session has time, offer an honorable out called "knot first aid." Indicate that actual hand and arm knots do materialize in this jumble of anatomical parts, and that it occasionally becomes necessary to effect a cure by deciding which grip needs *knot first aid*, i.e., which pair of hands should separate and then re-grip. Solutions are often quickly achieved after the group decides on the best break point.
- Don't be too preliminary in offering aid if time allows and the group seems inclined to continue the struggle. Some groups get so involved they have to be sprayed with a garden hose to loosen their grips–just kidding.

Variations

- If you want to include more people in the original people-knot, offer two lengths of short (4') rope to each person. Rather than holding hands, the ropes (called Buddy Ropes), act as an extension of a participant's arms, allowing more people to be a comfortable part of the action.
- Try using knee-high stockings as people connectors because of the stretch available. *Come to think of it, a short length of surgical tubing would work also.* Hold on, I take that back; a three-foot length of tubing would make a perfect length for snapping someone and there's too many available posteriors around to take a chance. (I could have easily deleted that italicized sentence above, but I wanted you to appreciate the creative process and how all creative ideas are not necessarily good ones.) It gives some credence to the aphorism indicating that, "If you know what you're doing, you're not being creative."

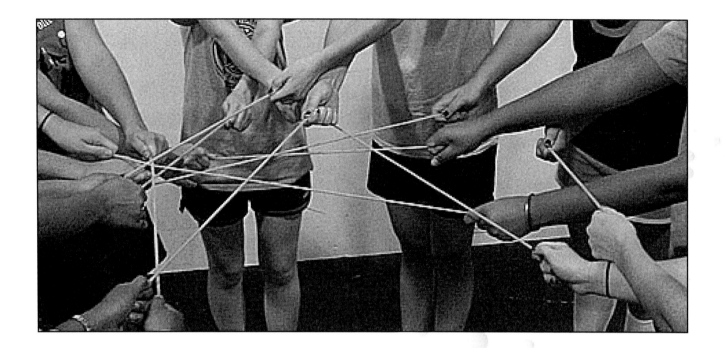

Maple Leaf Drop

I've written various expository pieces over the years on how to use scrap paper as the available prop for different initiative problems. In fact, one former write up is very much like this one, dropping a couple of pieces of paper from a height of about 10 feet and seeing which team can guide their paper closest to an **X** marked on the floor/ground directly below the release point. (*Funn 'n Games*, page 113)

This particular challenge (Maple Leaf Drop) is different in that a couple of extra props are allowed, with success based on the biological notion of seed dispersal . . . "the seed farthest from the tree."

Objective

To drop your delivery package from a minimum height of 10 feet (the higher the better), with the criteria for success being the team that has their package land the <u>farthest</u> from the released plumb line.

Props Provided

Two pieces of unfolded scrap typing paper, one penny ($0.01), and 12" of ½-inch masking tape. Each team of three will have shared access to a scissor.

Rules and Considerations

- Teams of three have 10 minutes to construct their descent package. There is no benefit to finishing early other than the time made available for practice.
- All practice must be accomplished within the limits afforded by simply standing and dropping, i.e., no ladder or balcony can be used for practice.
- At least one full sheet of the two provided must be part of the descent package. If the other sheet is not used, there is no allowance for a second drop.
- Cutting and/or tearing the paper is allowed.
- The penny must be part of the descent package, start to finish.
- Teams should be aware that since this is a competition involving a considerable amount of money and prestige to the winner, practice attempts should be as covert as possible due to corporate spying attempts.

- Establish a plumb line to the floor so that you have a point to measure from. If you have someone in your group named Robert you can ask him, "Is that line Plumb, Bob?"
- Have a measuring tape available to determine a winner (corporate contract provider).
- When released, the package cannot be propelled in any way other than the acceleration provided by gravity.

As with other initiative scenarios of this genre (be the best corporate team in order to win the lucrative contract), you can ask each team to make up a name and sales pitch to go along with their creative "maple leaf." Make sure to provide time for each team's presentation.

If you wish to make the exercise less competitive, i.e., noncompetitive, emphasize the biological benefits of having the seed land as far from the parent tree as possible. (That's why maple seeds spin like a helicopter—you knew that!) Do cheer each effort no matter how inept. You might consider offering the Edward Abbey Seed Dispersal trophy (an empty Blatz beer can) for best attempt.

Mohawk Walk

Interested in the history of the Mohawk Walk? Check out the **vignette** box.

Objective

For a group (ad hoc team) to move across 5–7 tautly strung sections of low cable that are connected from tree to tree, or pole to pole, with the intention of getting the entire team safely from start to finish without touching the ground.

Rules and Considerations

- Unless you are an avowed do-it-yourself type, contact a professional challenge course company to do the installation of your Mohawk Walk. If you decide to buy the gear and carry out the installation yourself, make sure you follow the guidelines made available by the Association of Challenge Course Technology (**ACCT**).

- As you step up onto the first cable (approximately 18" off the ground) know that all the ground under all the cables consists of gelatinous toxic material. If you fall off, or step off, into this miasma of carcinogenic waste, your only chance for survival is to walk back to the start where an environmentally acceptable herbal cleaning solution is located, then begin again from that point, i.e., start over.

- If returning all the way back to the beginning as a default penalty is proving too time consuming, have the offender return only to the support (pole or tree) of the previous cable completed.

- Participants are allowed and encouraged to make physical contact with one another while attempting to cross the cables.

- No props are allowed other than the ones provided.

- Short swings, taut double cables, and strategically placed stumps provide variety as part of the total crossing.

Mohawk Walk

The low-ropes course initiative, now known as The Mohawk Walk, used to be called The Soft Walk (see *Silver Bullets*, page 140). During the early years at Project Adventure, as the staff attempted to "show the world" what we were doing, portability of events was key. One of the low portable challenges we used to set up between trees was a series of taut ropes that allowed moving a balanced group from tree to tree without touching the ground. It was much like the modern Mohawk Walk with shorter sections between supports and experienced as a much "softer" walk, i.e., the ropes exhibiting considerably more slack. As time went by, taut cable replaced rope, longer distances between trees became the norm, more people could participate simultaneously, and portability became a nonfactor.

I remember how quickly the change took place. During an adventure workshop (in Byfield, Massachusetts, for you history buffs), the staff was demonstrating how to tighten a cable between trees. With a cable thus tightened, it was obvious that the benefits of using cable rather than rope rendered the Soft Walk immediately obsolete.

With a new "event" on our hands we asked the present group what we should name it. Two of the workshop participants were Mohawk Native Americans (Kahnawake tribe from the Montreal area of Canada). They jokingly indicated that they represented a minority group, didn't get much notice, so how about naming it after them? I played with the alliteration, came up with the cognomen *Mohawk Walk*, they liked it, and so it's been ever since.

About five years later, also during an adventure curriculum workshop at the same venue, Project Adventure caught some flack from a couple of participants who were very politically correct (PC) about everything. Their contention was that we were demeaning the Mohawk Nation specifically, and Native Americans in general, by frivolously using their tribal name in conjunction with an initiative problem. We kept our cool and were backed up by none other than *the same two Mohawk Native Americans* who had come back for a refresher course. The timing could not have been more perfect or extraordinarily apropos. Their comments and opinions about the PC concerns were classic; I wish I had a recording of what they said. Needless to say the specious concerns and comments about the Mohawk Walk were dropped and not mentioned again . . . by anybody . . . ever.

- If you KNOW that you are about to fall, step off the cable. Slamming into the ground is not going to benefit anyone and is certainly not going to enhance your commitment level.
- Do not try to move swiftly (run) across a cable. If you complete the crossing, there's a good chance you will make fast/hard contact with the support tree. If you do not make it, there's also a good chance you will get "dinged" from hitting the cable on the way down.
- If an attached rope is provided and you decide to tension traverse your way across the cable, you must have two spotters.
- The Mohawk Walk is not a stopwatch event. Allow the group enough time to think through their strategy.

Variations

- Make two crutches* available at the start. A crutch can be used by anyone in the group to help maintain balance on the cable by leaning on the crutch while it's placed in the toxic waste (the ground). However, the contact point of the crutch (the tip) must never be moved backward, i.e., from where it is placed on the ground. If the crutch is moved backward, even $1/8$ of an inch, continued use of the crutch by the group is immediately lost.
- Start two smaller groups at each end of the Mohawk Walk with the intent of having the groups pass one another while on the cables.

Debrief Questions

- What was the leadership situation?
- Did you feel like part of a team, or did you operate as an individual?
- What was the best and worst feelings you had while on the cables?
- Did you learn anything about yourself?
- Do you know what *center of gravity* means and how it applies to this event?
- Was there much laughter during the crossing? If so, why so much humor?

---

*crutches—It seems like most everyone has either broken a bone or knows someone who has broken a bone. Check around to see if any of your damaged acquaintances has an old crutch in the garage or attic that you can use. The use of a crutch is nicely symbolic, but if you can't find one, a stout sapling provides a usable substitute.

Nitro Crossing

How many swing ropes do you think are suspended from tree limbs around the country? Probably tens of thousands, eh? Or is that just me wishing there were that many? When I was younger there sure seemed to be a lot of swinging tires and swing ropes. Most of the swing ropes I see now are on multiple video game screens when I'm at Wal-Mart or the like. Is manipulating a cartoon figure on a swinging rope over a contrived electronic chasm considered an adventure experience? Troublesome questions . . . but I've got tons of experiential proof that real swing ropes are still popular, as evidenced by the comments and reactions of thousands of people over the years who have participated on the two swing-rope initiatives that make up the rubric above and are detailed below. People, young and older, LOVE swinging ropes!

If you have been looking for a couple of initiative situations that are just flat-out popular and which cost next to nothing to install, check out The Nitro Crossing and Prouty's Landing events. Having been a ropes-course installer for decades, I have strongly suggested in the past that people who want a challenge course contact a professional installation company to obviate the hassles of safety, insurance, and equipment esoterica; BUT, in the case of these two elements I'd say, "Go for it!" and do it yourself. All you have to do is hang a swing rope from a convenient limb. Now, having blithely committed you, here's what you really need to know.

- Buy a proper length of synthetic rope. I'd suggest 5/8"-diameter Multiline rope; it's immensely strong, essentially rot proof, and it's kind to your hands, i.e., no yarn splinters.
- Create a round turn with the rope, around the chosen stout limb and tie a backed-up bowline knot. (The round turn helps to keep the rope from chafing.)
- If you are operating in a high vandalism area I'm afraid your very attractive rope won't make it a week before being ripped off or cut. In that case you either need to take in the rope every night (a

huge hassle), or drill the limb, place a bolt, and hang a length of eye swaged cable into which you clip a short length of Multiline rope, (said rope goes in with you each night). And in that case, you will need some installation help. Email either Project Adventure, Inc., or ACCT for assistance.

Objective

To swing the entire group over an active pit of adhesive sulphuric acid (sticky, nasty stuff), without touching the miasmic gunk and without knocking off either of the "trip wires" (both attached to 25 pounds of G4 explosives) located at the beginning and termination of the swing. In addition, a #10 tin can with bail, seven-eighths filled with nitroglycerine (water), must be transported across the pit via the swing rope without losing ONE DROP of the nitro. (You can also set up the rope swing scenario involving life saving herbal supplements, etc.)

Set Up

- The swing rope ordinarily has a loop spliced into the end of the rope. If this is not the case, tie a couple of overhand knots in the end of the rope.
- The nitroglycerine container is filled with water if this initiative is being tried outdoors, or filled with confetti if being attempted indoors. Wooden gym floors don't like water.
- The distance between trip wires shall be determined by the facilitator as to the perceived adeptness of the group. Too hard = frustration; Too easy = boredom.
- The trip wires are installed by balancing a section of rug-roll bamboo (about 12') between two upright soft drink cans at the beginning and end of the swing arc. If bamboo is not available, any fairly straight, stiff, rod-like material will do; a sapling perhaps.
- Make sure the area outlined by the swing arc is free of rocks and punji-like objects that could put holes in people.

Rules

- No knots may be tied in the rope other than the ones already there.
- No props allowed other than what the group brought with them.

- If a loop in the rope is available for use, do not allow people to put their leg <u>through</u> the loop, as disentangling at the end of the swing is difficult and dangerous.
- Get rid of anything in your pockets that could hurt you or injure someone else: keys, pocket knife, pens, and pencils.
- If someone makes even the slightest contact with the ground during a swing attempt, that person must return to the start.
- If either of the trip wires is knocked off, <u>the entire group</u> must begin again. You mean even those who have already made it across? Correct, G4 is unforgiving.

- If any of the water (nitro) is spilled at any time after the start, everyone must begin again. If the spillage noticeably reduces the crossing challenge, the container must be topped off at seven-eighths capacity. Carry along a separate water container to top off the #10 can.
- At the beginning of the challenge, the swing rope must be initially obtained without stepping into the area between the trip wires (see Travesty Concept in Glossary). Do not allow diving for the swing rope; rope burns and worse will result. How about using clothing, shoelaces, or shoes to gain the rope? Yes, yes, and yes.

Nuclear Fence

If you are currently working in the field of adventure/experiential education, you are probably aware that The Electric Fence initiative problem is no longer utilized because of the accident rate associated with its use. Project Adventure's well-known, and often referred to, Adventure Programming Safety Survey, offers ample evidence that accidents occurring on The Electric Fence more than justify black balling the event. Fortunately, a former intern at PA, Brahm Schatia, came up with a creative way to maintain the challenge and excitement and virtually eliminate the danger. I tacked on a new name, obviously without much thought, and the basic Electric Fence initiative continues being used now as *The Nuclear Fence.* (And if anyone thinks of a catchier more appropriate name, please use it.)

Objective

To move your entire group up and over a taut section of small diameter rope, tied at approximately 40" above and parallel to the ground without touching or "breaking the plane" beneath the rope.

Rules

- Everyone in the group must maintain constant contact with someone else in the group <u>at all times</u> so that a proverbial "electric current" could pass through the entire group. If contact anywhere is broken, the person attempting to cross over must return to the start and try again. This essential rule prevents participants from being thrown over the taut rope, the cause of so many injuries in the past.
- If anyone touches the taut rope at any time, the person making an attempt must return to the start and try again.
- The same is true if anyone breaks the plane of the area under the rope.

Considerations

- The height of the taut rope can obviously be varied according to the age and skill of a particular group, just make sure it does not get tied so high that contact between people is consistently being broken in the group's attempt to get someone over. I'd suggest not going over 3½ feet.
- The Electric Fence allowed the use of a board as a prop. The Nuclear Fence allows no props.
- The Electric Fence was often set up as a triangle of ropes. The Nuclear Fence allows only a single strand.
- Stick with the Nuclear Fence rules and you should have negligible problems with injuries.

- As facilitator, you are there to establish and maintain the challenge. I'd strongly suggest not "looking the other way" if the rope is touched, even if that means eventually not getting the entire group over the rope. Challenge courses are not (should not be) designed or built to provide a series of entirely successful completions. Dealing with and learning from occasional failure is essential to **experiential learning.**

Prouty's Landing a.k.a. Swing Aboard

Objective

To see how many people you can swing onto a 3' × 3' platform from a designated starting point approximately 20' away from the platform.

Rules and Considerations

- Before the students show up, try a few swings yourself before locating the platform. Don't be too kind concerning the presented challenge, but remember, the plan is to eventually get everyone onto the platform so place the platform realistically.
- When initially hanging your swing rope, be aware that the higher (longer) the rope, the more gradual and gentle the swing. Short hanging ropes cause a rapid, hard-to-hold-onto swing arc.

- If your group is obviously too large to get everyone on the platform, either use an additional (and smaller) platform, or simply place a used auto tire next to the platform for additional standing area. Do this before you start so that it doesn't look like you are making changes midchallenge.
- If someone touches the ground during the swing or if someone falls off the platform, that person must return to the start. If you have ever played the table-top game "Skittleball," you can appreciate what happens when a substantial (well-covered) swinger comes zinging into a platform full of people; pretty funny actually.
- The swing can start from behind a length of rope laid on the ground perpendicular to the arc of the swing or from behind a "trip wire" arrangement, as in The Nitro Crossing. (Same rules apply.)
- The same swing rope can be used for either The Nitro Crossing or Prouty's Landing.

Punctured Drum

This "get wet" initiative is very prop and venue intensive. You need the right gear and the right place to allow this hilariously funny (I think observers have as much fun as the participants) water challenge to happen. Once those prop and place things are established, Punctured Drum is well on its way to becoming a school classic. "Hey, remember the class three years ago that spilled water all over the . . .?"

Objective

With an unlimited source of water, to fill a 55 gallon, multi-punctured, steel drum to overflowing.

Set Up

* This is the tough part. You need a well-scrubbed 55 gallon steel or plastic drum. Most drums of this type had contents not on the EPA's list of friendly liquids.

If you can find a drum that power washing or steam cleaning will cleanse satisfactorily, go for it.

* If you know someone with a cutting torch, ask them to "cut off" the top for you, explaining, "It's for the kids." Can openers, no matter how expensive or where they are from, are worthless; don't even try. I'm sure your friend with the torch knows not to cut open an unwashed oil drum, but you might want to mention it.
* You also need a fast-flowing source of water and at least a half dozen, one gallon, clean buckets.
* You need holes in the drum to number 10 times the number of participants, i.e., 10 participants = 100 holes (figuring an average of 10 fingers per participant.) You are better off having too many holes than not enough, figuring you can temporarily plug the holes not being used. Hobby stores sell corks in different sizes.
* I've seen the holes in the drum made with a hammer and nails (you're better off using a commercial spike), a geologist's hammer (very fast, but produces irregular diameter holes), and a 3/8" drill bit. Drilling takes considerably longer but makes the best looking holes. If you use a spike or sharp hammer you will have to grind down the interior sharp edges that are produced by the puncture blow; very time consuming.

- Don't make the holes in a pattern that is easy to plug with five spread fingers, encourage the participants to cooperate.
- Drill mostly 3/8" and a dozen or so 1/2" holes to vary the challenge.

Rules

- Pretty simple—plug those holes and keep the water flowing until the drum either overflows or the group's fingers give out.
- Holes can only be plugged with healthy flesh. There are certain anatomical areas of the body not to be used as plugs which I don't feel the need to identify . . . however, no tongues, please.

Considerations

- Establish a no-slip path from the water source to the drum, i.e., no mud.
- The distance from drum to water source obviously increases or decreases the level of challenge; your choice.
- Will the participants get wet? Totally.
- Take a look at your almanac planting calendar. In planting zone 6 do not try Punctured Drum outdoors from early October to mid-April, unless there are a few strong days of Indian Summer. Or, read up about identifying the various stages of hypothermia.
- Considering all the prep time involved, and your half naked participants, allow more than one attempt. And, where's the cameras?

Say What?

About five minutes ago I turned to page 130 in *Silver Bullets* to see if the write-up on Say What? needed additions or embellishments. Say What's quarter-century-old text is only a couple of paragraphs long and there's not much to the actual presentation, so, other than changing a couple of words I was about to move on, when I took a closer look at the illustration created by old friend Plynn Williams. I have no idea how many times I have glanced at that drawing over the past 25 years, but suffice to say, "a lot."

Most of the photos and illustrations for this 25th Anniversary edition are new, but I kept the one on page 130 so I could ask you this question. See anything wrong with the illustration? Check out the completed tangram* the woman is holding then try to relate the five pieces in her hands with the four incongruous balanced pieces held by the puzzled guy. Hmmmm? Maybe the birthday cake had something to do with the discrepancies. Or maybe

Plynn drew it to fit the space available. Whatever, Say What? is a decent exercise in communication. Give it a try.

Ask two people to sit back-to-back on the floor. Supply one of the individuals with an assembled tangram puzzle. The other member of the backward dyad sits, committed to being mute, looking at the jumbled pieces of an identical tangram. The person with the assembled puzzle then attempts to verbally explain to his/her silent partner how to put the pieces together to achieve a congruent solution, and no peeking over shoulders.

The talking/listening/doing procedure can be turtle-like or impressively swift. A joint working knowledge of geometric vocabulary makes the task much easier.

Debrief Questions

- Which seemed most important, the speaking or listening skill?
- Was there any particular stumbling block you encountered as a pair?
- Answering separately, what do you think your partner did to create congruent tangrams?

*tangram—A Chinese puzzle made by cutting a square into five triangles, a square, and a rhomboid and using these pieces to form various pieces and designs—a dictionary definition. For Say What?, as long as the pieces form some type of recognizable polygonal final figure, that's a tangram.

7-UP

There aren't many initiative games I recommend without hesitation . . . 7-UP is one of them.

Objective

For a group of about 12–15 circled players to catch seven sequentially thrown objects, with a new object being added every throwing attempt until all the objects are successfully caught. (I have used the word object here for the item being thrown, i.e., any soft throwable from Nerf Ball to knotted towel.) For this particular write up; object = ball.

Procedure and Rules

- Everyone (including the facilitator) stands in a fingertip-to-fingertip circle. The fingertip thing is just to size-the-circle; put your fingers down.
- The facilitator tells the group that he/she is going to toss a soft throwable object up to a height of about 10 feet so that the arcing ball will land approximately

in the center of the circle. The facilitator, with sincerity, indicates that every time he/she lofts an object it will be with the intention of having that ball land in the middle of the circle—every time.

- Instructions continue that the just-tossed object must be caught by anyone in the group. (People are allowed to step into the circle to make the catch.)
- After the initial catch the facilitator picks up another ball from the six remaining at his/her feet.
- The second ball in play (now about to be lofted by the player who caught the ball) does not need to land in the center and can be directed toward anyone else in the circle. A 10 foot minimum apogee must be reached for all thrown objects, i.e., the ball may not be tossed directly (no loft) to a person.
- Following a count of 1-2-3 by the facilitator, both objects are tossed up simultaneously on 3 and must be caught by different people. If either ball is dropped, the game starts over with the facilitator's initial toss into the center.
- If both balls are caught, the facilitator picks up another ball, then it's 1-2-3 again and all three objects are tossed up, following the previous rules bulleted above.
- This tossing and catching continues until all seven objects are simultaneously tossed and caught, to triumphant shouts of "Yeah!" or whatever.

Considerations

- To be safe, make sure your tossed objects are soft; no hockey pucks or shot puts, even tennis balls are too hard for this initiative.
- If you don't have any soft throwables at hand, distribute six sheets of scrap paper (all the same size), and ask those with paper sheet in hand, to **"origami"** them (a barely acceptable verb in this case), into a ball sized wad, i.e., crumple the paper. Why not seven wads? The final throwable object should be of a different color, size, and texture to identify itself as the final object and to increase the chance of dropping it; an additional challenge. A small stuffed or soft toy as a final object is ideal.

- As facilitator you will probably have to make mention of keeping all the thrown objects on a high arc, as the temptation of making a direct, low throw to another person is almost irresistible.
- As facilitator, keep up the pace of the activity, at the same time allowing and suggesting brainstorming and discussion among the participants.
- This initiative game seems initially easy but will soon test the group's physical skill, group cohesiveness, and sense of repetitive endurance.
- Remember, you are involved as a quasi-participant. Your role as initiator and thrower is to establish and maintain the challenge. Resist the temptation to offer advice or help. Maintain your role as cheerleader and support mechanism.

Debriefing

- If you attempt this initiative game with more than 15 people, someone will probably find themselves without an active hands-on role. Talk about the various roles within a group that are essential toward solving a problem.
- Talk about multitasking and diminishing returns as pertains to the number of balls in the air simultaneously and how many are not being caught. What can be done about achieving the task of catching all the balls (answering the phone while talking to a client, while looking for a file . . .)?
- What's the pragmatic application of lessons learned to school, home, or in-the-office situations?
- Ask questions to cause questions. Probe for specific answers without having to ask the questions.

The Spider Web

The Spider Web is probably the most popular and best known of all challenge course initiative problems; pretty heady stuff when you consider the number of activities available. The "web" is inexpensive to build and install, fits almost anywhere, can be made portable, and has an acceptable mix of challenge and fantasy.

Objective

To maneuver your entire group through a fabricated spider-type web without touching the ersatz web material ($^3/_{16}$" diameter bungee cord). "To maneuver through" means physically passing individuals from one side of the vertical web to the other side.

Rules and Considerations

- Most webs are fabricated with 12–15 web openings. As a participant passes through a web opening, that particular opening closes for the remainder of the attempt, i.e., a body can only pass through a web opening once. If a person touches a section of web and has to return for another attempt, that particular web aperture remains open.
- During an attempt, if any part of the web is touched by <u>any</u> participant, the person trying to get through the web opening must return to the start and try again. To make the challenge considerably more difficult, require that everyone who had already made it safely through the web to also return.
- Timing this event, I believe, is counterproductive.

Fabrication Tips

Or, to save time, you may want to check out the Spider Web Kit available at Project Adventure. Call 1-800-468-8898, Ext. 4556.

- Find two trees about 15' apart, or firmly sink two 4 × 6 boards vertically about that same distance apart. Make sure the area between the two uprights is clear of all rocks, sticks, roots, etc.
- Place $^3/_8$" staples, or $^3/_8$" eye screws (pre-drill before placing) on the inside of the uprights at the following three heights—7 feet, 4 feet, and 1 foot above ground. Place the staples as pairs facing

Spider Web

From the years 1979 to 1995 I authored and distributed a quarterly periodical called "Bag of Tricks." I don't think I ever had more than 500 subscribers, but the discipline of "getting out the copy" every three months kept me on top of my game and allowed a satisfying level of sharing to take place. Most of the material that made up the text of the original *Silver Bullets* (publishing date 1984) came from "Bag of Tricks."

During those years of creating and recording ideas, I occasionally received a tip or trick from a subscriber that I would pass along. I can't remember the year, but I received a letter and two poorly focused photos of something the writer called The Spider Web. The letter's content consisted of a couple of paragraphs explaining the faded photographs and honestly, held little interest. So I stuck the letter and photos in my "holding" area, a back-of-the-drawer slot just short of the "circle" file.

A couple of years went by and during one lean quarter I found myself a bit weak on "Bag of Tricks" content, so I went to the file and pulled out the Spider Web info, tried to make the letter content seem more attractive, and hoped the readers wouldn't complain about the fuzzy photographs. The rest is experiential education history as the Spider Web became, and continues to be, one of the most popular low initiatives ever offered. So much for my keen sense of play, fun, challenge.

The author of that letter was a guy named John Jarboe. If you ever run into him offer a "Nice Going!" and tell him to drop me a line.

directly toward one another. You will need a total of six staples to do this. Horizontal orientation of the staples is best.

- Reeve a length of ³/₈" Multiline rope (or any decent rope of that diameter) through all six staples and secure the two rope ends together with your favorite bend. (Try eye splicing one end of the rope then reeving the other end through that eye splice; pull the rope taut and finish off with two half hitches.)
- Cutting sections of ³/₁₆" bungee cord, tie one end of the cord (use a Prusik knot or a taut line hitch) to the frame rope (anywhere on that rope) and tie the other end of the bungee to the opposite side

of the frame rope. To make sure your web strand is taut, cut the bungee length about a foot short of the distance required and stretch the bungee before tying the Prusik knot. Tying a Prusik knot (or taut line hitch) allows you to adjust the size of the web openings by moving the Prusik up or down the frame rope.

- Continue cutting and tying bungee lengths until you have the number of web openings that best accommodates the number in your group. Bungee cord of this small diameter can often be found in a fabric shop.
- (optional) To keep the frame rope taut on the bottom, drive two eight-inch staples over the bottom rope and into the turf. Make sure you drive (mallet or hammer) the staples flush with the turf to prevent injury. Finish fabricating the web openings before whacking in the staples.
- If you want to make your web portable, use small rapid links (or those "toy" carabiners that seem so ubiquitously popular) to clip into the six vertically oriented staples. At the end of a session unclip the color coded links (red link to red staple, etc.) and remove the entire web. To keep the web from getting tangled, place the web on a section of sheet and roll up the sheet with the web inside, labeling top and bottom. Seem like a hassle? Wait 'til you try to undo an upside down tangled web!
- Try to find one of those horrible looking rubber spiders to dangle from your web for that just-right touch of organic surrealism.

Implementation and Safety

- Require that all participants remove pencils, pens, keys, etc., from their pockets.
- Do not allow diving attempts through web openings.
- People can be passed through a web opening but only head first; a safety consideration.
- Participants should not consider going over the web.
- It's OK to relax and enjoy the attempt, but do not allow physical or verbal horse play when passing someone through the web.
- Coats and shoes can be removed if temperatures permit.
- Remember—you don't have to succeed to be successful.

Variations

- Attempt to weave a 75' length of rope back and forth through the web openings without touching the web. Use a longer section of rope to increase the challenge and vice versa. All participants start on the same side of the web.
- For greater numbers of participants, build another vertical section of web at right angles to the first web.
- Handicap high-performing groups: blindfolds, loss of speech, only one person allowed to talk, one person to be completely limp, (not the group's largest!).

Processing Questions

- Did you need a leader? Was there a leader?
- Were you pleased with your group's performance? Why or why not?
- Why call this activity *The Spider's Web*? Why not call it *The Bungee Break Out*?
- Was there fear involved with the attempt? Fear of what?
- Were the handicaps unreasonable?
- Why didn't you just disregard the rule about touching the web?

Spinner

Objective

Using <u>only</u> the provided materials, to create a spinning top and to spin that top longer (duration of spin) than any of the other teams attempting to accomplish the same thing.

Materials Provided

2—small marbles
2—large round-headed push pins
Modeling clay (enough to make a 1½" diameter ball)
Access to a set of Tinker Toy-type props, particularly the hub and spokes
18" of ½" masking tape

Rules and Considerations

- After providing the objective, the materials, and the rules, allow eight minutes of hands-on prep and practice time.
- Each team of 3–4 players is allowed two official timed spins, attempted sequentially.
- Each team can attempt as many practice spins as they like during the allotted eight minutes.

- Time starts when the top is spun. Time ends when the top ceases all movement.
- All spins for record are attempted on an identical flat surface. That flat surface cannot be moved.
- If spins are attempted on a table top and the spinning top falls from the table, that attempt is void.
- All team spinning devices must be placed within a secure area before the official spinning attempts begin. Once in the secure area, no practice attempts or physical alteration of a top are allowed.
- Spins of over 30 seconds have been achieved.
- There are obviously other props and materials that lend themselves to creating a spinning top. Be creative. Be safe.

- It's up to you whether to allow blowing. A dedicated team can cause a top to spin for over five minutes. Are you ready for that?

Questions

- What was the curriculum objective of this activity?
- Did the competitive aspect add or detract from the exercise?

- What did you like most and least about the activity?
- What was your incentive for building the best top?
- Was everyone on your team an active part of the team?
- Did you try to copy what another team was doing?
- What's the difference between cooperating and cheating?

Stickum Up

I was messing around with a roll of gym tape one day and this is what happened.

Objective

To retrieve a handful of quarters from a plastic tumbler located in the center of a 12' diameter circle, using (or not using) the available props that may (or may not be) essential to the coin's removal.

Props Needed (Maybe)

- A 12-foot diameter circle, (which happens to exactly duplicate the dimension of a painted-on basketball jump circle)
- Plastic drinking tumbler
- About 15 quarters to place in the tumbler (or nickels, but quarters are more impressive)
- 25 additional quarters . . . or nickels
- A 4-foot length of 1-inch plastic gym tape; 1" blue painter's tape is also a good choice.

Rules

- The tumbler, with about 15 quarters therein (arbitrary number—what's in your wallet?), is located in the center of a 12-foot diameter circle.
- The cup may not be touched by the provided tape.
- The tape or quarters may not touch the area within the outlined circle.

- Participants may not touch the area within the outlined circle, or the cup, with any part of their body, clothing, other materials in the room, or any other organic or inorganic substance in the Universe.

Considerations

- The cup must be placed on a smooth surface, i.e., not a Berber rug.
- If this problem is being attempted for time, any touching within the circle results in a one hour penalty. If not being attempted for time, a simple "That's illegal!" is sufficient.
- Make up a funny or gripping story about why you need to retrieve the quarters from the cup (ex., for use at a casino (slot machines) to win the money necessary to save the local animal-humane-society's-state-subsidized-building from being razed).

Solution #1

Lay the tape on the floor sticky side up. (Stickum Up!) Take the 25 loose quarters and stick them individually onto the gummy side of the 1" tape so that a file of well-adhered side-by-side quarters is made available. (Did you notice that quarters are also 1" in diameter? A good thing to know if someone asks you how many quarters in a foot.) Have two, tall, meso/ectomorphic participants stand opposed to one another at the outside diameter locations of the circle, one of the individuals delicately holding an end of the taped quarters. Each of these two participants need to be supported by at least one endo/meso participant in such a way that the "ecto" participant can be lowered cantilever style (feet remaining outside the circle), into the circle's space.

This support-by-hand, Mission Impossible ploy is similar to the way people retrieve Twirlies from center circle in the initiative Twirlie Bulls Eye. (*Funn 'n Games*, pages 80–82)

The participant holding the taped quarters is lowered first, immediately followed by their cross-circle partner. The free end of the pendulumed taped quarters is adroitly grasped by that second, inclined, person. The now jointly held, well-quartered tape ($6.25 worth) is positioned by the cantilevered holders so that the <u>quarter side</u> is gently swept toward the cup—don't touch the floor—until contact with the cup is made. The sweep/slide

continues until the cup and quarters within can be retrieved by one of the other team members. Done!

Solution #2

Stick enough quarters on one end of the tape so that a loop can be formed (like a cowboy's lariat). One supported person then leans into the circle and slips the lariat loop over the tumbler and pulls it to the edge of the circle. This is not easy, but I've seen it done and feel obligated to alert you to the fact that it can be accomplished so a group doesn't blindside you with their creativity.

TP Shuffle

I have to admit to naming this low-ropes course activity; an obvious double entendre depending upon your interpretation of TP as either *Telephone Pole* or *Toilet Paper*. Interpretation aside, it is, after all, just a log lying on the ground.

In the 1984 version of *Silver Bullets* I spent quite a few sarcastic sentences explaining how easy it was to install a TP Shuffle log. Twenty-five years later it hasn't gotten any harder. To wit, check out this quarter-century-old quote defining how to "build" a TP log.

> "With a conscripted class, or a few strong friends, arrange the chosen telephone pole (TP) horizontally on a flat, level, grassy or nongrassy area. Done! Yahoo . . . I could build ropes courses all day."

Objective

To have about 12–14 people standing on top of a 30' log, exchange places so that one half moves to the other end, and the other half takes their place . . . and without falling off the log.

Set Up

- Ask 14 people to balance on top of the log so that seven people on the right, and seven people on the left, are all facing toward the middle.
- To increase the challenge and make the facilitator's job of spotting ground touches easier, support each end of the log (about two feet in from each end) on a perpendicularly placed short (3 foot) section of log. **Do not cut these 3' sections from the 30' log!** Drill through the top log and into the shorter log beneath with a ½" diameter extension bit. Then using a sledge, drive a ⅝" × 16" machine bolt through the top log into the log beneath. Drive the bolt head flush with the top log's surface. Well done Sir Builder.

Rules and Considerations

- If exchanging ends is used as a timed event, it is considered a penalty (20 seconds) if someone touches the ground. If the event is being attempted just to see if it can be done, and in the event of a penalty, have the person suffering a ground touch return to the position where he/she started.
- As with all timed initiative problems, it is important to allow more than one attempt to allow the magic of trial and error to make more of failure, and less of quitting.
- People can be lifted off the log. Sitting or lying on the log is also allowed.
- If you chose to support the 30' log on two short log sections (as outlined above), you are not allowed to stand or balance on those short perpendicular logs.

- Characteristically, participants really get into this challenge and do not want to be told their time is up. If you recognize your group as being very motivated, it's easier to set a time limit at the beginning than limiting time at the end.

Variation

Try the basic change of positions challenge with eyes closed and/or not talking.

Traffic Jam

Traffic Jam and Two by Four are both decent no-prop initiatives, but frustrating to write about again, as the solutions to both are immutable and after 25 years, haven't changed much. So, don't expect much different from me in the next couple of pages, because there's not much different to tell you, as Traffic Jam and Two by Four continue to confound and frustrate generation after generation of experientialists . . . like you!

I forget the moves to this scratch-in-the-dirt problem every time I use it with a group, but I've yet to see a group who did not eventually come up with THE (there's only one) solution. Don't worry about remembering the jump-here, step-there moves as long as you get the rules straight. If the group asks probing questions, offer an occasional "Hmmmmm," or "What do you think?" Nodding your head affirmatively also helps, particularly when you are Hmmmming.

Objective

The objective of this largely trial-and-error problem is to have two columns of people facing one another, change places on a line of squares (one person per square) that has one more place than the number of people participating. See boxes-in-a-line at top of next page, with arrows representing people. When completed, the group on the left will have changed places with the group on the right. This activity is not ordinarily done for time.

Set Up

- The boxes illustrated can be rubber or plastic gym spots, paper plates, squares scratched in the dirt, taped squares, circles etched with sulphuric acid in the polished gym floor, etc.
- Eight people represent a decent challenge. More people rachet up the challenge to the point of frustratingly difficult; not where you want to be.
- Both groups (must be equal number) start off facing one another with a blank space separating them.

Rules

- The following represent legal moves:

1. A person may move into an empty space in front of them.

2. If two people are face to face, one of those persons may move around the person he/she is facing if there is an empty space to move into.

- The following are considered illegal moves:

1. Any move backward.
2. If you are facing someone's back, you may not move around that person.
3. Any move that involves two people moving at the same time.

Considerations and THE Solution

- This is a difficult initiative problem so don't present it 15 minutes before lunch. Be prepared for considerable frustration, even anger. You may have to call a temporary halt and suggest that the group talk about not so much the solution, rather what they are trying to achieve by working together on this problem.
- I don't blame you for wanting to know the solution, notwithstanding my cavalier suggestion of how to respond to student questions. So here's the solution, and I'll bet you forget it before you present it. Remember the solution below or remember to say,

"Well . . . what do you think?"

X	X	X	X		O	O	O	O
1	2	3	4	5	6	7	8	9

When the first person moves, notice whether she moves into an odd or even space. If she moves into an odd space, she and her teammates only move into odd-numbered spaces until each member reaches their final destination. The other team moves only into even spaces until each member is home.

Variation

If the group proves to be one of those high performing types that blasts through all your carefully planned and calculated initiative problems, try the following. After the group comes up with a solution to *Traffic Jam*, ask them to try it again, just to prove they really knew what they were doing, and maybe even a third time to solidify their performance as a team. After the third successful completion, ask if there is anyone in the group who has it down cold, that is, someone who could lead a new group through the various necessary maneuvers. By this time there is bound to be some hotshot who thinks he/she has the solution "nailed." Ask that person to lead the group one more time through the shuffling, twisting turns that end up with everyone in the correct position. Then, hit 'em with the REAL challenge.

Ask the committed participants to hold their collective breaths for the time required for the leader to maneuver the anoxic group to a solution. The leader is allowed to breathe, the group is not. It's interesting to see how external stress can play havoc with confident performance. Ready . . . GO!

Trolley

If you don't have at least one set of Trolleys you don't have much of an adventure program. (Author's specious and sarcastic comment in a weak attempt at in-the-know humor.) But it's partially true; it seems there are Trolleys of every shape, size, and consistency: long ropes, short ropes, alternating ropes, thick boards, skinny boards, fabric velcroed boards, inflated boards, Duct tape boards, gellin' boards, and virtual boards. Virtual boards? Sure, just stand there within a column of in-tune people, think good thoughts, intone Ommmmm and soar, hover, or glide (your choice) to your destination. Happy landings and you can't beat the price. Kidding aside, The Trolley is a classic and highly useable initiative problem that participants enjoy and look forward to trying more than once.

Objective

To move a group of 3–12 people over a designated 30'–50' span of "poison peanut butter" using only the two provided rope-festooned sections of 4" × 4" lumber.

Trolley Construction

Before getting into the potential hassles of a handyman Trolley, you might want to buy a pre-made pair sold currently by a number of companies that specialize in adventure programming gear. Contact the folks at Project Adventure, Inc. (See contact information on one of the last pages in this book.) But, if you like to saw, drill, fabricate, and do it yourself—here's how . . . and it's not difficult, just time consuming.

- Trolley 4 × 4's can be as short or as long as your group needs dictate. A set of Trolleys four feet long with room for two people might be useful for a special needs population, or for younger students who have trouble cooperating beyond a one-on-one situation. Trolleys up to 16 feet, and even longer, have been built for large groups.
- For the Trolley boards, buy the least expensive 4 × 4 stock available. Don't try fabricating Trolleys from 2

× 4 boards because the 2" measurement (actually closer to 1½") isn't thick enough to countersink the hand line knots, and if you leave the overhand knots on the surface of the boards it makes "walking" attempts difficult beyond challenging.

- Using a try-square tool, draw a line across the 4 × 4 board every 12", and on this line find the center of the board. Using a 1½" drill bit, drill each one of the center marked lines to a depth of 2". If you have access to a drill press, use it and save yourself a heap of effort. If not, use a <u>new</u> spade bit (Speedbor) in a powerful enough portable drill to handle the work load. These holes can also be drilled with a bit brace. I mention this only as a veiled challenge, having drilled a few 4 × 4's this way some time ago. If your boards measure 12' long, that means you have 20 1½" × 2" holes to drill; a substantial physical commitment for one person, but, if you have students helping who want something "meaningful" to do, a bit-brace and elbow grease will add considerably to their I-helped-build-it sense of satisfaction.
- Using a ¾" drill bit, drill through the center of each 1½" countersunk hole. To keep the drill bit from splintering through the far side of the board, watch for the tip of the spade bit to just break the surface of the board, then turn the 4 × 4 over and, using the break-through pin hole as a guide, drill all the way through from that side to obtain a "clean" hole.
- Cut 20 five-foot long sections of ½" Multiline rope. This type of synthetic rope costs a bit more, but it will be kind to your hands (no poly splinters) and will probably last longer than the boards. By the by, a sharp cable cutter cuts rope cleaner and easier than any knife I've owned. There's not much image associated with a cable cutter, but . . .
- Reeve (thread) one of the 5' sections of rope through each hole. It will be necessary to tightly tape one end of the rope to get it to pass through the ¾" hole.
- Tie an overhand knot in the rope end exiting from the large countersunk hole. Tighten the knot as close to the end of the rope as possible without dissolving the knot.
- Pull the knot into the countersunk hole by jerking on the other end of the rope. Any part of the knot that sticks above the plane of the board must be tapped into the hole with a hammer.
- Using a propane torch, burn each inserted knot sufficiently so that it partially melts in the hole

and cannot untie itself accidentally. Moderate the pyrotechnics to control smoke. Do the burning outside and don't breathe the fumes. Considering the number of things that are bad for you now-a-days, I'm sure acrid-smelling smoke from burning synthetic rope must be in that category.

- Either tie another overhand knot in the free end of the rope or, if you have the time, inclination, and skill, perform a back splice in each rope end. The end knot, or back splice, provides the participant with a handle and it looks better than just taping the end.
- Using a medium rasp, chamfer (bevel) all sharp edges of the board. Finish off with 100 grit sandpaper. Better yet, at the beginning of this project, remove all sharp board edges using a router.

Implementation and Variation

- If you want to add a bit more challenge, drill the first and last hole 2" in from the ends of the board. This provides rope for two additional people, but less board feet to stand on.
- During your initial presentation about the "peanut butter challenge" do not set the Trolley boards on the ground parallel to one another, as this reveals the most efficient technique for Trolley travel.
- If the group asks if they can lay the boards end-to-end then walk the boards, be prepared with a confident answer based on the validity of out-of-

the-box problem solving, the inherent value of creative thinking, and knowledge of the travesty concept. In other words, whatever you think fits the situation best at the time.

- Tie another overhand knot about ⅓ of the way down the available rope. After the group has mastered (is somewhat capable of) the 1-2-3 RIGHT, 1-2-3 LEFT quasi-military technique, suggest that they try to make progress while holding onto the lower knots. This bent-over "spoon" position makes the group more vulnerable to the **domino phenomena.**
- If you have a hot-shot, I-can-do-anything leader-type who might need a bit of compassionate humbling, suggest that he/she take the lead position on the boards and call signals from there. Why? Try it . . . be experiential, you'll see.
- Try placing an undrilled length of 4 × 4 on the field to act as an obstacle that must be crossed. The results of this attempted crossing (usually the perpendicular approach) can be very humorous as the group gets stuck halfway, with all efforts translated into simply rocking back and forth. Don't point out the efficient side-step technique of crossing over the 4 × 4 until the debrief. Be aware that if a group tries to "walk" a long Trolley over (perpendicular to) a 4 × 4 there is a good chance the Trolley might crack. This perpendicular (+) crossing is usually safe with a 12' Trolley.

Two by Four

Of the two initiatives being considered here I'd have to say that Two by Four is the one I use most often, probably because there are only four moves involved to complete the problem. If a group is struggling I'll often supply the first move and announce there's only three remaining, and it's STILL challenging. I like that.

Two by Four is historically a tabletop problem attempted with black and red checkers, or nickels and dimes. In this case substitute male and female participants for black and red checkers. It's a quasi-cerebral problem that usually requires more **trial and error** than thinking. Hold on, speak for yourself Rohnke. Sorry, it's true, some people have the capacity to think through this kind of challenge. Trouble is, most groups won't listen, as trial and error continues its sequential wont until the various failures point the way.

Objective

For a line of eight people, standing shoulder to shoulder and alternating male/female, to end up with four males on one side of the line and four females on the other side, in four appropriate moves.

Rules and Considerations

- Don't announce the minimum number of moves until an initial attempt has been made. Very seldom will a first attempt be completed in four moves. If a group does achieve completion in four moves, congratulate the group and move on to the next challenge, and make sure it's a tough one . . . unless you think their four-move completion was stumbled upon, then ask them to give it another try.
- All moves must be made as pairs. Anyone next to you constitutes a potential pair, male or female.
- As a pair moves they leave an empty slot in the line which must eventually be filled. There is no solution if a gap remains in the line.
- Pairs may not pivot or turn around, i.e., they must maintain their forward orientation.
- If a group is suffering from terminal frustration, offer them the first correct move (make sure it's correct!). Such largesse increases the group's belief that the solution is imminent, and depending upon their outlook (glass half full or half empty), that's either one less than four, or three, to go.

If you forget the solution or neglect to reproduce the numbered male/female hieroglyphics on your forearm, don't panic, just appear slightly amused or sagely intolerant, coupled with an occasional smile and supportive nod, until they hit on the correct sequence.

Facilitating Tip

Remember the first two moves, which means there's only two to go.

Both of these initiatives require thinking, communication, and sharing with an excellent opportunity for someone to manifest a leadership role. Talk about it.

WORDLES

I have to admit up-front, I am not a fan of most word games or puzzles, like cryptograms, anagrams, crossword puzzles, etc., with the exception of Scrabble and Wordles. My wife and I play Scrabble on a fairly regular basis and have score cards that date back a couple of decades, (bragging rights have to be based on accurate historical records, particularly when you are married). Scrabble tip—If you get stuck with a Z and an X tile, try the word **ZAX** (a slate working tool). Slip ZAX onto a triple word award and you're cruisin'.

I can't remember who introduced me to WORDLES, but I initially didn't like them; probably a knee-jerk reaction of my anathema toward most word games. But the logic and creativity of juxtaposing words within a phrase gradually won me over. And when I realized how useful they could be toward encouraging a disparate group to begin talking among themselves and sharing ideas, I was sold. Some *WORDLES* just make me smile, like this one: HIJKLMNO. That's it, that's all there is to it, and the answer is *water*! H to O; get it? Come on, stay with me here.

A *WORDLE* is a representation of letters and words that because of their location, separation, proximity, and orientation symbolize a simple, and usually well-known, statement or phrase. Example: SIDE SIDE, would be interpreted correctly as *side by side*. True, not profound, but interesting. Another example: YOU/JUST/ME reads as, *just between you and me*.

Get started on the following list of WORDLES when you have some leisure time and see if they don't start

to get under your skin, or become like really good crunchy peanuts, i.e., you can't eat just one.

WORDLES? Where's the adventure? We have already talked about adventure being in the eyes of the beholder, defined as "An activity of uncertain outcome characterized by risk and excitement." Remember? So just because it's printed material doesn't mean there isn't the potential for adventure, particularly on a miserable rainy day when even you (Oh, revered survivalist) would rather stay inside.

Try this. Reproduce ten WORDLES on separate 3 × 5 cards, i.e., one WORDLE per card. Write the answer on the back of each with a #1 pencil (so that it doesn't show through.) Write down another 10 WORDLES, and then do that two more times so that you end up with 40 cards, and 40 different WORDLES, in four separate stacks. Color coding helps you separate the cards afterwards.

- Place a single stack (10 cards) in each corner of a room; WORDLES up, answers down.
- Separate your larger group of participants into four smaller groups. How do you get four equal groups? Try this: Carefully rip out four advertising pages from a magazine and put them congruently on top of one another. Use a scissor to cut straight lines all the way across and through all four sheets. Make the cuts (considering you are cutting through four sheets) so that there are a total of cut pieces to equal the number of people in your group. Mix the pieces thoroughly and have everyone grab a piece, then suggest getting together with those folks who's piece will help finish your puzzle. Four equal groups? Rrright! You might want to edit your advert sheets as Camels, Viagra, and Kotex probably don't fit the tone of what you had in mind.
- Each group must have a paper and pen and something like a clipboard to write on.
- Each group is assigned a corner in the room. After arriving there and on a GO signal, each group

attempts to correctly translate and write down as many of the 10 WORDLES as they can decipher in two minutes.

- At the two minute signal (be strict), each group rotates clockwise to the next corner, and has two additional minutes to work on the next 10 Wordles.
- This continues twice more until each group has seen and tried to figure out, all 40 WORDLES.
- The facilitator then takes all 40 cards, shuffles them, and indicates that there will be an additional three minutes made available for all four groups to share their combined information with the intention of getting as many of the 40 Wordles correct as possible. How they share the collected information and use the cards is up to them. The cards may not be turned over . . . yet.
- After three minutes (again, be strict with the timing), turn the cards over one at a time, and see if a correct interpretation has been made; be lenient, remembering that the process is more important than the results.
- Variations and adaptations of this activity can obviously be made to allow more of a competitive or cooperative approach.

1. SIDE SIDE

2. YOU/JUST/ME

3. BAN   ANA

4. $\dfrac{\text{ONCE}}{\text{A TIME}}$

5. *NOON LAZY*

6. DEAL

7. FRIENDS STANDING MISS FRIENDS

8. NME NME NME SURROUNDED NME NME NME NME NME

9. ECNALG

10. 2UM
   +2UM
   ‾‾‾‾‾

11. HO

12. HIJKLMNO

13. TIME

14. ABDE
   △
   /MAT\

15. ED
   +ED

16. TIMING TIM ING

17. MCE
   MCE
   MCE

18. WHEATHER

19. ME NT

20. ALLWORLD

21. OHONLEE

22. IECEXCEPT

23. BJAOCKX

24. H A N D

25. PAS

26. DO I'OR

27. YOUR PAANNTTsS

28. GESG

29. ONE
   ONE

30. ISSUE ISSUE
   ISSUE ISSUE
   ISSUE ISSUE
   ISSUE ISSUE
   ISSUE ISSUE

31. NAFISH
   NAFISH

32. _____ IT

33. STOMACH

34. PROMISES

35. ∠AL

36. MOTH
CRY
CRY
CRY

37. ME QUIT

38. $\dfrac{O}{M.D.}$
Ph.D.
L.L.D

39. i i i i
O O

40. $\dfrac{STAND}{I}$

41. DICE
DICE

42. O - 144

43. CYCLE
CYCLE
CYCLE

44. KNEE
LIGHT

45. GROUND
FEET
FEET
FEET
FEET
FEET
FEET

46. HE'S/HIMSELF

47. DOCTOR
DOCTOR

48. K
C
E
H
C

49. R
ROAD
A
D

50. LET'S GO
NOV. 11   NOV. 23

51. THHAENRGE

Answers to WORDLES

1. Side by side
2. Just between you and me
3. Banana split
4. Once upon a time
5. Lazy afternoon
6. Big deal
7. Misunderstanding between friends
8. Surrounded by enemies
9. Backward glance
10. Forum
11. Half an hour
12. Water (H to O)
13. Long-Time-No-See
14. Matinee
15. Added
16. Split second timing
17. Three blind mice
18. A bad spell of weather
19. Apartment
20. It's a small world afterall
21. Hole in One
22. i before e except after c
23. Jack-in-the-box
24. Hand in hand
25. Incomplete pass
26. One foot in the door
27. Ants in your pants
28. Scrambled eggs
29. One-on-one
30. Tennis shoes
31. Tuna fish
32. Blanket
33. Upset stomach
34. Broken promises
35. All mixed up
36. Mothballs
37. Quit following me
38. Three degrees below zero
39. Circles under the eyes
40. I understand
41. Paradise
42. O—gross
43. Tricycle
44. Neon light
45. Six feet under ground
46. He's beside himself
47. Paradox
48. Check up
49. Cross road
50. Let's go on a double date
51. Hang in there

52. Thought ~~thought~~ <u>on</u>

53. H–O–P–E–S

54. DICE
    –DICE

55. Performance
    "

56. AAGGEENNTT

57. COLOWME

58. . _____

59. Close
    Close
    Close
    Close

60. W,I

61. oLDER

62. XQQQME

63. YUO'ER

64. NIRENDEVOUSGHT

65. KEY KEY KEY KEY KEY KEY KEY KEY KEY KEY (arranged in a ring)

66. Copi Coppy <u>Copy</u>

67. LEAN
    REVO

68. H/E/A/D

69. MOMANON

70. HAIR _____

71. LOI'MVE/YOU

72. TRN

73. HARM
    ON
    Y

74. 1,2,SAFETY,3,4,5

75. <u>HEAD</u>
    LHEOEVLSE

WORDLES Answers

52. On second thought
53. Dashed hopes
54. No dice
55. Repeat performance
56. Double agent
57. Low income
58. Point blank
59. Foreclose
60. I'm upset
61. Growing older
62. Excuse me
63. You're confused
64. Midnight rendevous
65. Key ring
66. Copyright
67. Lean over backwards
68. Headquarters
69. Man in the moon
70. Receding hairline
71. I'm in love with you
72. No U turn
73. 3 part harmony
74. Safety in numbers
75. Head over heels in love

Zig Zag

![sun icon] [one person icon] [two people icon]

Zig Zag is typical of most low-ropes course elements. Its presentation allows an immediate visual, and in some ways visceral, response from a group.

"Gimmie that board!"

"Here, grab my arm and I'll fit this end into that notch."

"OK, now what?"

You can almost count on an abundance of random action before much thought is applied to a solution. Basically, what needs to be done physically to solve Zig Zag is conceptually easy ("Truth is obvious after its discovery."); the real task is making it happen.

Objective

To transport a group across a designated area without touching the ground with either of the available boards or any part of the participant's body.

Rules

- To be used safely and appropriately, the prop boards must be fitted into the designated slots of the permanent upright posts, i.e., prop boards may not be turned flat and placed on top of a post. If stood upon in a flat orientation the boards will break.
- If a participant's body part, or a board, touches the ground:

1. a time penalty may be assigned.
2. the individual at fault is required to return to the start.
3. the entire group must begin again from the start.

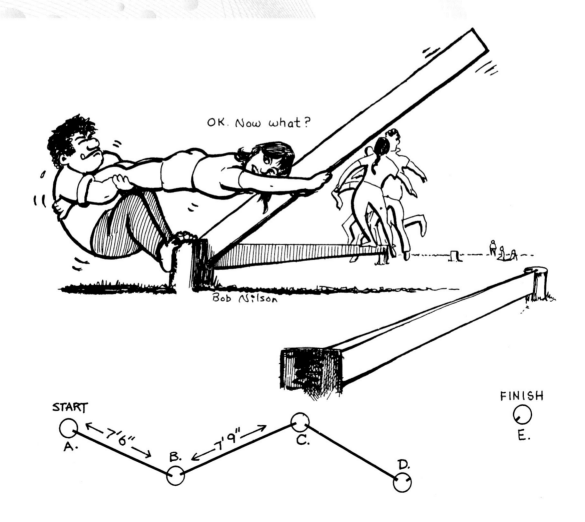

OK. Now what?

Bob Nilson

START
A. ←— 7'6" —→ B. ←— 7'9" —→ C. D.

FINISH
E.

4. the group loses use of that board and as a default, must bivouac for 24 hours on site before beginning again. You know I'm kidding, right? Come on, this stuff is not that serious.

Construction Tips

- 2" × 6" boards should be used as crossing boards. (I just noticed that the old *Silver Bullets* write-up indicates the use of 2" × 6' boards—WRONG!)
- Do not substitute 2 × 4's for 2 × 6 boards, they will break.
- Board BC should be equal to the space DE.
- Boards AB and CD should be less than the distance between DE, so that only board BC will fit in the space DE.
- Boards AB and CD measure 7' 6", and board BC measures 7' 9".
- Rout or rasp the board edges, and sand if necessary to remove splinters.

- Use non-pressure treated boards if possible. In most cases, untreated boards are lighter.
- Posts are sunk in the ground so that approximately 12" of the post is above ground.
- The top of each post is notched to a depth (about 5.5") that will fit the depth of the board. Make sure the board/notch fit is not too tight, and not too loose. Use a chain saw to fashion the notch if you are in a hurry, otherwise take your time with a sharp chisel—much neater.

Debrief Topics

- Did you need a leader for this challenge, or did the group come up with a solution?
- Is a leader necessary for all challenges?
- What did the group do first after the challenge was explained—think or act?
- Did you consider Zig Zag a comparatively easy or difficult challenge? Why?

Funn & Stunts

The Balance Broom a.k.a. Witches' Broom

Have you ever made yourself really dizzy from spinning, like when you were a kid whirling around and around on a lush grass field? Well, if you were left out of the dizzy-izzy games line then, or more recently backed-out at Six Flags, let me introduce you to The Balance Broom.

Before we get into this any further, I'm not going to try to convince you that The Balance Broom fulfills any particular curriculum need or purpose;

it's just fun. Oh sure, there's some trust built into the essential spotting and being able to handle dizziness might help in an athletic sense, but basically it's just an out-of-body experience that makes people laugh and be more willing to try something that's failure oriented. (Don't announce that.) When you can encourage a whole group to try something where failure is imminent and accepted, the participants have taken a big step toward functional use of trial and error as exemplified within the cycle of experiential learning: Try—Fail—Learn Something—Talk and Share—Try Again.

Objective

To hold a broom overhead with your arm extended, fix your gaze on the broom, turn 360° in either direction 15 times, place the broom on the ground in front of you, and step casually over the broom while maintaining an upright position.

Set Up

- Use of a broom increases the difficulty of completing 15 rotations because the weight of the broom head, unless held perfectly straight up and down (not going to happen), begins to spin out of vertical and becomes much harder to control. Try using a Boffer or a rolled up and taped newspaper. Stick with a broom if you are looking for a physical challenge.
- Perform The Balance Broom on grass or a gym mat, as spinning out of control is frequent.
- Establish a minimum of four spotters surrounding the broom spinner with instructions to step in and grab the spinner if they lose control and start to fall. A disoriented person should not be released by a spotter until they have regained a semblance of balance.

Procedure

- If a spinner has reached only 6–7 rotations and is beginning to lose control, tell them in a loud voice to drop the broom and step over it NOW. Spotters, be diligent.
- If someone seems reluctant to try, suggest that they make the turns with a partner. In this case, two participants face one another with hands on each other's shoulders, with one of the pair holding the broom overhead. When the looking-up rotations are completed the pair attempts the broom crossing together. Have plenty of spotters available.
- Don't count on the spinner to count his/her own rotations. Assign a person or let the group do the counting. Remember you are counting rotations, not seconds.

Contraindications

- Let people know that dizziness will occur as the result of attempting The Balance Broom. If someone honestly indicates that dizziness makes them nauseated, allow that person to become a spin counter or observer. Also, be aware that dizziness has been reported to trigger epileptic seizures.
- If you introduce The Balance Broom and decide not to use spotters, someone will eventually get hurt. Take advantage of an activity that encourages enjoyment and spotting practice.

Balance Practice

I'm not sure if this use of three-foot dowels came about just because we were using them for other activities (Human Ladder), or because we needed something (a prop) to help emphasize the importance of balance on the ropes course . . . and in life. Serindipitously the dowels happened to be there so we used them. Balance in life? Where did that come from?

Objective

To balance a 3' × 1" dowel on the tip of your finger, the palm of your hand, your nose, or any other part of your anatomy that presents itself as a balance challenge.

Set Up

- Buy some dowels, as above, or more frugally cut up some old broom or mop handles; don't forget to rasp and sand off the rough edges after you make the cut. Try using a hack saw, as the fine teeth result in a smoother, albeit slower, cut.
- I remember seeing and trying the following dowel tricks using peacock feathers. The feathers,

because of their inherent lightness and wide surface area (resistance to air), provided ideal tools for beginning balance practice. Got any peacocks around?

Remember how a circus performer could balance spinning plates on the end of a stick and then place the stick on his/her chin or nose and continue the spin? That kind of balance skill takes a huge amount of practice and commitment, but almost anyone can gain immediate satisfaction by getting rid of the spinning plate and just attempting to balance the stick (dowel). Such simple balance efforts, particularly when first attempted, require subtle hand, arm, and body movement, and in some cases jogging this way and that to keep the dowel somewhere near upright. Therein lies the fun and the desire to repeat what you were trying (called practice), but you don't have to say that.

As skill or luck increases, try balancing the dowel on your chin, forehead, or even nose. Have different lengths of dowels available to provide a range of challenges. And speaking of greater challenge, ask

two people to vertically balance a dowel on their respective palms, then carefully toss their dowels toward one another simultaneously in an attempt to catch their partner's dowel; a catch represented by a vertically balanced dowel on each receiving palm. If a traded catch is eventually accomplished, see if the dynamic duo can include a 360-degree spin of the dowel (end-over-end) before the catch is made—extraordinary. Too easy? Try it with three people—watch your heads!

Contests (self or group) to measure maximum vertical time balanced or for time and distance covered, are natural incentives for continued practice. Why practice something as intrinsically useless as balancing a dowel on your fingertip? (Why practice golf?) Letting your body know what it is capable of accomplishing and what that level of confidence can do for a person is reason enough. Additionally, knowing the potential of your energy equilibrium and being able to coordinate sequential balanced movement is another step toward creating a confident, self-assured individual on the ropes course of life. Did I say that? Help!

Beau Coups Balls

Read the bulleted section in the game Frantic (page 24) to clue in on where and how to come up with beau coups tennis balls, because you're going to need heaps of them for the activity Beau Coups Balls.

Objective

How many tennis balls can be held off the ground for five seconds by a person standing (not squatting) with both feet on the ground?

Rules

- A two-minute time period is allowed to cram and/or balance tennis balls into whatever anatomical nooks and crannies seem available for stuffing. Remember, these are tennis balls, not marbles.
- Clothing cannot be used nor can any other type of prop other than those portions of the anatomy deemed appropriate, and you better deem carefully.
- This trust exercise can be attempted as an individual, i.e., one person, does his/ her own stuffing or Beau Coups Balls can be attempted as a pair; one person does the holding, the other does the ram/jamming.
- The five second holding time starts when the final ball is placed and announced, or when the two minute time limit is up.
- Make sure all extraneous balls are off the floor because when the stuffed person lets go, balls will be galore.

I'd suggest having at least 100 tennis balls on hand for a varsity pair's attempt, and somewhere around 75 for the solo shot.

Variation: Garbage Galore

Rather than using tennis balls, which, as stuffing fodder doesn't require much imagination, provide a congerie of <u>clean</u> recyclable trash (plastic containers of various sizes and shapes, aluminum cans, egg cartons, etc.). Following the guide-lines above, attempt to compartmentalize and redistribute your trash stash and see how much rubbish (weight) can be held off the floor. You will need a small fish scale,

or produce balance, and a lightweight plastic bag to compare attempts unless you and the players would rather judge a winner more subjectively, i.e., aesthetics of placement, crushing creativity, alacrity of distribution, etc.

Does that mean crushing cans and flattening plastic is OK? Could this be considered an example of experiential/adventure (recycling) education? Whatever floats your environmental/adventure boat! Procedural GREEN tip: Deposit the crushed aluminum cans in an approved recycling container, i.e., don't just stick them in the trash.

There aren't too many activities where a camera seems a must, but Beau Coups Balls along with Fire in the Hole, Silvia's Silly Sequence, Funny Face, and Orange Teeth all seem to qualify for whatever photo-of-the-month contest you plan to enter.

Boffer Bonkers

At one time the word *Boffer* meant something in the gaming world. A Boffer was a foam sword (actually shaped like a sword) with a wooden handle, offered as a commercial package along with goggles, ear protectors (I'm not kidding), and a book of suggested play instructions. The ear protectors (no cauliflower ears at this school!) were a bit much, but I assume someone's legal counsel suggested their inclusion as part of a "risk free" package.

As far back as 25+ years, PA players used Boffers for a number of activities but basically people just liked whaling-away at each other. Getting hit was no big deal and the satisfying sound of Ethafoam-on-skin was worth repeating. Drawbacks included cost, broken sword tips (causing incrementally shorter swords), and the possibility of getting hit with the other end of the sword, i.e., the wooden handle!

So we sought out a commercial supplier of the sword material (Ethafoam), and bought a "plank" or two. A plank was a rectangular section of Ethafoam that allowed the fabrication of about ten "bats." A bat consisted of a rectangular cut section of Ethafoam (a sharp knife did the job); each bat measuring 4 inches by 4 feet. We trimmed foam material off all four edges at the end of a bat (about ten inches worth), reducing the diameter of that end and making it easier to grip. Colorful plastic gym tape was then wrapped around and around the trimmed end to fashion an ersatz handle. We found that the 4" flat part of the bat, when applied with alacrity to a fleshy part of another person's anatomy, made a hugely satisfying sound, and, it didn't hurt!

If all this purchasing, measuring, cutting, and taping sounds like too much of a hassle, buy a few foam Noodles from a store like Wal-Mart. Noodles are the popular, colorful, and inexpensive foam cylinders used primarily for fun and flotation in backyard pools. Cut a Noodle into thirds, providing three sword/bat/cylinders. (This will give you three bat-like implements measuring about 2' 9" each.) Either tape the ends or don't tape the ends to designate a handle; it doesn't seem to matter functionally, but some people like handles.

Having spent too many paragraphs telling you about the playing implements, I'd say it's about time for some Boffer Bonker action. This simplistic, blatantly competitive game is one of the most aerobic and least serious one-on-one, wildly kinetic confrontations I've ever played. Competing against someone about your own height and level of fitness, wielding swords and whacking balloons can easily elevate your heart rate to a building-aerobic-fitness level.

Boffer Bonkers can be played as team vs. team, but the pure form is one balloon, two players; i.e., mano-a-mano. Attempting to whack a balloon past your opponent is sure to maintain your involvement, but observing from the side lines remains interesting for only about a minute. If you want to play Team Bonkers, simply supply more people with foam bats, and keep the rules simple . . . as follows.

Blow up a couple of 12" balloons and tie them off. Place one inflated balloon on the floor in the center of a gym. (The gym is probably lined for basketball so put the balloon right in the center of the jump circle.) From that location, both players back off in opposite directions until they are standing on their respective free-throw line, facing the center court balloon. Kneeling on one knee, each player in concert with their opponent slams their bat three consecutive times on the floor then dashes toward the balloon. The contest has begun.

Objective

Using the bat only, to strike the balloon past the opponent's end line (the line just past the overhead backboard), so that the balloon hits the floor beyond that line, in which case a point is scored. A player on offense is not allowed to cross his/her opponent's end line.

Rules and Considerations

- A player can only strike the balloon with a foam bat. Players cannot purposefully hit one another unless one of the players is obviously about to score a point . . . no head shots please.
- No purposeful physical contact is allowed at any time, i.e., shoving, etc.
- If a balloon breaks there is no time-out. The ref will throw in a pre-inflated balloon at the juncture of rupture.

- When explaining the game objective above, I made it sound like scoring multiple points was necessary to win a game. Almost without exception, whoever scores the first point wins. Gasping opponents, experiencing substantial oxygen debt, often desperately agree to end the contest as a tie at mid-court. It's an amazing biological fact that the body's need for oxygen can totally overcome the need to win.
- If Team Bonkers is played, limit the number of participants on a side to four, for a total of eight playing at one time.
- Aggression Bonkers allows a player(s) to cross their opponent's back line. To score a point in this game the balloon must make contact with the back wall. If you are playing on an outdoor court (not a great idea if there is any wind at all), the back wall rule is waived. A winning shot in this case puts the balloon off the court. Try using a beach ball (heavier than a balloon) if wind is a problem.
- As I suggested tongue-in-cheek, those many years ago, "Do not substitute 2 × 4's for regulation Boffers (or bats, swords, etc.) because splinters may cause the balloons to burst."

Bottoms Up

This improbable juxtaposing of bodies has always seemed to me a hands-on lesson in kinesiology and physics. If done well, with a partner about your own weight, achieving the sought after posteriors-off-the-floor positioning is only moderately difficult. If you try to make it happen using strength alone, and ignoring the body as a lever, Bottoms Up will remain bottoms down.

Objective

For two people sitting on the floor, facing one another, to achieve a "bottoms up" positioning with only the soles of the feet connecting and four palms on the floor; the photo says it all.

Procedure and Considerations

• For both "glutes" to clear the floor, positioning is key. In preparation, skootch your posteriors as close together as comfortably possible, concurrently positioning your sole-to-sole feet juxtaposition as high as possible.

• Consider Bottoms Up as a one-on-one warm-up exercise, warming up both the muscles, joints, and psyche.

• If done well, even poorly, you are going to feel a poignant tightening in the triceps area. If you don't know where the triceps muscle is located, you soon will.

• If your bottom remains permanently part of the floor, blame it on your partner and find someone more your size to blame it on next time.

• Try Bottoms Up using three people, obviously more difficult. If you make four-up with separated feet let me know, 'cause I've never seen it done. A three-second hold is considered an official attempt.

If you are planning on using Bottoms Up for the main part of your class, better plan again. Bottoms Up is a unique warm-up ploy that allows participants the chance to talk, touch, discuss, and problem solve amidst copious laughter—ten minutes max, or you're milking it.

Chronological Line-Up

PASS!

Lining up according to . . . something seems to hold a fascination for most folks. I suppose it's because people like to compare things they have done, age, height, years of marriage, practically anything that's comparable. Most of these topics are not brought up in polite social conversation so this spontaneous sharing provides an opportunity for either a just-met group or band of veterans to compare what's on their minds, if not on the tips of their tongues.

I tend to use an exercise like this whenever I ask a group to line up for something . . . anything really. Ordinarily when someone lines up for an activity they do just that, it doesn't take much thought or preparation to form a line. But why not take the time and offer a reason for creating a line, even if there is no particular reason? At the least, it's fun to compare and share, and what's the hurry? A purposeful line-up also tends to separate best friends or joined-at-the-hip adolescents.

For example, particularly with an older group, ask everyone to line up according to their relative venerability, i.e., by age. (There are some age associated words that are negatively profiling and that no one wants to hear associated with themselves, particularly if the words fit: caducity; hoary; elderly; senescence; curmudgeonly.) So I say, " . . . youngest line up to the left, the more *venerable*

to the right" (*venerable* sounds more venerated than elderly*), but . . . you must place yourself in the line where you think you should be without saying a word or giving any indication of what your actual age is. Remember your place in line is where you should be, not where you want to be.

There ensues much shuffling around and laughter, particularly in the middle of the line. The youngest and oldest know where they belong and move right or left without much hesitation. When the maneuvering is about done, announce that it's time to declare, or not declare, your age by either (1) saying how old you are, (2) offering something that happened in your birth year of some historical significance (other than your birthday!), or (3) simply saying, "I pass."

You will find that most people just blurt out their age and could care less what other people think. The occasional "I pass" is usually surrounded by declarations of 34, 35, 37—I pass—38, 40 . . . so there you are.

After the declarations, indicate that the chronological line they just established could be considered a trust activity. Everyone has an age and everyone jokes about their age, but it seems to be a social gaff to either ask about, or announce an age. So why not just go for it in an enjoyable format that almost seems to have a reason. Ages were revealed

*elderly—I read last week in a national news magazine that the concept of elderly begins at age 70! How can they say that? Elderly! Excuse me while I drool.

(mostly), laughter was shared, whatever kidding occurred was good-natured, the venerable end of the line was applauded, and you got to hear something personal about someone that brought you all slightly closer. Well done! Next . . .

Caveat   Chronological Line-Up does not work well with school groups, as everyone is usually close to the same age. Instead, line up by the two middle numbers of your SS#, your height in inches, how many books you have read this year, the number of calls you make (or receive) per day on your cell phone, how many push-ups you think you can do, etc.

Heads Up   Check out the write-up on Hog Call (pages 78–79) to see how Chronological Line-Up supports that particular time span of hog hollerin' disharmony.

Coming and Going of the Rain

Has anyone NOT seen or experienced this classic outdoor education activity? Every time I say that to a group about an activity, 90% of the people raise their hands. So I guess that means I'm either getting older (a given), or all these adventure based activities are generational, i.e., just wait around a couple decades, then reintroduce all the old stuff as new stuff.

Author's Aside—"Stuff?"   I've got to go look that up . . . wait there. Didn't take long, as I have a dictionary near at hand. Wow, there's a lot of stuff listed under STUFF, so I'll just give you the #1 definition of at least 18 descriptions. "The material or substance out of which anything is or can be made." Doesn't that cover just about anything and everything? *Stuff* is such a useful word.)

A few years ago I wrote and compiled four books (*Funn Stuff*, Nos.1–4; creative, eh?), and since I had already made up an acronym for FUNN, I thought making up another acronym for STUFF wouldn't be too hard—it was; I never did come up with anything that made sense. "Serious Teachers Understand Fannie Farkel" or "Solipsistic Troglodytes Utilize Finger Food" . . . see what I mean?

Objective

For a circled group to audibly and tactually experience the sounds of a summer rain approaching and leaving an area. If the group cooperates and performs their individual roles well, there is the distinctly rewarding experience of hearing and feeling the increasing wind, the pitter-patter of raindrops, and eventually the heavy drumming sounds of a summer rain.

Set Up

- Ask your group to make a circle then all turn to either their right or left. Have them tighten the circle by side-stepping toward the center until everyone can easily touch the person's back in front of them.
- Using the person in front of you (yes, once again you are part of the action), demonstrate the sequential movements necessary to achieve the sounds and movements desired, as follows:

1. With the palms of your hands held flat against the shoulder (scapula/trapezius) area of the person in front of you, make rotating movements with your hands (wax on-wax off) to achieve a swishing sound—the increase of wind preceding a shower.
2. Change to a slapping motion on his/her back with your fingertips—beginning raindrops. These are not subtle motions, nor are they retaliatory; play nice.
3. Change to a heavier finger slapping action with the fingers held together—larger drops, more volume. Maintain the trust, don't hurt your partner.
4. Return to the motions in #2.
5. Return to the motions in #1.
6. Stop, and wait for all sounds to cease.

When you begin #1, at the onset of this exercise, as soon as your partner feels you initiating an action on his/her back, he/she passes that identical action on to the person in front of them, and so on, until that motion makes full circle and is returned to your back, at which juncture you begin #2.

Considerations

- I'm sure you can appreciate how quickly this fragile and fleeting exercise can weaken or dissolve during its trip around the circle. Emphasize sequence and attention to task, but maintain the fun. Also, try to keep your group comfortably small, although there is admittedly an exciting dynamic to larger groups. I've seen this exercise done impressively with more than 100 people, but, 100 committed people.
- Coming and Going of the Rain can be a completely different experience if attempted with eyes closed.
- Pick your location with some forethought. Don't ask a group of students to attempt this sensitive sequence in an area with other people wandering by. A quiet location is also necessary, as chain saws and leaf blowers tend to interrupt the fragile sound sequence you are trying to establish.
- If your group is too young or too immature to handle the overt touch necessary, reproduce the rain sounds by:

1. Rubbing your palms together vigorously
2. Snapping your fingers out of sequence
3. Snapping fingers of both hands rapidly
4. Slapping your thighs
5. Pounding your chest—then reverse the order

The greatest benefits result from achieving the cooperation and trust level necessary for the elements to be realistically heard and felt.

Historical Aside

The full-page photo on page 92 of the original *Silver Bullets* depicts a poorly contrasted, not very well focused picture (I took it) of a young guy getting hit in the head with a lot of water, and obviously enjoying it. At the time, he and I were standing on a catwalk near the top of a 100+ foot water tower in North Carolina in anticipation of rappelling off the tower; note the Goldline rope and non-locking carabineers in the lower right corner. The water was pouring from an overflow tube off the top of the tower. I'm not sure why I used that photo to complement this activity other than the fact there was water involved and a happy face, because what was happening on that tower had absolutely nothing to do with Coming and Going of the Rain.

The Compass Walk

I've presented The Compass Walk activity so many times I'm sure the initial presentation has become embellished to the point of hyperbole. Nonetheless, what I try to pass along in keeping with the activity itself and the parallel justification of enjoying what you are doing, is a front-loaded narrative that's true in essence.

Front Loaded Vignette   A volunteer was placed by helicopter in a trackless arctic tundra setting (there had been a recent local light snowfall) and asked to walk to an unseen destination one mile away without use of map or compass, i.e., by instinct alone. The individual was oriented in the correct compass direction and told their destination was identical to the blue painted X they were currently standing on. After walking for an hour or so the person was retrieved and aerial photos were taken of his clearly defined tracks in the snow, which revealed

he had not come within a half mile of the distant X. The photos plainly indicated he had walked in confident concentric circles, much like Winnie the Pooh had done while trying to find his way in that classic A.A. Milne tale, *Pooh's Perilous Peregrinations*.

With this visual fresh in mind, ask for a volunteer who thinks he/she might have the Daniel Boone instinct that would allow them to walk a straight line without the aid of map or compass, and in this case because we can't afford a trip to the Arctic or a helicopter, to make the walk blindfolded, or with eyes closed. I lean toward the simple, eyes closed method which avoids the hassles associated with blindfolds and allows peek-by-choice.

With the group located at the edge of a large field, the volunteer announces his/her distant goal (a tree, automobile, backstop). The members close their eyes, and begin purposefully walking toward that objective. Another volunteer (typically a friend) responsibly agrees to follow closely behind the walker to protect him/her from injury. Usually within 50 feet of having started, the walker begins to veer either right or left and usually continues in that same arcing direction. Sometimes the arc becomes so severe and continuous that the misdirected, but totally oblivious, person actually comes close to returning to where he/she started. If you can get a giggling group to be quiet long enough, the look on a person's face when he/she is finally stopped is priceless. The extent of misdirected walking observed is usually enough to tempt the remainder of the group to believe they can do better. Ask the group to pair up, pick a destination and see how honestly accurate they can be.

Procedure

- Most people do not use blindfolds anymore and I'd have to go along with that choice, blindfolds are a hygienic and procedural hassle. Younger groups need to "sneak a peek" occasionally (see 2nd paragraph above), and that's OK as long as Compass Walk doesn't dissolve into a travesty of spot-on attempts. We're working on trust here; trust that they will be kept physically safe by a partner, trust that everyone will keep their eyes shut, and trust that no one will make fun of another's attempt.
- Make sure the person acting as spotter understands his/her role as protector.

1. Ask the spotter to stay behind the walker so that direction is not compromised.
2. Once it's obvious that the walker has missed his/her destination (or made it!), the spotter should tell the walker to open his/her eyes. Strongly emphasize that taking advantage of people with their eyes closed is not acceptable.
3. If it's obvious that the walker is going to make physical contact with something (tree, fence, car) or step in a hole, the walker must be verbally alerted well before the danger becomes imminent.

- Talking between walker and spotter is OK as long as the conversation does not involve the destination and/or how to get there.
- After the two participants have walked downfield toward a destination, suggest switching roles on the way back.
- If the group enjoyed their one-on-one forays with compass walking, suggest the following variations:

1. Try to pair up people who tend to walk in opposite directions. The ensuing push/pull interaction is worth talking about. Don't forget to send someone along for protection.
2. Have a pair (all eyes closed) attempt to operate piggyback style, however only the top person offers direction; the bottom person is for transportation only. The predictably poignant conversation shared during the walk is worth disclosing and sharing with the group afterward. A third person is obviously necessary for safety back up.
3. Try jogging rather than walking. The usual result of increased speed is going wrong faster.
4. Walk backward.

Bring the entire group together at the end of the exercise (after the variations) and suggest that they try to accurately accomplish the Compass Walk as an entire group while maintaining some kind of physical contact with one another. This type of mass walk usually proves to be more accurate than the methods attempted above, which, honestly has very little to do with why you are presenting this activity, but . . . may be interesting to someone.

Comments about the Large Group Walk

- Sightlessly orienteering as a large group is a functional way to conclude the Compass Walk activity, usually resulting in a "feel good" finish. I do need to warn you though, splinter groups can become physically fragmented, i.e., not be able to agree with one another about their direction orientation and split off in separate directions. Not a problem as long as there are enough spotters to stay with the bifurcating groups. Afterward, make sure the group is provided enough time to talk about what happened and how to handle that kind of conflict in the future.

- Follow directly behind the large group (making sure there's a proctor in front with his/her eyes open as the group meanders down the field), dropping a brightly colored plastic ball, like the colored balls in a McDonald's playground pit, about every five steps. After the group has opened their eyes at the end of the field, looking back at the winding path of balls provides an interesting visual of where and how much the group strayed off a straight compass course.

- Just before starting their walk, tell the group that you will not say anything on the way downfield unless there is a safety problem. Upon arrival, at or near the destination, they will hear you say "Stop!" After stopping they are to keep their eyes closed, then *slowly* point toward where they think the destination is located. (Point *slowly* so no one gets a finger stuck into a closed eye, or open mouth!) Then have them take a look and share excited conversation. Don't interrupt for at least 30 seconds unless you are asked a question; let the excitement roll.

Dog Shake

I can't remember if it was Jim Schoel or myself that started doing the Dog Shake back in the early days of Project Adventure, but it has become one of those classic icebreaker activities that novice facilitators talk about, want to observe, are willing to try in a workshop setting, but are often reluctant to use with their own students. Maybe after reading through this detailed description you will be confident enough to at least try your routine alone in front of a mirror. Quoting directly from the original *Silver Bullets*:

> "Don't present this exercise until the group has had a chance to figure you out. You may want to practice a few times before demonstrating it. Pick your practice site wisely."

Right . . . like your bathroom, with the door closed, and nobody home!

The Dog Shake takes its name directly from the way a dripping wet dog shakes (right next to you), kinetically demonstrating a biologically ideal way to

initiate the drying process. You will never be able to duplicate the unhinged, explosive wriggling movements a dog achieves, but in relative slow motion the human miming attempts can be fun and not inhibiting, particularly if shared. (See photo of shaking dog—*Bijou*, for those of you who remember her.)

To convince an obviously dubious group to join you in a spasmodic Dog Shake is largely dependent upon existent rapport with the group and your current level of **chutzpah**. The following running commentary should at least get you ready for your closed-bathroom-door, canine tremors debut. Pay attention now and follow closely. The instruction in quotes are what you say (or something close to that). The sentences in *italic* are what you actually do.

"A Dog Shake always begins at the tip of the nose."

Begin wiggling your nose.

"See how hard it is to wiggle your nose without including your cheeks and mouth?"

Exaggerate your mouth and cheek movements.

"If you are worried about what other people are thinking, relax because here go your eyes."

Roll your eyes randomly in their sockets and keep 'em rolling.

"Now move consistently down from one body part to another. (This has got to remind you of the old camp song about this-bone-connected-to-that-bone.)"

Your whole head begins to bounce around, which starts the shoulders bopping, continuing down the arms, to the fingers.

"Don't leave behind the head and eyes, keep 'em moving. And the chest is part of the shoulder movement, which continues right on down to the waist and hips. Your patter can include any body part I've left out, within reason, of course."

If you have ever played with a hula hoop you're home free with this part of the anatomy, but *also try to slip in a bit of Tahitian hip gyrations.*

"Can you feel the water flying off your body?"

Wham! There go the hips. The thighs are next which starts the knees a-shakin', then right on down to the toes.

"By this time you are almost 100% convulsive. Don't stop. Do it! Do it! Do it!"

Continue the total shake for a few more seconds.

People are usually laughing and nervously enjoying your antics by this time . . . as your chutzpah meter goes off the scale. Don't give them time to lose the laughter … or leave. Ask them to join you in a similar sequence and immediately begin as above. Tell them not to worry about what to do, you'll be there to help them all the way.

Caveat   Make sure you do not present the Dog Shake in an area where other students can stop and casually watch. It's hard enough to get a participation commitment from people you have been working with,

but an audience of gawkers who have no idea what experiential education entails is not going to help.

Talk them through what you just demonstrated, joining them in the shaking. The whole sequence should last no longer than 45 seconds.

At the finish, the "dog shakers" usually applaud themselves, a nice gesture really; there should be more of that spontaneous self approval. The good athlete and adept student usually get the kudos, here's a chance for the average Jane & Joe to hear applause and feel good about what they did. Move on to the next exercise amidst a feeling of shared spontaneity.

Final Observation

If you watch a dog shake after getting totally wet (check out the photo) the shake moves quickly from nose to tail. As a finale, see if you and your students can make that happen. Start your nose twitching and let the movement transfer immediately and directly to your hips—kind of an impulse manifested in a torso twitch and subtle hip shake. It's hard to verbalize but I can feel it, and if it feels good it's probably right.

Dollar Jump

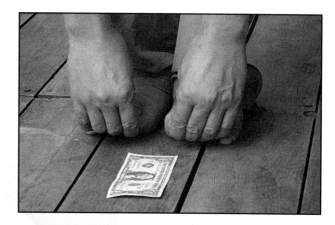

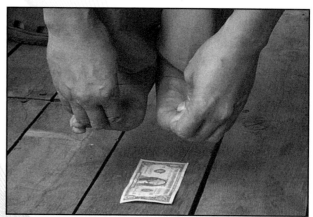

If you were to measure the distances of all the times I have demonstrated hopping over the length of a dollar bill I'll bet it wouldn't even be close to a single trip to the moon, probably wouldn't even make the bottom cable of *The Two Line Bridge*, but even so . . . I've done it lots of times. Here's the point, depressing as it might be; I can't even make a $.75 jump now, and maybe even a 50-center is out of reach. Age? You bet. Ever hear of the book titled *Growing Old Is Not for Sissies*? You better read it.

Objective

To jump over the length of a dollar bill placed flat on the ground.

Rules

- The jumper must grab their toes (end of the shoe) and hold onto their toes for the complete jump. Letting go at any time during the jump or landing voids the attempt.

- The jump starts with the jumper's toes as close to the end of the bill as possible. The jumper must clear the bill with their heels for the jump to be considered successful.

- Only a forward jump over the bill is allowed. (Backward jumps are easier.)

- After clearing the bill, a jumper must maintain a finished position on their feet for three seconds. Falling forward, backward, or sideways nullifies the attempt.

- Place one official (jump for cash) dollar bill on the floor, but encourage practice jumps in other parts of the room. Be aware that some people (predominantly males) become so eager to complete the jump and win the dollar, that they will not let go of their toes even considering the obvious consequence of making facial contact with the floor.

Cash Comment   Offer the bill as a reward for anyone who can successfully (see above) jump over the bill. Try the jump a few times yourself before you start handing out dollar bills. Over the last 25 years I've probably given away between 7–10 dollars, well worth the money for the enthusiasm generated. When you put that dollar on the floor and announce the challenge, notice the shift in interest and eagerness to try.

Dollar Jump is a filler activity, but it can also be used, as mentioned above, as a ploy toward generating enthusiasm and encouraging individuals to try something new, something they have never tried before. This is also another opportunity to demonstrate, without having to say it, that failure can be fun.

Facilitating Tip

Be strict about the rules and maintain the challenge. It bothers me that so many instructors and teachers are willing to give away dollar bills to make sure the students feel good about themselves. They don't need spoon-fed success, they need satisfying challenge, tinged with a real chance for failure.

Fast Draw

Some of the activities in this book, and others I've authored, are admittedly marginal in their application toward achieving an explicit educational goal or developing curriculum, but I don't want to seem apologetic. There are all kinds of activities currently available designed with serious and crucial intent, so I've purposefully written in a big chunk of whimsy associated with the games in this book, and why not? Fast Draw and its variations allow some of the proverbial inner child to hold sway before rules and mature intent "adultrate" the game. There's a salient quote you need to read before continuing; it's obviously meaningful to me, I hope it holds some meaning for you.

> "For he knew, as all students did, that the basic purpose of instruction was not so much to teach young people good things as to fill up all their time unpleasantly. Adults had the notion that juveniles needed to suffer. Only when they have suffered enough to wipe out most of their naturally joyous spirits and innocence were they staid enough to be considered mature. An adult was essentially a broken-down child."
>
> Piers Anthony

Gear Needed

A pocket mirror for everyone in the group. When mirror shopping try to find the plastic encased type, i.e., no edge of glass exposed. Round or square, a "pocket" mirror indicates a size of about three to four inches in diameter.

Objective

Just about anything you can think of that involves a mirror(s), bright sunshine, and a child-like sense of creativity. To wit:

#1—Hold the mirror on your hip in flash mode, as if getting ready for a Wyatt Earp-like fast draw. Pair off with another mirror wielding, slow talkin', cigar chewin', tough lookin' hombre, and set up for a *High Noon*, middle-of-the-street showdown . . . I reckon. Stand about 10 yards apart facing one another with the sun potentially hitting each mirror at about the same angle. Then the two combatants can trade benign invectives (let's not go overboard here), and when one "draws," the other immediately responds in kind. The idea is to cause the other person to experience the "retinal flash" first, indicating a win for the person causing it to happen.

Players are honor bound to . . .

. . .yell loudly and kinetically respond when they experience the flash, and believe me, there's no doubt when the flash hits.

. . . keep their eyes open and directed toward their opponent.

The winner swaggers off looking for another dude to challenge. The loser, in an attempt to readjust their ego, also swaggers off (albeit with somewhat less panache) looking for someone with a slightly slower draw.

#2—If the thought of symbolic gun fighting does not appeal, have the two flashers stand side-by-side, and up-sun (sun in their eyes) of a shaded wall. Using an agreed upon target on the wall (different color spot, a pipe, knot hole, etc.) these fast draw target contests are considerably less sanguinary . . . much more Aquarius. It's also fun to have the entire group (with mirrors) stand in that up-sun position and flash a light spot from their mirror somewhere on the wall, concurrently trying to figure out which bobbing and dodging sun-dot is from their mirror. With 15–20 dancing sun-dots on the wall the effect can be dizzying . . . and well worthy of continuing. Multi light-dot contests with this many people playing are laughable because of the difficulty in trying to determine whose fast moving sun-dot belongs to whom.

#3—If you concentrate ten sun-dots on an outdoor thermometer will the temperature increase? How about 20 dots? or 30? What if your group is standing 10 feet away? How about 50 feet? After determining these bits of very significant data through the scientific method, will anyone in the group commit to having five sun-dots concentrated on their exposed mid-section from

about 10 feet away? How about 10 dots at 15 feet? Now try increasing the dots, one at a time. Is this fun? Is this a scientific experiment? How can you be academic with so much laughter involved?

"I was playing when I invented the Aqua Lung. I think playing is the most important thing in the world."
Jacques Cousteau

Did you know that Archimedes, in an attempt to protect Syracuse from the Romans in 214 BC, is said to have set a ship on fire with polished bronze mirrors from a distance of one bow shot? Archimedes notwithstanding, if you didn't learn anything else from this exercise, remember to protect your amidships, i.e., belly button, in this case.

Try to bring a large mirror from home (say 2' × 3') and experience what the heat from one large mirror feels like.

Caveat   Do not flash the sun's rays from a mirror this large into anyone's eyes, unless there is a considerable distance between the mirror and a targeted person.

#4—How many mirrors can you set up (handheld) in a zigzag pattern and still read a notice tacked to the far side of a tree? Also using handheld mirrors, how many times can you zigzag the sun's rays to display a sun-spot on a shaded wall?

#5—Consider team flashing, the object being to try and move your team from one designated location to another as fast as possible and without experiencing the retinal flash. Such a contest could begin in an open field and spill over into a wooded or building area, but remember, you need sun. If someone experiences a retinal flash during their attempted crossing they must stand in place for 90 seconds (honor system) before attempting to reach their home base or flash an opposing player. The first team to get all their players into a designated base area (rope in a circle) have identified themselves as flashers of a high order. As such, each player is encouraged to look directly into his/her own mirror, wink, and say, "Nice going (their name), you are one heck of a flasher." Speaking of that, have you ever been retinally flashed from behind a Shag Bark Hickory? I didn't think so; better get busy.

5-5-5

I'm not sure what makes this exercise so appealing, maybe the unselfconscious touch, the competitive posture, the uncompetitive approach . . . no, I think it's the "feeling:" the feeling after each 5-5-5 exercise is completed, a sense of satisfaction and release; the satisfaction from doing something cooperatively and well; and the physically relaxed feeling associated with ending a tense exercise. Sounds like I'm trying to sell you something, but give it a conscientious try with an emphasis on cooperating with your partner and see if you don't agree.

Objective

From a variety of stances and making palm contact, partners begin to apply equal pressure against one another so that the pressure increases very gradually as one of the partners counts slowly, out loud, to five. When maximum pressure against one another is achieved another count of five is made as that upper limit pressure is maintained. Finish off with a final count of five as joint pressure is slowly released. Attempt to do this so that the counting is consecutive and smooth. Increase pressure for 5 secs.—Hold pressure for 5 secs.—Decrease pressure for 5 secs.

Considerations

- If you are using palm-to-palm contact, face one another squarely remembering that the objective here is to achieve the 5-5-5 sequence cooperatively. If one of the partners is obviously stronger than the other, the stronger person has to adjust the pressure he/she is applying so that this does not turn into an arm wrestling contest. Ideally, where the palms meet, both hands should not move one way or the other during the 5-5-5 counting sequence.
- Left hand, right hand, press upward, press downward, press ankles against one another; it's up to you and your partner how and where you want to apply the 5-5-5 count and resistance.
- Facing one another, and with both hands extended, ask students to put both palms on each other's shoulders. Partner's try to gradually (5-5-5) push each other into the ground, then release.
- This is not a contest so if you see students twisting or leveraging their bodies to gain a physical (competitive) advantage, the value of the exercise is being compromised.
- As an additional challenge for mature groups, ask the two participants to maintain eye contact throughout the 5-5-5 sequence.
- Don't rush through this series of exercises; allow pairs to experiment with various pressure tactics and positions.
- After a few one-on-one attempts, suggest pairs get together and share what they have tried with their partners, then combine those ideas as a quad 5-5-5 team. The more you allow people to be creative, the more they will want to pursue your agenda.

Funny Face

The outlandish histrionics associated with Funny Face have their place, and that place is not immediately after a group has gone through a "storming" session or just before attempting a climb up The Pamper Pole. Give Funny Face a try when you think the group is comfortable with your interpretation of zany, i.e., when they have seen enough of the "real" you to know that your Dog Shake (see page 124) demo isn't a manifestation of a canine neurosis. Funny Face seems to function best when group members need a break from being sophisticated teens, office workers, executives, administrators, etc.

Announced Objective

To make your partner smile and/or laugh before you do.

Funny Face

I've never been very good at this game, always breaking a smile at the worst time and I've even been known to slip a giggle . . . just not varsity material. But, it bothered me. I've always been good at things I want to be good at, so I thought a thought and came up with a technique for inciting my Funny Face partners to not only smile, but even occasionally flat-out laugh. I don't play Funny Face much anymore, so I don't feel too poorly about revealing my proprietary secret. There is a caveat though; if you have recently recovered from a head cold, for the sake of propriety and mucus retention, don't try to use this technique.

The set up and application are simple enough. Take a dime (a nickel does not work for me and a quarter is out of the question) and stick it up your nose, i.e., into your nasal cavity; either side, it doesn't matter. Notice I said, "into your nasal cavity," <u>not</u> your sinus cavity. That's all you need to know—you're ready.

When you are face to face with your opponent, wait about five seconds or until you are sure they are giving you their best serious face and are glaring right at you. Slowly bring a cupped hand, palm up, to just under your nose (not too cupped, and not too close, because you want them to fully observe what is about to happen). Then put the thumb of your other hand against the nostril that <u>does not</u> have the dime in it, and snort OUT forcefully. The dime will fly out of your open nostril into your cupped hand (often bouncing off your palm because of its velocity . . . if so, back off the snort a bit).

Now the tough part; you have to remain serious. Don't laugh until your partner does; you won't have to wait long; works every time. You're welcome.

Not-So-Obvious Objective

To break down some inhibitions, embellish the word *zany*, and have some spontaneous funn.

Procedure and Various Rules

Funny Face can be used either vis-a-vis, or with silly sets of say 4–7 players. The rules, recently established and constantly being amended, state that after the GO signal everyone in the small circle tries to make everyone else either smile, chuckle, giggle, laugh, guffaw, etc. If you slip and display the slightest sign of humor you are eliminated. (There are usually lots of self-appointed judges standing around, so don't worry about you having to make lots of smile/no smile decisions.) Participants are not allowed to touch one another, and all eyes must stay open and looking in the general direction of the action. As all true funny-facers know, "He who looks away, faces funn another day."

Galloping Feet or Footsie

Galloping Feet is a variation of Galloping Hands. (*Small Book About Large Group Games*, page 9)

Sit your group in a circle on some lush, verdant turf, on warm sand, or perhaps snuggling your tush onto and into a two-inch pile shag rug (be aware of the current slang use of shag). Your choice, but make your posteriors happy. Create the circle tight enough so that participants are almost hip to hip.

Start a movement with your foot (wiggle just your foot . . . yes, you are part of the sitting circle), indicating that you would like the group to pass that movement around the circle with dispatch, i.e., fast, clockwise or otherwise. Really, any foot movement is OK, but try to be creative and initiate more than just one motion.

There is something fascinating and functionally attractive about sitting in a circle, watching and taking part in the sequential antics of the group's feet. Hand movements can be subtle, flowing, lambent and ethereal (like the Hawaiian hula!); foot movements, however, are mostly jerky, robot-like, and distal to the point of being out-of-body. I'd bet whatever below-the-waist challenge you come up with is upstaged by the herky-jerky movement of feet trying to respond to a neuronal command center at least five feet distant from the source; think anatomically, or don't think at all . . . just keep moving those feet . . . and reading.

Dismissing that last outré paragraph as more of Karl's contorted cognitions, ask the group to pass a demonstrated sequential foot movement AFAP (as fast as possible) around the circle. This speed task works better (looks better too) with groups of thirty-plus participants than with smaller groups. Whatever movements(s) you or the group initiates is not necessarily integral to anything else (unless it turns out that way). You are doing this to initiate creativity, fun, and some spontaneous laughter with the idea of creating a useful, pleasant, play segue to whatever comes next.

> " . . . we take chances, risk great odds, love, laugh, dance . . . in short we play. The people who play are the creators."
> Holbrook Jackson

If you can't figure out why you are frantically trying to establish a reason for sequentially flipping and flopping your feet in concert with a bunch of other smiling foot fetish folks, loosen up some; let play mode overcome curriculum mode. Remember the acronym FUNN? Let IT happen occasionally.

Human Camera

There aren't too many low key activities like this one that allow situational trust to develop so quickly and easily. Having said that, make sure you sequence Human Camera so that at least a minimum of unselfconscious touch/trust activities have already been attempted: examples–*Tag* games; Compass Walk; Hand Jive; Bug Tug.

Objective

To demonstrate how to use a partner as a functioning camera, with each partner having the alternating opportunity to be either the photographer or the camera.

Procedure

After having listened with patient attention to well meaning facilitator comments about how a camera is like the human eye (or vice versa), partners for this trust activity are either assigned or chosen. Indicate that initially one of the pair will act as a camera, the other person as photographer.

The photographer asks the "camera" to shut his/her eyes, then leads the surprisingly mobile "camera" to a location where there is an interesting object available for recording on retinal film. Using the human camera body as an infinitely mobile tripod, the photographer maneuvers his/her partner's head (the camera) in such a way that his/her closed eyes are positioned directly in front of the object to be photographed—a close-up in this case. Gently pull your partner's ear lobe to activate the shutter (eyelid). With this tactile encouragement, the "camera's" eyelids open and shut <u>quickly</u> in order to record the scene. The photographer can, at this juncture, tell the camera what shutter speed might be needed, giving the camera some guidance as to how long to keep their lids open; longer for panoramas, rapidly for action subjects.

Lead your partner from scene to subject, recording maybe three photographic possibilities, which will establish the basis for a later discussion between the two of you. Switch roles after having talked about the experience. Human Camera as a shared experience lends itself to trust and developing a pair's rapport.

There are two kinds of trust being established here, physical and emotional.

- The "camera" is physically trusting the photographer not to put him/her in harm's way with their eyes closed.
- Being photographically positioned in a socially awkward posture is not a common problem while Human Camera is being shared, but occasionally a creative instigator might unfeelingly position their partner's face near where it should not be. Fleeting humor? Perhaps. Building trust? No.
- Since there is some mature decision making associated with being the photographer, give some thought to proper sequencing of this activity.

Inch Worm

If you're looking to get serious grass stains on your shorts in order to try out some newly purchased, environmentally benign, super biodegradable cleaning soap, here's the butt slider you've been looking for . . . and it also serves as a decent one-on-one warm-up activity.

Objective

With a partner, to move inch-worm style on turf or mat by sitting on each other's feet while alternating push and pull moves with the upper body, attempting to accomplish this in a cooperative, somewhat coordinated fashion. Or, more succinctly, move like an inch worm with your partner.

Set Up and Procedure

- Sit on the turf facing your partner, then skootch toward one another until you and he/she are close enough to sit on the top of each other's feet. (Big feet offer an advantage, or at least a certain comfort factor.)
- Grasp your partner's elbows, or the fleshy, sometimes muscular, distal end of their humerus.
- Decide which direction you would like to travel. Lateral movement is out, so it's either toward or away from your partner.
- After deciding, the partner in whose direction you are headed lifts his/her derriere off the ground and shifts that part of their anatomy 12"–14" toward whatever goal you have in mind; be reasonable considering it's a backward transfer.
- The second partner then lifts his/her posterior off the ground, and in a cooperative, rocking, bug-like movement duplicates the step above, moving toward the partner, i.e., forward.
- Repeat the rocking, butt shuffling, push/pull movements and try to gain some momentum as your skill and confidence increases.

After your various pairs of bug shufflers have had some impromptu fun inch-worming around the field, call them over (encourage walking) and indicate, because of their rapid and impressive increase in skill and dexterity, that the opportunity for a grand inch-worm/bug-tug competition has presented itself, but only for those pairs who feel they have it all together.

After a few minutes of training time to get the "bugs" out, set up the volunteer pairs on a starting line (rope), aiming them toward another section of parallel rope about 20 feet away. Then it's ready, set, GO! Be prepared to observe gyrations, twisting, and competitive zeal beyond the typical Wide World of Sport's fare. And, if a slower pair happens to grab a more coordinated duo while being passed, well, that's just an unfortunate misinterpretation of what cooperative competition really means.

What does the winner get? Grass stains . . . lots of grass stains.

InVisible Jump Rope

If you think skipping rope is for dweebs-only, try jumping into a "hot pepper," staccato-like, *Double Dutch* set up, turned by a couple of street-wise young women, who could, BTW, turn and jump you into the next county. Most students, male and female, respond well to jumping rope if presented as a means of having fun <u>and</u> achieving fitness.

(Author's Aside) *On a recent flight I was caught without reading material, so, once again found myself totally immersed* in the buy-it-here-for-big-bucks catalog, conveniently located in the seat-back pocket directly in my line of sight. I was on my second thumb through (it's either that or perusing the in-flight American-Delta-U.S. Air-United magazine, reading about "Three Days in Someplace-I'll-Never-Travel-To," or "How to Drink Red Wine With Chicken and Still Feel OK About Yourself"). At least the "buy me!" catalog presents itself as what it is, a blatant commercial series of advertisements, rather than the bland and predictable Muzak-like subliminal text of the in-flight mag.

However, I did find an interesting fitness item in the catalog that seemed a bit beyond the pale, and that you need to know about. It was an advert for a ropeless jump rope. True, all you buy is two handles that sport a pair of small digital read out windows, each indicating how many times you swept your arms up and down. The big selling points were that the handles beeped if you did not keep up with your chosen work out pace, and they packed really well in your luggage. I'll bet they would have worked swell as a prop for Invisible Jump Rope.

Now, don't get me wrong, I like jumping rope, it's just that I get bored quickly with something so repetitious. So someone tells me, "Do tricks while you're jumping and spinning the rope." Interested, I try a few tricks and continue missing, i.e., stepping on the whirling rope or having it whack me in the shins. What we need (the royal WE), is a rope jumping, warm-up series of tricks that will allow us to emulate the good guys without having to look bad. Enter The Invisible Jump Rope, just pretend . . .

Measure the length of your pretend rope by standing on the rope and bringing the ends up to under your armpits, cut there. You obviously can't expect to do all these tricks if your pretend rope is too short. Mime with me here! Step off the rope (the one you were just measuring and cutting) and holding the ends, flip the bight portion of the rope over your head . . . nobody begins jumping with the rope in front, it just isn't done.

Begin slowly, jumping and casually turning the rope in sequence with your hops, being careful not to miss. See how easy it is to coordinate the hand and foot movements? Try a trick! Cross your hands (and your arms up to the elbow) vigorously in front of you each time you jump. This crossover move isn't that difficult and will definitely impress your friends, particularly if you're holding two digitally enhanced, beeping handles with no rope attached. Unbelievable!

You recognize by now that almost anything is possible within this playful format, so use your imagination in context with this anything-goes workout.

1. Try a double jump, a triple, maybe even six turns! If you make it you have just broken a Guinness world's record; five turns in one jump—really!
2. Try some fancy footwork, any old dance step you can think of will do; a jig, a fling, an entrechat, etc. Don't forget to keep turning the invisible rope.
3. Entice someone near you to jump at your pace and initiate some follow-the-leader moves. At the end of a few wildly impossible turns together, spin/hop away from one another and with a nod of agreement, both throw your ropes high in the air toward one another. Grasp the falling, flailing rope and continue jumping and turning without missing a beat. Fantastic!
4. Hop toward someone and try jumping as a pair. (Your rope or mine?)
5. End with some kind of Brogdingagian group jump . . . and not one person has missed a beat.

A Lightweight Idea a.k.a. Balloon Steeplechase

I've had some fun over the years with this balloon activity, and I believe the amusement resulted from my having to create and establish a balloon obstacle course almost every time I presented the activity.

Objective

To move an inflated balloon through a steeplechase of obstacles as quickly and efficiently as possible; this is a timed event.

Procedure

- Haul out your stash of 12-inch diameter balloons and ask each member of your group to blow up that balloon to about its advertised diameter and tie it off. Smaller balloons don't allow the whack it/smack it action that makes this game both challenging and fun.
- As the balloon festooned group hangs on your every word, point out a steeplechase route that you planned and tried before they showed up. Actually take them through the course to reduce the number of "Yeah, but . . ." questions; there are always questions.
- In laying out the course, think OBSTACLES; bleachers, in and out of doors, fences, windows, through the front seat of a car. Also think SAFETY. Don't create obstacles that put people in jeopardy.

Rules

- The balloon must remain airborne the whole time, start to finish. The balloon can be whacked, bumped, blown, and tipped, but never gripped or held.

- If a balloon touches the ground (floor) the player has 15 seconds added to their final time, or, they must repeat the previous obstacle—their choice. The balloon is allowed to touch the various obstacles, but may not rest on them. In other words, the balloon must be moving all the time.
- If a balloon breaks, the aggrieved player shouts for a new one (delivered with alacrity by the facilitator, you, in this case), blows it up, ties it off and continues without penalty, except for the time taken to get back in the game.
- If the second balloon breaks, that player is disqualified for the time being. "Time being" according to the bureau of weights and measures is 150 seconds, (151 seconds in a leap year).

Comments and Considerations

- Try using a staggered start (a participant every 15 seconds).
- Have the students time themselves. This takes the onus off you, and it gives them the opportunity to make another attempt to better their own time.
- Considering that so many activities are done for time, you might want to present this lightweight idea as simply something to try, i.e., "See if you can do it."
- If your group numbers more than 15, set up an additional obstacle course.
- As a variation (be ready for chaos), start one group at the beginning and one at the end of the obstacle course. If you strongly suspect your group can't handle the predictable bedlam, postpone introducing this activity until they can.
- If your group is unusually adept (or needs some good solid failure and/or laughter), ask them to complete the obstacle course by hitting the balloon with only their _____ (insert an acceptable portion of their anatomy other than a hand).

Mirror Image

Mirror Image allows an acceptable entree (acceptable to the students) into unconventional (read wacky) quasi-curriculum activities. How's that for an I-can't-wait-to-try-this intro? Or, what in Heaven's name are you introducing?

Objective

With one person acting as initiator, his/her partner attempts to become and respond as his/her mirror image.

Procedure

- Ask the pair to face one another about 18" apart from a toe-to-toe position.
- Have the pair decide who is going to be the movement initiator and who will be the "mirror."
- The initiator makes controlled movements (including facial gyrations) that their partner must try to duplicate.

Thoughts and Considerations

- All movements should be in slow enough motion to allow the "mirror" both the time and desire to want to try to duplicate the initiator's actions. Fast, and/or unrealistic movements result in a quick breakdown of the desire to cooperate by the follower.
- The enjoyment level of sharing these actions and reactions is largely dependent upon your initial low key presentation of the whats, whys, and hows.

1. What—Offer a demonstration with a volunteer.
2. Why—We "play" toward developing greater levels of communication, cooperating at a higher level, and trusting one another physically and emotionally.
3. How—See Procedure above, and (1).

Variations

- After each member of the dyad has had the chance to be both initiator and "mirror," ask the pairs to try the anti-mirror set up, i.e., the follower tries to do exactly the opposite of what they are being shown. This antithetical switch can produce some classic action/reaction moves with resultant laughable confusion, and where the words "Slow Down" becomes a mantra.
- Just for a change of pace, have one person as initiator being followed by two, three, or more "images."
- And for the ultimate, existential Mirror Image experience, ask a person to stand in front of a large mirror and follow his/her own image; an Olympic performance every time, guaranteed. Be sure to move slowly as not to get ahead of yourself.

Mrs. O'Grady

Mrs. O'Grady is a typical summer camp stunt, but is useful as an adventure curriculum ice breaker. "Did you know that a good laugh is so strong you can break ice with it?"

Objective

To join a group in performing a disjointed, sequential series of non sequiturs for no other reason than to see if you can keep up, and eventually determine where and when the zaniness will end.

Set Up

Six to 8 people standing in a comfortably loose circle, with you as part of the circle.

Procedure

- Ask the person to your right or left (once chosen, continue in that direction) the following sequence of questions, also demonstrating what their physical and verbal response should be.

  You—"Did you hear what happened to Mrs. O'Grady?

  Them—"No, what happened?"

  You—"She died!"

  Them—"How did she die?"

  You—"With one cocked eye."

- At this juncture you close one eye tightly and keep it closed for the remainder of the game. The person next to you who has been answering your questions then asks the identical series of questions to the person next to him/her. This continues around the circle until everyone sports "one cocked eye."

- When the questioning role is once again yours, continue to add embellishments to the way Mrs. O'Grady expired. (examples: ". . . with her mouth awry." (twist your mouth grotesquely to one side); " . . . breathing a sigh."; ". . . with her leg held high."; and " . . . waving goodbye."
- By the time all of these movements, sounds, and postures have been initiated, copied, and continued by all members of the circle, physical fatigue and a certain hysterical monotony allows an unselfconscious abandonment to the game.
- I don't think I need to say this, but . . . I'm going to anyway. Part of your role is obviously as initiator. Your other function is as a person obviously not afraid to take a chance and have fun at the same time. Please don't present these various off-the-wall activities by the numbers, and with limited enthusiasm.
- If things are progressing too slowly, the next time the questioning comes around to you, include two things to do in your expanding obituary.
- If you have student leaders who feel comfortable with the initiator's role, have them begin other *O'Grady* circles. Don't include more than eight people in a circle for obvious reasons of fatigue and tedious repetition.

I'd suggest not debriefing this "theater in the round," simply enjoy it with everyone else.

Orange Teeth

The last sentence of my write up on Orange Teeth in *Silver Bullets* (1984) reads, "This idea is straight from the 4th grade via my son Matthew." Matt is now 35, lives in Salem, MA, and works in a clinic there as a hyperbaric chamber technician, and I'd guess has not thought much about Orange Teeth for some time . . . but I have.

Want or need to impress your 4th grader? Want to try something that will make you smile, citrically? I think you'll like this, particularly as a shared experience.

Objective

Forget the objective, just try it.

Set Up

- Cut an orange (thin-skinned oranges work best) into quarters and eat the edible part down to the whitish rind. Eating the orange isn't part of the experience, but don't waste it. Speaking of the word *orange*—did you know that the word orange does not rhyme with any other word? Now you know.
- Slice the quartered peel to form "teeth," as indicated in the photo. Don't cut too near the edge as it's too easy to rip the rind. Use a cutting board.
- After making the cuts, position the rind in your mouth so that the exterior of the rind (orange color) faces in; this will take some manual lip manipulation as you fit the edges of the rind between your lips and gums. I'll admit, not too tasty, but come on, this is experiential education

and you'll be pleased (entertained) by the results.

- Your noticeably ascorbic false teeth should now be in place. Look in the mirror and stick your tongue through the teeth for a touch of bizarre realism. See, I told you this would be fun.
- Take digital photos of each other for later sharing with unbelieving friends and family.
- Thanks again, Matt.

People-to-People Surfing

Cowabunga! I always wanted to say (write) that in a purposeful way. So, there you go! I know it's a west coast, surfer-dude term, but have no idea what it means, probably just an exclamation of feelin' good about being a surfer. As to this activity, if you're looking to create a situation where some unselfconscious touching is going to happen BIG TIME, you have found it.

Objective

To create a land-based, people-to-people "surfing" situation where the "surfer" rolls on top of, and is propelled by, a base of self-rotating people lying perpendicular to the surfer-dude.

Set Up and Procedure

- Situate the group (as many as possible) lying face down on a grassy area so that bodies are parallel to one another and about two feet apart. Forward progress of the surfer is determined by the rolling-over commitment of these whitewater volunteers.

- Ask a volunteer surfer-dude to lie face down on top of, and at right angles to, the first two or three lined up bodies.
- As the entertainment director (That's you!) Shouts, "Surf's Up!", the people under the surfer roll over in a direction that everyone has agreed upon, downhill is certainly easier and results in a much wilder ride.
- If the surf-machine is well-controlled, the surfer will travel swiftly (albeit somewhat clumpy-bumpy) toward the "beach," i.e., whatever destination was chosen.
- Each member of the surf machine performs one roll as soon as the surfer reaches him/her. It is here (there) that the term "unselfconscious touch" becomes manifest.
- After the ride, reinstate the surf mechanism, making whatever position changes are necessary or desired, and repeat with another "Hot Curl" sequence for the next *malihini*. (Quaint Hawaiian term as applied to a newcomer to the islands, usually a dweeb.)
- It's best for the surf people, and surfer dude, to keep their arms extended forward during the exciting ride to preclude a rolling elbow massage.

Pole (Sapling) Vaulting

When I was a kid (couple of years ago) there were two things I really enjoyed doing when there seemed to be nothing else to do and nobody to do it with; vaulting and throwing spears, both activities utilizing whatever the woods near my home had to offer.

The spear throwing eventually moved from flights of fantasy (Trojan wars, hoards of attacking Mongols and, of course, aliens of various description), to intercollegiate javelin competition (over 200' on a good day). The vaulting never got past the play stage, as I educationally dressed up what I used to do as a kid and made it more pedagogically acceptable; it's amazing, as an author, what a few chosen words and some level of respectability allows.

Objective

Using an 8-foot long sturdy sapling as a vaulting pole, to run forward, place the pole into the turf, and hold onto the other end as it completes its predestined arc with you along as a rider.

Simple field vaulting offers a just-fooling-around activity that generates a decent upper body workout and a sense of reasonable risk-taking that encourages continued efforts, plus it's fun. There is a unique free-of-the-earth weightlessness and sense of swift movement that can be achieved without much effort or skill by using a simple vaulting pole, and a commitment to try.

Procedure (Including an Approximate How-to)

Provide a number of hardwood saplings that measure about 8' long. These poles need to support someone's weight plus the momentum of the vault. Don't use skinny, flexible poles made out of aluminum, bamboo, PVC, or conduit. Find some hardwood saplings growing in an area that needs a touch of environmental selective pruning.

- Do not sharpen the ends of the pole.
- Here's the part I think you'll like. Don't teach the students how to vault, reverting to the tenets of experiential learning which strongly indicates that some failure is not only OK, but lends itself to eventual success. If the vaulter jogs forward holding the pole, plants the pole solidly in the turf, and holds onto the other end of the pole, there's a good chance that forward progress free of the ground will occur in a more or less arc-like fashion. If not, there's plenty of grass and attempts to be had.
- How about a demo by the facilitator? Sure, go for it, but remember not to look <u>too</u> good.
- If the vaulting pole continues to end up between a vaulter's legs (not comfy), you might want to assist with some basic technique suggestions like, "Don't let the pole end up between your legs."
- As in all that we do within the realm of experiential adventure education, how far and high someone vaults is not as significant as the consistency of attempts. Make absolutely sure that everyone who tries gets the same amount of encouragement and praise.
- Let's be honest, there are some folks who just aren't going to clear the ground. Suggest that they try a standing vault, i.e., no runs up. It is not the distance achieved that's important, rather an attitude toward trying.

As expertise is gained, and the pole no longer ends up between their legs, the desire for self-testing or vaulting over obstacles might be the logical next step. Try vaulting for distance on grass, or set up a vault over a small gully. If the situation presents itself, don't ignore a wet or muddy area as incentive for a grand challenge. Don't attempt vaults on the ground that may leave holes in your epidermis—rocky, woodsy, littered.

Ok, now for the spears. I'm kidding. No spears . . . leave the spears alone.

Popsicle Push-Up

I enjoy presenting this initiative problem then watching the puzzled looks on the faces of the participants as they try to bring order and comprehension to the simple but enigmatic instructions. If you have never heard of, or participated in, the initiative Popsicle Push-Up (hard to believe these days), read the objective and rules below and perhaps you'll appreciate what I'm saying.

Objective

To support the entire group two inches off the floor (ground) for two seconds.

Rules

- Only palm contact is allowed with the floor.
- No props.

See what I mean? That's it. That's all. Is that great, or what?

Do you think someone will suggest having everyone do a handstand? Great theoretical solution. Will it work for everyone? Next idea please.

How about the Yoga frog stance, where each person squats down, rests their knees against their forearms while balancing on their palms? The obviously experienced Yogi-type person suggesting this method gives an impressive demo. How many can do that? Next . . .

What if everyone jumps up in the air at the same time, like in the Toyota advert? Do you know how long Michael (air) Jordan stays off the floor in one of his patented leaps toward the net. You don't want to know. Next idea . . . and how about some realism.

During this rash of **impossiprobability** there's often someone actually thinking. That person may even hit on a solution that works (there's more than one), but there's still something missing—credibility. The quiet thinker in this case nails it, but does not have the "ear" of the group or doesn't have the "gym" voice needed to be heard over the spate

of ideas being offered. Since you are the sage facilitator in attendance, take note of *who* and *what* for the eventual debrief, but let it ride for now, i.e., don't offer, "Hey, why don't you listen to . . ." In other words, let the group stumble, and operate inefficiently; maintain their right to fail.

Because the name of the game is Popsicle Push-Up, here's the solution based on that name. But, considering the cocktails of thought involved, be aware, if you offer this problem to half a dozen groups you may end up with variations of half a dozen acceptable solutions.

You mean accept pretty much any solution that comes close?

No. Be liberal with interpretations, but be tough in sticking to the stated rules. Nobody really wants the solution to this or any initiative problem as a gift. (There's a reason they call it a challenge course.) One of your primary responsibilities as a facilitator is to maintain the challenge. If there is anything that will quickly degrade the validity of this kind of experiential approach it is an instructor/teacher who wants/needs their group to be successful so badly that they consistently revert to their years of training as a teacher, and end up teaching, rather than allowing the group to come up with their own techniques, answers, and mistakes. There's more validity to what can be learned by screwing up, and trying again, than having the answers spoon fed in the guise of "successful" completion.

A Solution

- First set up the classic four person push-up called The Popsicle Push-Up.*
- Ask for four volunteers who can do one push-up, then invite one of those people to lie prone on the floor as if he/she were about to do a push-up.
- The second person lies down at right angles to the first person, with the tops of his/her feet (instep) on top of the first person's upper back. Because of the inherent weakness of the lower back (4th & 5th lumbar), readjust people's feet off that area.
- The third person repeats the prone procedure, using the second person as his/her foot rest.
- The fourth person fits into this weave as to connect everyone in a square configuration; his/her insteps are on top of person #3. The square is complete when person #1 puts his/her feet on top of person #4. All four players should now be face

*popsicle push-up—The popsicle portion of the game name came from the square configuration of wooden popsicle sticks that we used to weave together as kids.

down in a push-up position with their insteps on top of someone's back. Check out the photograph.

On a count of 1, 2, 3—all four prone participants attempt to do a push-up on three. If done well and together there will be four raised bodies with only eight palms touching the floor—impressive. If one of the push-up people has trouble getting up (pressure on their back might be a problem), indicate to that person to start their push-up on the #2 count rather than 3, offering a leveraged head start; it works sometimes.

After your various eager groups of four have had some fun with this quartet push-up (it looks and feels good when done well), ask the group to try to connect the quad arrangements in an attempt to include the entire group in a mass popsicle push-up. If someone just can't physically manage to squeeze out a push-up, locate that person on top of an

already formed prone quad so that the person on top can reach down to add whatever strength they have to the joint push-up, at the same time being lifted by the combined strength of the group.

Popsicle Push-Up is a time-consuming event; not from the standpoint of actually putting the people together and doing it, but because it takes a long time for a group to decide on a realistic solution. This group attempt obviously needs a leader, and that leader has to emerge, not be assigned.

People who have back problems, or for whatever reason opt to not participate, can be official photographers or prejudiced referees for the next WORLD RECORD attempt.

I mentioned there were other successful ways to solve this problem, so don't be surprised when you see them. Your response to the "successful" group–a knowing smile coupled with an affirmative nod.

Red Baron Stretch

When Project Adventure was still in the process of establishing and defining itself in the early 70s (the majority of our work then was with physical education students), staff were constantly trying to come up with creative, zany, and colorful ways to do what had been accomplished in the past with repetitive uncomfortable exercises. The Red Baron Stretch was one of those creative ways.

Objective

To encourage a group, at the beginning of a P.E. class, to participate in a stretching exercise.

Caveat Be aware, to make this "work" the facilitator must be comfortable with the imaginative patter associated with the exercise, and have the chutzpah to demonstrate what he/she expects the students to try. Experiential adventure education is not clipboard teaching, (Do this, do that, and I'll stand here recording grades).

Procedure

- Pretend that each of your hands (salute position) is an airplane engaged in aerial combat. Right hand = The Red Baron. Left hand = Snoopy.
- The "planes" can chase each other anywhere that your body, arm, and contortionist inclinations allow. Keep your feet comfortably separated and stationary.
- Don't forget the occasional burst of oral gunfire for authenticity.
- To add a bit of cooperation to the aerial combat ask one person to be The Red Baron and another person to be Snoopy, right hand to left hand for example.
- All movement must be in slow motion so that the flyers can stay in sync with one another.
- The RBS is not meant to be a few desultory arm movements this way and that. Take your partner to where they have never been before, make this activity a STRETCH.

The RBS is a madcap, come-join-in-play stretching exercise–not meant to be competitive.

Rodeo Throw

Try the following activity on a wooden gym floor; a rubberized gym floor provides too much friction.

Throw a hula hoop away from you with an underhand wrist flick, and in the same whipping motion impart a backward (clockwise) spin to the hoop. The hoop will travel—rapidly spinning and gently bouncing—away from the thrower until the backward spinning motion overcomes forward momentum, causing the hoop to spin in place for a couple of seconds, eventually returning in the general direction of the thrower.

For some arcane reason people like putting a backward spin on hoops. As such, the rubric above covers a bunch of what you might call "minor events," but they are things people like to do, and there's some physical skill associated that can be practiced and improved upon.

One skill that comes to mind is: stand on the gym floor, hoop in hand, facing a blank wall about 30 feet away (more or less, depending upon the age and throwing adeptness of the participants). Throw your hoop toward the wall with the characteristic backward spin and see how close you can come to the wall without making wall contact and still have your hoop spin back to you. A single pivot step is allowed to grab the returning hoop.

- Or try, with many hoops at hand, to see how many hoops you can throw and spin before the first one falls over.
- How about the ultimate flamboyant throw and catch? Spin the hoop away from you and when it comes back don't move, just let it park itself right next to your side where your casual hand awaits. Of course, just as the hoop arrives at your hand, you look distractedly away. As always, looking casually competent requires practice.
- Standing at one end of the gym give a hoop a maximum spin and see

who can record the longest reverse roll, i.e., how far out and all the way back.

FUNN aside, practicing this type of throw is preliminary training for the next event; the classic Rodeo Throw. Try to have lots of hoops on hand to include as many people as possible.

Two participants stand next to one another at one end of the gym; one as the runner, the other as thrower. The thrower reverse spins the hoop on the floor, as above, and the runner attempts to sprint out and scoot through the vertically spinning hoop without knocking it over. Timing is important, as the best chance to scamper through the hoop is when it briefly spins in place. Two trips through the hoop are possible but require a good throw and a committed runner. The best throw-and-scoot I ever witnessed was five trips back and through the hoop. The thrower was excellent, the runner was small, fearless, and nimble . . . and they practiced. An easy way to improve—use bigger hoops.

Variations quickly present themselves from this simple beginning as people align themselves differently (opposite ends of the gym for nearly simultaneous throws and dives), or try increasingly difficult tricks—feet first through the spinning hoop. Or just have fun spinning the hoops by yourself and ignore the various challenges. Sometimes getting up in the morning is enough of a challenge, and it's funn just to have fun.

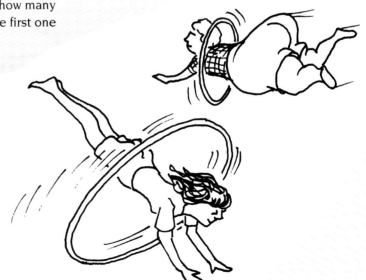

Scooter Slalom

Scooter Slalom reminds me of what I used to do as a kid . . . make up something that was difficult to accomplish, something that made you breathe hard, and where regular rule changes seemed to make sense. I like Scooter Slalom.

Objective

To be pushed by a partner, while tentatively perched upon a pair of gym scooters, through a challenging slalom course made up of creatively-arranged orange cones (pylons). This is a timed event. See illustration.

Set Up and Procedure

You will need at least two gym scooters. Check out the scooters to make sure the wheels turn freely; use wheels with ball bearings if possible. If the wheels don't spin freely (360° laterally <u>and</u> vertically) they are going to cause hard-to-remove friction streaks on the gym floor. Does this concern you? It better, because most custodians feel toward their newly polished gym floor as parents do toward a first child—beautiful, one of a kind, and irreplaceable.

This aerobic activity requires that the students work in pairs. They will be "scooting" through an ad hoc slalom course set up on the gym floor in an attempt to establish a fast time. Emphasize pair satisfaction because time comparisons with other scooting pairs are inevitable, and occasionally detrimental to what you are trying to achieve.

The rider sits on one of the scooters and places his/her feet on the second scooter. (See illustration.) The second member of the pair stands behind the rider and provides the GO by pushing. The slalom course (see illustration), should include a few right angle turns, a couple of "hairpins," and a straight-a-way; be inventive (tough but realistic) as you create the course.

As the pair attempts to make their fastest trip through the pylons, it becomes obvious that the pair who works together (the rider uses his/her hands as

outriggers to aid balance and turning), shows the most improvement. There is an infectious quality to this activity as each pair is convinced they can "do it faster next time."

Rules

- One pair on the course at a time.
- For each pylon touched, a second is added to the total time. If a pylon is knocked over, add another second.
- If a rider's foot comes off the front scooter and touches the floor inadvertently, the ride may

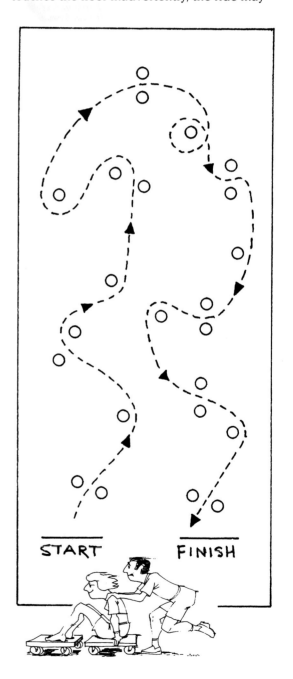

continue. If both feet end up on the floor (no scooter support), the ride ends. If a rider's posterior ends up on the floor—game over!

- Sling-shotting the rider is not allowed . . . but sure is effective.
- Rider and pusher must maintain physical contact throughout the run, particularly over the finish line where sling-shotting a rider is so tempting.
- Riders should wear helmets.
- Riders should also wear gloves to protect their palms during turns.

Considerations

- Try to set up the slalom course (using the entire gym floor) so that the START and FINISH lines are at the same end of the gym.

- As this activity uses up a good deal of energy, a pair should be encouraged to switch roles as rider and pusher. This suggestion is typically well-received by the pusher.
- Try to have more than one pair of scooters available to keep things moving.
- As the pushing efforts become more competitive, fully half the attempts will end with the rider polishing the floor with their posterior. Have the next couple ready to start.
- A couple of students in the group should act as timers until their turn comes up; this frees you up to be in the right place at the right time, however you want to interpret that.

Self-Testing Tests

Many years ago, (decades actually) when LIFE magazine was much more a purveyor of news, I read an article, which at the time had a profound effect on how I saw myself as an athlete and how I wanted to see myself. I can't remember the name of the article now, but the author was Dr. Thomas Cureton, a researcher well-known for his groundbreaking work in physical education testing, particularly in the 1940s and 50s. The article outlined 10 physical tests, indicating if you could pass them all you were aspiring Olympic material. To back up that claim, Dr. Cureton applied the 10 tests to three well-known Olympic contenders at the time, and all three failed to pass all 10 tests. In fact, only one person passed eight of the 10 tests. Dr. Cureton, then in his 60s, passed them all. (It was his test after all.)

I was in college at the time and a self-avowed jock. I took the test and only passed half the challenges; I was shocked and chagrined. The test was a fitness epiphany of sorts, inspiring a personal physical regimen aimed at passing those tests, all of which I eventually accomplished and went on to garner many sports awards. But what I'm leading up to is the fact that these tests were effective as an incentive in my case because no one else knew about them, and no one was testing me. I was under no pressure

to perform, experiencing a personal pursuit of excellence (Cureton's tested and well-documented levels of excellence).

Years later I borrowed a couple of Cureton's tests that seemed most applicable and used them as part of Project Adventure's growing adventure curriculum. I've found that most people like to be challenged in a way that allows some choice and Cureton's tests allowed that choice. In addition, all his tests are self-graded. If you do well, pat yourself on the back because there's no one else there to do any patting, and if you do poorly, you don't have to make a wild guess to access who's at fault.

There's another thing I like about these self graded tests; the ability to check progress over a period of time. This week I'm going to test my balance and flexibility. Next week I'll try the same tests to see if my training has allowed any improvement.

I suspect by this time you get some inclination that I like Dr. Cureton's tests. So here's an example; try it, see how you do. Have all your participants stand separately a few feet apart and raise up on their toes (way up) to a tenuous balanced position. Arms are then extended to the front, hands together, palms down—like a person about to dive. Feet are closely juxtaposed. Try to hold this tippy position for 20 seconds with your eyes closed, and without falling from your tip-toe stance. If someone loses balance and tippy-toes out of position, suggest they return

Other Cureton "Tests"

- From a kneeling position swing your arms forward, jump to your feet and maintain balance, i.e., do not shift feet after landing.
- Hold your toe, or tip of your shoe, and jump through the hoop/loop formed by your arm and leg, without releasing your toe or shoe (see photo).
- Sit on the floor, legs straight in front, with heels 18" apart, fingers laced behind the neck. Bend trunk slowly forward until your forehead is 8" from the floor. Maintain for two seconds. Do not bounce.
- Run in place for 120 seconds at 180 steps per minute, then take one deep breath and hold that breath for 30 seconds. (This was the toughest test for me!)

Do these tests remind you of the tedious and predictable pull-up, push-up, sit-up routines of your gym class? Does the word play come to mind? No answer necessary . . . it was a rhetorical question anyway.

*"All other species play to play. We're the only species that **plays** to win. Maybe that's why there are so many losers."*
Lily Tomlin

immediately to their balanced posture. While on your toes, count the number of times a balance lapse occurs during those 20 seconds. In this way, a means for future comparison is recorded and the number of lapses are known only to the participant.

If you are interested in learning more about Dr. Cureton and his physical fitness tests, check him out on the Internet under *Thomas K. Cureton*. Be prepared to sift through a plethora of fitness information; this was a very well-known individual.

Shark

There are books dedicated to the use of parachutes and games, but I want to tell you about just one that plucked my appreciation of macabre humor and sense of sanguinary anticipation; an on-the-edge experience, part of the horror/humor genre.

Objective

To sit in a circle, holding with both hands the peripheral edge of a large (32-foot diameter) parachute, waiting for an assigned SHARK, patrolling under cover of the chute, to grab and gobble the totally exposed, sausage-like legs of the circled players.

Set Up

- As a group, stand in a circle holding onto the circumference of a parachute, then sit down, pulling and adjusting the edge of the chute up to everyone's waists. Legs remain beneath the chute as tasty, wiggling "sausage treats" for a designated SHARK.

- Ask everyone to close their eyes and raise one hand if they would like to be the SHARK. Explain that you will be coming around to tap one of those volunteers on the shoulder. The tapped person will immediately open their eyes and scoot under the chute and begin patrolling the periphery of the "shark pool."
- Ten seconds after designating who the SHARK will be, ask everyone to open their eyes.

Rules and Considerations

- When the SHARK spies a pair of juicy feet that look delectable, he/she grabs those appendages, alternately squeezing and relaxing their grip (chewing motion) for a few seconds before pulling their victim under the chute to also

become a SHARK. All this is accomplished amidst considerable shouting and thrashing about by the victim. (When pulled upon, and encouraged to come under the chute, it is the victim's responsibility to acquiesce not resist.)

- These two marauding SHARKS then continue their patrolling of the "pool" looking for more wiggling sausages.
- Indicate to all potential SHARKS, at the beginning of the game, that cruising the pool without touching anyone or touching lightly, adds considerably to the angst and anticipation, i.e., don't grab and squeeze every leg as you silently and menacingly slip by.
- I would not attempt to play this potentially frightening game with a young group. Honestly, I don't know what I mean by *young*, but certainly pre-school and kindergarten would be included. A one day experience for mid-elementary? Go for it.

The Six-Member Pyramid

This was one of the activities I was going to delete because of the potential for injury, but as I looked at Plynn's 1984 illustration and saw the 15 person pyramid arrangement in the background, and the shaky 10 person pyramid in the foreground, I realized there was another (smaller) symmetrical pyramid still within the illustration, the six person pyramid. It's obviously up to you, and if you have been presenting the 10 person pyramid with no hassles or close calls, then you're doing something right, go for it. But the six person pyramid will achieve the same "thinking vs. reacting" result. One group of 10, or two groups of six?

Objective

To build a symmetrical six person pyramid as quickly and efficiently as possible.

Rules

Timing begins when the facilitator finishes presenting the problem. Do not allow time for discussion. Time ends when the final person tops off the horizontal or vertical apex.

- In the event that people choose to build a vertical pyramid (99% of the time), make sure that either a gym mat or soft ground is available as the base.
- Only a 3-2-1 person pyramid is considered to be symmetrical.

Considerations

- In your presentation, make no mention of having to form a hands and knees pyramid. The problem can be solved and performed in fewer than five seconds by a group that lies down on top of one another in the 3-2-1 sequence, or even more functionally, simply stands together in that same 3-2-1 arrangement.

The problem of physically stacking six people is not that much of a big deal, but still requires people getting down on all fours and receiving a

kidney massage from someone's knee. When the
challenge is presented, and no time is allowed for
discussion, the first suggestion is usually accepted as
the only logical solution, and participants revert to
the "playground" kneeling pyramid . . . concurrently
remaining well inside the conceptual box.

Snowflake

If you are looking for an activity that will challenge your students to become more introspective, identify leadership, and tax their physical endurance . . . Snowflake is not what you're looking for. Snowflake is an I-Can't-Believe-I'm-Doing-This, one time activity, based on FUNN, and not much else. Shared zaniness? For sure. Here's the deal and how it works.

Objective

To catch a Styrofoam peanut (lightweight packing material) on the tip of your tongue, after it has been dropped from a substantial height. If you are worried about the oral aspect of Snowflake, give each person a paper cup as the catching device. Hold the cup in your non-dominant hand. Big cup = Easy Catch; Little cup = Not-So-Easy Catch

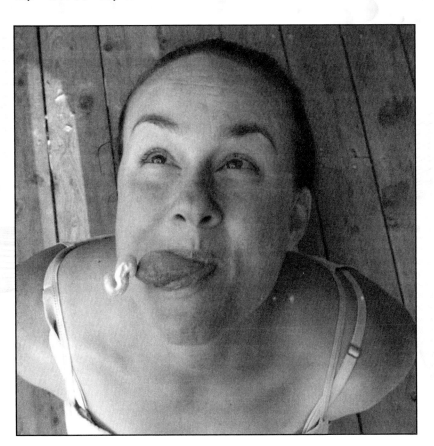

Set Up and Superfluous Comments

- Get hold of some loose, peanut-type Styrofoam packing material; the kind you have lots of around the house during Christmas time. These ultra-lightweight objects are your "snowflakes." Did you know that no two pieces of Styrofoam are ever exactly alike? No, really, that's true . . . I read it somewhere.
- Climb to the top of something (staging, tree, ladder, Astrodome) and launch a "snowflake" or two. Watch their slow and erratic descent. I'll bet it would be difficult for a person standing below to catch one on the tip of their tongue; oral adventure at its best.
- As you launch a "snowflake" or two from a balcony, check out your release technique. Look familiar? Ever watch the folks at Sea World feed the dolphins?
- Tell your group, with all sincerity, that the "snowflakes" being used are unadulterated "flakes," i.e., they have never been dropped or tongued before.
- Finish off the FUNN with a mass delivery of a few hundred "snowflakes" to the assemblage below.
  - For you potential aficionados of snowflake morphology, the cupped Styrofoam shape is the most predictable floater and therefore the easiest to "tongue." The S-shaped sky-scooter (see photo) represents, by far, the toughest descending target.

Caveat   The "catch" is made with the tongue only. Stick out your tongue and keep your mouth closed to prevent inhaling a piece of Styrofoam. Snowflake is not meant for use with young participants unless paper cups are used as the catching device.

Space Counting a.k.a. Finger Figures (Figgers)

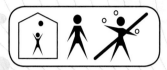

Some time ago I was sitting on an exercise bike, winding down a spinning sequence and looking for a way to maintain my interest long enough to stay on the bike for at least that extra minute of cool-down pedaling. I'm not sure why, but I started counting spins, simultaneously space writing the sequenced numbers with my index finger, promising myself that I'd stay in the saddle and keep pedaling until I reached one hundred; the strange rituals we follow in search of fitness.

I actually stayed on the bike considerably longer because I became fascinated with the finger manipulations involved in space counting. It was an honor system thing; if I made a mistake I felt honor bound to go back and do that number again, (the 50s were particularly troublesome). Then, of course, I just had to know how long it took me to reach one hundred, so I *finger figgered* again for time. (My personal best is 1:30 and change; a veiled challenge?)

Split up into pairs and ask the two self-chosen ersatz competitors to extend their index finger (writing hand) toward one another, tips of fingers almost touching. Then, maintaining eye contact, start finger counting as fast as possible toward an agreed upon number. When the number is reached, swiftly retract your finger to make a fist, definitively stating your completion. At some point, talk about competition, honor system, and what each person felt like while finger counting.

On a less competitive plane, ask one of the pair to accept the role of leader with his/her partner attempting to duplicate the leader's movements; mirror image kind of thing. Try the cooperative attempt with a third partner and even more if the group is into it. Don't forget to switch roles. Also, don't forget to "write" slowly enough so that your partner(s) can follow. Which was most fun, competing or cooperating? Don't lay a value judgment screed on their responses; let them decide.

Variations

- For more *serious* mano-a-mano competitions, have a competitor's "second" hold the opponent's wrist, attempting to keep movement of the *figgering* hand immobile, allowing only finger mobility. Hold your own wrist to see what I mean. Considerably more difficult, eh?

- Just for the fun of it, try competing against a blank computer screen (open a new file to get a blank screen). You get the same multiple image strobe-like phenomena as when you wave your open hand from side to side in front of a lit computer screen. The more rapidly you wave, the more strobe effect you get. So what causes that? Must be a science and/or physiology lesson there that I somehow missed in Physics 101 . . . those many years ago.

Sylvia's Silly Sequence (SSS)*

Looking for a segue to nonsense? SSS will help you get there, acting as a five-minute filler at the end of class, as a funn-filled emotional warm-up, or to remind your players that life isn't all that serious. You think curricular laughing is not important? Think again.

Primary Objective

To officially allow and coax students to try something that will not add to their school-cool factor, but will allow a shared zany and humorous interlude, camouflaged as curriculum.

Secondary Objective

Try to dislodge a penny balanced on top of your nose using only facial contortions (see rules below).

Rules

Ask the penny person to lie down on their back; that's *supine* for those who care. Lying on a wrestling mat is more acceptable than the school parking lot.

- Balance a dry penny on top of the supine person's nose; sweat and/or mucous should be avoided.
- No movements of the body or head are allowed. Nose and facial (mostly lips and cheeks) movements are allowed, encouraged by supportive shouts of "Get crazy!" or "Topple the Copper!"
- Blowing the coin off your nose displays such unbecoming gaucherie no further comment seems necessary.
- Adept tongue manipulation, however, displays a rare and admirable bent for extreme adventure.

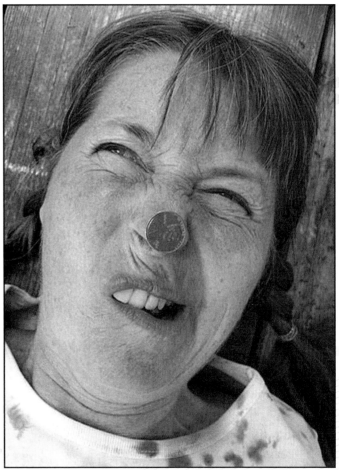

Considerations

- Set your own time limits, considering that two minutes of facial contortions could cause cramping and a trip to the school nurse . . . and who's going to explain THAT!
- If you have two players who have experienced "the thrill of victory" and would be amenable to some head-to-head competition, ask the two to lie down (again, supine) so the tops of their heads are juxtaposed, even lightly touching, and begin the penny manipulation from that shared cranial position.

*Sylvia's Silly Sequence—Twenty-five years ago I stuck Sylvia's first name on this silly stunt but never assigned a last name. So, 25 years late, thank you Sylvia Shirley (who was, at the time, offering adventure activities at William and Mary College in Virginia) for telling me about and demonstrating this zany challenge.

Tattoo

During the early years at Project Adventure I consistently manipulated my time with students toward letting the next magic moment happen. Tattoo was one of those spur-of-the-magical-moments. I know, sounds hokey, but it's true; the undiscovered moments were floating around (in my brain?) as if waiting for someone or something to let them happen. Also, good things happened during those early years because there were good people piling on the compost of creativity to allow the burgeoning curriculum to take root and flower. Too metaphorical? Here it is straight. People like me would have never had a creative impact if it were not for prescient people in administrative roles that quietly understood or sensed good things were happening, and had the conscience, perspicacity, and fortitude to let it happen.

> "Play is the exultation of the possible."
> Martin Buber

If you were to ask me, "What is the game of Tattoo?" I'd have to initially respond, "It's not a game, more of a directed happening, and secondly, I'm not sure you can understand Tattoo without having experienced the action associated with just . . . doing it." I'm still not comfortable when someone asks me to explain (what, how, why, etc.) concerning an experiential situation without retreating into excessive detail (communication, self efficacy, cooperation, fun, trust) and still the question remains. "Yes, I see, but what . . .?" And therein lies the ongoing problem of explaining experiential education to those who have not been part of the experience. Considering that you bought this book and are probably part of the adventure "choir" I've been preaching to over the decades, convincing you that experiential education is a valid educational approach seems a tad redundant. So, considering all the white space already taken up in the Introduction, Preface, and Foreword to this book, in addition to the highly suggestive, insinuating segments of the various activities I've rewritten that have to do with the theory of adventure experiential education, without further ado, here's Tattoo.

Objective

To have the opportunity (even if not immediately understood) of throwing multiple available tennis balls in a gymnasium, at one of the basketball backboards as to produce a drum-like tattoo sound.

Procedure

- Offer each participant (numbering 10–100) two tennis balls,* then ask the participants to arrange themselves on the mid-line of the basketball court, facing toward one of the backboards. (For this throwing sequence to work there must be a wall located a few feet behind the backboard, i.e., not bleachers or open space).

- The participants should arrange themselves on the gym floor so they can make a full throwing motion downcourt without making physical contact with other throwers. Prior to saying "GO," the facilitator dumps one hundred or so tennis balls randomly on the court to provide additional ammunition.

- On a GO signal, everyone throws their hardest in an attempt to hit the basketball backboard with a tennis ball and continues throwing with accuracy and rapidity trying to produce a drum-like tattoo sound on the backboard.

- After "firing" their initial tennis balls, throwers should attempt to nab a rebounding ball or two and continue their assault on the backboard.

- All the tennis balls will obviously not rebound directly back toward the throwers, so 2–3 volunteers must position themselves somewhere under the backboard to retrieve stray projectiles. Being a retriever is not as strange or as scary as it sounds since all the throwers are aiming at the backboard, well above the downcourt volunteers' heads. If your group is too young, immature, or untrusting to allow your volunteers to feel safe from intentional hits, DO NOT PLAY TATTOO.

- Allow the fire-at-will action to continue for at least a full minute of frenetic throwing. The sound and movement are rewards in themselves. In addition, those people who like to throw, and throw well, have the opportunity to "chuck" as many balls as hard as they like, cheering their own efforts and accuracy because no one else is paying any attention. In contrast, those folks who can't throw well can either fling a few balls or none at all without fear of censure or disregard because,

*tennis balls—See the game Frantic in this book about where to find an abundance of used tennis balls.

as above, no one is watching or monitoring their efforts or lack of effort.

- After things slow down a bit, ask each person to retrieve and hold onto 2–3 tennis balls. Indicate that you want to start Tattoo once again, but this time by throwing with the opposite (non-dominant) arm. The results are humbling and humorous, and if a retriever happens to be hit with a poorly thrown ball, the direction of the ball is apt to have nothing to do with intended direction or a trust issue. Almost everyone throws badly with their non-dominant arm except the ambidextrous few, so reluctance to try is usually put aside. Still don't want to throw? S'ok , it's their choice, but be sure to make that choice solidly available.
- After about 30 seconds of high arced and poorly aimed throws (and much good-natured ribbing), let the throwers finish up with a few good hard ones to polish their diminished egos.

Variations

- Ask a group, balls in hand and standing at one end of the court, if they can hit the far wall with a ball thrown with their "opposite" arm. After a few attempts (some hits, mostly half-court shots) let them finish up with a few throws with their "good" arms. You will be surprised (and so will they) at how many good athletes cannot throw a ball the length of a basketball court using their non-throwing arms.

- Request that everyone pair up for the next activity, The Howitzer Throw. The object of this command/ response bit of cooperation is to have one participant tell his/her blindfolded (or eyes simply closed) partner where to throw a ball in order to hit a target (backboard, championship banner, wall buzzer). Pairs may not touch one another, responding only to words of directions from their sighted partners. Six shots at one target is suggested, then another target is chosen and roles are reversed. Although it's tempting, considering the task at hand, try to keep the directed shots at non-living targets. Don't keep score, keep it fun instead.

Debrief Questions

- Considering that the only thing asked of you was to make a drumming sound on the basketball backboard, why play Tattoo?
- And throwing with your non-dominant arm? How come?
- What were you thinking of during the most active part of Tattoo?
- Was there anything particularly satisfying about the activity?
- Did you feel any sense of "team" associated with the activity?
- Were you surprised by any part of what you did or experienced during Tattoo?

Tube Hockey

A Historical Perspective

Tube Hockey isn't played much anymore; not because it isn't fun or physical, rather it's becoming more difficult to find large truck inner tubes, as tubeless tires have become the norm. But I'd like to take the time and space here to acquaint you with THE game that started the Project Adventure, **adventure games** revolution. Tube Hockey was the first off-the-wall, made-up game I used with classes during that initial year (1971) of PA curriculum development.

One of my responsibilities that fledgling year at Hamilton-Wenham Regional High School was to develop curriculum for the sophomore physical education classes. Since our staff was hired from Hurricane Island and North Carolina Outward Bound, the types of activities we were comfortable teaching were necessarily those that emphasized hiking, sailing, rock climbing, fire starting; i.e., those things associated with OB. Some of the students were enthralled by what we did (as above) and what we didn't do (pull-ups, jumping jacks, basketball drills). But some of the "scholars" thought we were elitist, esoteric, and even subversive. (Esoteric? We were so esoteric we didn't know what esoteric meant.)

The daily expectation during those nascent days was coming up with something that was not only acceptable to the majority of the students, but fit the paradigm of Outward Bound, their physical education prospects, and our own developing curriculum. Honestly, I wasn't initially having much luck with any of the above until I decided to have some fun myself.

Thinking back to what I did to entertain Karl when I was close to their age, I nostalgically recollected kicking around a solidly inflated inner tube; can't remember why, but nebulous memories indicated fun, physical and bizarre. So what follows here as rules, procedure, and objective resulted directly from my kicking and chasing an inflated inner tube a couple of decades earlier. And the Hamilton-Wenham students? They loved it. As the result of their enthusiastic kicking, more tubes were needed, as "flats" increased beyond what our patch kit could handle.

Objective

To score a goal by pushing or kicking your team's tube past the opposing team's goal markers. (Use pylon goal markers about 12' apart for people who seem to care about who wins, or just indicate a team direction for the pure players.)

Procedure

Facilitator—Divide up into two equal teams.

Student response—"Yeah, right I've heard that before . . . equal what?"

Facilitator—Equal doesn't necessarily refer to number of players, does it?

Student response—"I don't want to be chosen last again."

Facilitator—Try this. . . . Fold your arms. Fold 'em, like this. If your right arm is on top, go over there. If your left arm is on top, come over here. That should give us two teams, with numbers about even? Right! Let's play *Tube Hockey*. (If this choosing-up-sides technique seems interesting, check out the activity *Categories* in the PA book **QuickSilver**, page 85.)

Ask the two teams to walk to either end of the playing field, (about half a football field or soccer pitch). Place two tubes in the middle of the field about ten yards apart. Each tube needs an identifying mark that can be easily and quickly identified. Tie colored strips of fabric around the tubes, or use two colors of spray paint.

Each team then chooses a runner from their number. At the GO signal, the two runners (red and blue) take off toward the tires. As soon as a blue or red runner makes contact with their blue or red tire, the entire blue or red team can dash forward and try to kick their tube over the goal line.

Rules

- The first team to forward their tube over either goal line receives a point and all play stops. Both tubes are set up on the mid-field line and play (as above) begins again. This is a very aerobic game, and as such, the down time after a goal is scored is well appreciated.

- The tube may be forwarded by any anatomical means (kick, push, knee, arms), but cannot be touched by the hands. Inadvertent hand touch is inevitable—play it loose ref.
- *Hooking*—Putting your foot/leg through the tube in an attempt to either pull the tube, or keep it stationary. Hooking is not allowed. If a foot or leg hook continues for more than two seconds after the referee shouts HOOK, a point is subtracted from that team's score. If the team has no score to subtract from, the other team gets a free kick.
- If a pile up occurs (no movement of the tube for 15 seconds) it is up to the ref to stop play, retrieve the tube from under the pile of bodies, spin it like a discus, and throw that circled sausage as far as possible.
- There are no boundaries, therefore no time outs. If a team is put in danger (highway, swimming pool) because of this rule, modify the rule.
- There are no goalies, per se.
- Hockey-type checking is not allowed, but setting dynamic picks is definitely OK.
- To score a point the tube must cross the goal from the field side of play.

- The penalty for unnecessary roughness is removal from the game.

Considerations

- The more air in the tubes, the more action on the field.
- *Tube Hockey* is suitable for all weather, but the ideal field condition is a glazed snow surface, which causes a well-kicked tube to scoot like a humongous hockey puck.
- Keep a patch kit and pump available for the inevitable small punctures that occur.
- Wrap copious amounts of duct tape over the valve stem to prevent bare skin injury.
- *Tube Hockey* on a wet field is a grand introduction to mud wrestling.
- Players should recognize (you too coach), that each team needs a designated offense and defense that operate concurrently and independently.

If you have a copy of the original *Silver Bullets*, on page 71 is a photo taken in 1971, or maybe 72, of a group playing *Tube Hockey*. That's my posterior at left center trying to instigate a pile up, so I can catch my breath!

The Turn-Style

Popular? You're looking for popular? The Turn-Style is popular.

Objective

Quite a few, and that's one of the reasons why The Turn-style is so popular with both students and facilitators. But initially, let's stick with the basics. Using an 18'–20' jump rope of retired 8 mm Kernmantle rope,* ask the group if they can get through the spinning rope from one side to another by (1) entering one at a time, (2) making one jump while in the spinning arc of the rope, and (3) not missing a beat of the rope between participants.

I've included a proposed graduated sequence of *Turn-style* (as to degree of difficulty), to indicate how much can be accomplished with a single jump rope.

Rope lying on the ground.
- *Challenge:* get the group from one side of the rope to the other in sequence as fast as possible.
- Consequence for touching the rope: five-second penalty for each touch.

Rope suspended one inch off the floor (by two turners).
- *Challenge:* same as above.
- Consequence for touching the rope: four-second penalty for each touch.

Rope suspended loosely 12" off the floor.
- *Challenge:* same as above.
- Consequence for touching the rope: three-second penalty for each touch.

Rope clearing the floor by a minimum height but swaying back and forth at least three feet from side to side.
- *Challenge:* get the group from one side of the rope to the other in sequence.
- Consequence for touching the rope: group starts over.

Rope being turned 360° with rope moving toward the group.
- *Challenge:* Get the group from one side of the rope to the other in sequence.
- Consequence for touching the rope: group starts over.

Rope being turned 360° with rope moving away from the group.
- *Challenge:* get the group from one side of the rope to the other in sequence.
- Consequence for touching the rope: group starts over.

Rope being turned (turning direction up to the group).
- *Challenge:* get the group from one side of the rope to the other in sequence with each person individually making a single jump before exiting the rope.
- Consequence for stopping the rope: group starts over.

Rope being turned (turning direction up to the group).
- *Challenge:* get the group from one side of the rope to the other in sequence with each person individually making a single jump and without allowing an empty turn of the rope.
- Consequence for stopping the rope or allowing an "empty" turn: group starts over.

Rope being turned (turning direction up to the group).
- *Challenge:* get the group from one side of the rope to the other AFAP. Each person must make a single jump but more than one jumper at a time is allowed. Empty turns are allowed.
- Consequence for stopping the rope: three-second penalty for each person who is part of that attempt. Each of those participants must jump again.

Two parallel ropes being turned in opposite directions (Double Dutch).
- *Challenge:* move the group in sequence through both ropes (ropes are separated by at least ten feet), so each person makes one jump within each turning rope.
- Consequence for stopping either rope: group starts over.

---

*Kernmantle rope—See Glossary; but whatever rope you have that has some weight to it will suffice. Lightweight polypropylene rope does not turn well and can leave yarn splinters in your palm.

Rope is turned only twice.

- *Challenge*: to see how many people en mass can make two successful jumps (no misses) with two consecutive turns of the rope. Everyone jumps at once. Ready? TURN!
- No consequence; unlimited attempts allowed. See Double Max Jump below.

The reason for offering so many different methods of moving over or through the rope is primarily because multiple tasks that increase sequentially in difficulty, allow the challenge to be spread out over a series of days. It also allows the facilitator to choose from the challenges as to the perceived skill level of the group, thus precluding boredom and/or frustration; i.e., seeking the **flow state.**

Double Dutch

Use two lengths of 18' rope as above. With one end of each rope in the hands of two experienced turners, have them spin a Double Dutch tattoo on the floor or street. If you don't know what Double

Dutch consists of, ask any streetwise student for a demo, because verbalizing the sequence is more than I want to take on.

DD is the stuff of pure nostalgia for some, aesthetic appreciation to others, and flagellating frustration for most. I have observed young women perform feats of skill and endurance among, on top of, and underneath those spinning double ropes that would make a Sports Illustrated photographer's finger itch. Try stepping into those whirling ropes for a bit of "hot pepper"—it's a humbler.

Using this difficult rope jump sequence allows some students to display an impressive level of individual performance that they may not have achieved in more traditional sports and games. Strokes and ego burnishing—we all need it.

Double Max Jump

Objective

Using a 75-foot section of retired $^3/_8$" (9 mm) climbing rope, ask a group to see how many people can make two consecutive jumps without anyone missing, What do you think; 5 turns? 10? Try two (2), and see what happens.

Set Up and Considerations

- The starting position is with the rope on the floor, and a turner at each end. All the potential jumpers stand on one side of the rope. Turning direction of the rope and standing position are up to the group. Considering that a missed jump results in a foot or leg tangled in the rope, it's immediately obvious who missed; a humorous incident the first 2–3 times, deteriorating to "can't-you-lift-your-feet" protests and grumbles.
- One of the turners calls out, "Ready, TURN!" and the rope comes sweeping around. Both turners need to be alert so that if the first jump is successful they are ready to immediately initiate the second turn.
- Allow multiple trial and error attempts as the group works through the necessary problem-solving dialogue.
- Change turners when necessary to combat arm fatigue and give someone else a rest from jumping.

• •

Warm Ups

What do you think of when someone mentions "warm ups"?—jumping jacks? stomach crunches? a second cup-a-joe? maybe just a general term for doing something physical that you would rather not do, considering it's not cool to be warmed up? I think the secret to offering a decent warm up session is two-fold: first, make sure the action doesn't look or feel like a warm up session, and second, apply your edutainment talents to warm up people both physically and emotionally.

Tag Games

You played some type of tag game when you were a kid, right? You had to! Tag was a prerequisite to growing up, a physical and social obligation. Well, take that old-time street game, change the rules some, tweak the boundaries, and change the lingo. Voila! . . . a unique warm up. The activity is active, the rules few, and play doesn't have to last any particular length of time. Play until enthusiasm wanes then wax-off to another activity.

Recently I've been spending more time trying to understand the social kinesiology of the tag itself. You are actually making contact with another person when the tag is made, so the tag (touch) should be appropriate. Someone recently told me (after I had used too many loaded words attempting to explain what appropriate meant), that the best way to explain what appropriate means, without getting into what appropriate *really* means, is to simply say, "If we were all wearing bathing suits, don't tag (touch) the bathing suits." Perfect.

So why not start off by demonstrating an appropriate tag? Do that; touch (tag) someone and reciprocate the tag, because that's the way of the tagging world, i.e., in a tag game nobody touches without anticipating a reciprocal tag. So now tag someone else near you in the room. No hurry, take your time, make it a conscious, quality tag. Good . . .

good, now tag someone and make a casual attempt not to be tagged back. As you glide around the room, tag as many people as you can (appropriately, of course) and swivel, duck, and jibe to keep from being tagged, but don't run; enjoy the tags and tagging attempts, no reason to run away.

If you get a chance, while the fun is swirling around you, take a look at what people are doing and what their faces reveal. This somewhat rare occurrence is called PLAY, and the faces reflect a sense of joy that play engenders. Is there a reason for what they are doing? No. Is anyone keeping score? No. Are there winners and losers? No. Are they having fun? Sure looks like it, which is fairly typical when people play. Seriously, when was the last time YOU played?

> "Play is where life lives, where the game is the game. At its borders we slip into heresy. Become serious. Lose our sense of humor. Fail to see the incongruities of everything we hold to be important. Right and wrong become problematical. The game becomes winning. And we lose the good life and the things that play provides."
> George Sheehan

Everybody's IT

Often called the world's fastest tag game and rightly so because everyone is literally IT. As with any tag game when someone is IT they chase someone else attempting to transfer the IT status to that person, so in this case everyone is chasing everyone else. Here are a couple of rules to reduce the confusion and coalesce the context.

The group spreads out within an unbounded area* and at the beginning signal, each person

attempts to tag someone else. If a tag is received before you tag the tagger, you are eliminated. (No big deal because Everybody's IT only lasts about 30 seconds.) Having been tagged, sit down or put your hands on your head to indicate your tagged status, or you will continue to be tagged appropriately. If you were lucky or skillful enough to be the tagger above, continue trying to tag (eliminate) the other swarming players. This fast action continues until one player remains, then just as he/she begins to feel good about themselves, shout GO again, and the fast action begins afresh.

*unbounded area—I no longer use boundaries for tag games, announcing that the fun is right around here and if you want to have maximum fun, here is where you need to be.

Sometimes players really care who wins and play becomes cautious rather than confident, i.e., the game begins to drag as the last remaining players shuck & jive trying to avoid one another. To initiate continued action, announce that anyone who takes a backward step in a confrontation is eliminated.

Help Me Tag

Tie knots in old towels to equal half the number of people in the group; the knotted towels are called "birds." If your budget and sense of whimsy allow, buy rubber chickens to equal half the number of people and replace the towels with chickens (birds). Assign 2–3 people to be IT.

Rules

- To be immune from a tag, a player must be in physical contact with a "bird."
- Since there are only 8 "birds" for 16 players (for example), there is much flipping of the bird. "Hey, help me over here!"
- There can only be one "bird" in the hand, as two in the bush has absolutely no function in this game.
- The "bird" cannot be thrown to the same person twice in succession.
- Remind people that the fun is HERE, obviating the need for boundary cones, outline ropes, taped areas, etc.

Hop on Tag

The fun in any tag game results from trying not to be caught by IT, coupled with the titillating excitement of the chase, or the more socially devastating situation of not being chased at all.

Rules

- The only safe area in Hop on Tag is to be supported off the ground on someone's back, piggyback-style.

- Being in this supported condition offers five seconds of immunity to being tagged, at the end of which time the pair must separate and run to find another partner to hop on or be hopped upon.
- IT may not stand next to a pair waiting for them to disengage.
- A player may not hop on the same individual twice in succession.
- If the group is larger than 15 individuals, designate two people as being IT. If this becomes the case, the two ITs must identify themselves by making a continuous sound, or running around with one hand on their head.

Sore Spot Tag a.k.a. Hospital Tag

Same rules as with Everybody's IT except the tagged person must hold (apply a bandage) to the appropriate spot where he/she was tagged. If that person is tagged again he/she must hold the second tagged spot with the other hand, limiting their ability to reciprocate a tag with only a foot (no kicking), or hip, or head—if it's a slow tag. It's hard to keep from laughing at yourself if you have been tagged twice in hard to reach places on your body.

Recognize that these tag games are not designed as aerobic exercises to promote fitness, rather as a brief warm-up activity that causes people to interact, cooperate and breathe hard. Now what do you have planned for the remainder of your scheduled session?

Triangle Tag

Ask three people to hold hands to form a triangle. One member of the triangle is the free person, designated to be caught; the other two members of the troika serve as blockers. The fourth person in this Tag-Quad is IT and tries to tag the free person in the triangle.

Rules

- The IT person can run around the triangle and try to lean across the triangle, but cannot purposefully try to break one of the three gripped contact points.

- The IT person must always have one foot on the ground.
- The triangle people dance, swivel, block, and jump around to keep the IT at bay.
- Change roles in a clockwise direction every 30 seconds, or whenever a catch is made.

Consideration

This tag game can segue from gentle to very rough, very quickly. Keep your eye out for a player that becomes too aggressive in order to make a tag.

Trust

Cooperative Competition

"Play is nature's training for life."
Frederick Froebel

As much of an oxymoron as "Cooperative Competition" appears to be, the rubric will make more sense once you have tried this useful one-on-one exercise of competing honestly while cooperating fully.

Objective

With two players participating (competing), trying to maneuver your partner (opponent) off balance so they have to reposition one of their feet. The not-so-hidden agenda, while competing at an agreed-upon level of effort, is trying to make the confrontation last as long as possible so that the competition becomes a cooperative exercise almost resembling a dance.

Rules

- Starting position: Stand facing one another assuming the foot-forward spotting position. One of the players touches the toe of his right foot to the toe of his partner's left foot, and subsequently the toe of his left foot to the toe of his partner's right foot. (Refer to the photo.) Palms should be touching.
- No other physical contact is permitted but the tips of the toes and palms. Be conscientious about not shoving with your body to gain an advantage.
- The two players can push against their opponent as firmly as they wish (palms only) but all movements must be accomplished in ULTRA slow motion. This allows your partner time to respond to your maneuver. No fast movements allowed, even to gain an advantage, or win.

Considerations

- Shorter participants have an advantage in this exercise because of their lower center of gravity.

This often allows females to present a formidable challenge.
- Most "contests" end with both players simultaneously losing, i.e., falling off balance together. When you are debriefing this activity at a later time, ask the participants what they did when both players fell off balance together. The answer is often "supported one another to prevent falling to the floor."
- It feels good to win, but it also feels good to cooperate with a former competitor (Squat Thrust). Cross-linked thoughts of "I'm winning!" or "I'm losing!" conflict with what the person honestly feels, with what they think they should feel.
- The best contest is the one that lasts the longest. There is more to this exercise than explanation allows; give it a conscientious try, remembering in this case it's not how it looks, but how it feels.

Come on Down!

Here's a high-ropes course, "forehead slapper" concept, that has been available from the very beginning but like most *obvious* ideas has been overlooked; seems like everyone was caught looking up when they should have been looking elsewhere.

Simply stated, "Why not start certain high-ropes course activities <u>from the top and climb down</u>?" Why not indeed? Everything on a ropes course is predicated on climbing or moving up, against the unrelenting pull of gravity. Why not heave students up to height via a Flying Squirrel arrangement, (including a slack belay rope that provides protection when the FS haul rope is unclipped upon reaching the top), then suggest that the rider become an active participant and climb down under control? Call it "Come on Down!" and apply the transposed direction to any high element that seems to make sense; like reverse climbing a Vertical Playpen, a Fire Cracker Ladder, a Dangle Duo, a Cargo Net, or a high stapled tree. This would allow a small but significant percentage of students to experience operating at height who might not otherwise get the opportunity (overweight, physically challenged, freaked out).

The pragmatic key is to require descending <u>under control,</u> their control. Everyone is aware that, on belay,* all a climber has to do is to let go at any time to get down quickly, safely, and easily. Knowing that gravity is working with you might be the incentive that tempts a reluctant student to try participating at height. Having climbed down, that person might want to try climbing UP the same element; what a concept!

The Flying Squirrel serves as a decent stand-alone ropes-course element, but even at its best (a haul system to help fearful or physically challenged participants), there was something missing. Being hauled up to 30+ feet on a pulley/rope system is a fun, intense experience that also engenders a sense of compassion and cooperation by the haulers, but other than requiring a yes/no response, the person being lifted up and down is strictly along for the ride. Come on Down would allow additional participation and choice on a number of already-installed events with a simple retrofitting of pulleys, ropes, and connectors.

In the sport of rock climbing, is climbing up or climbing down more difficult? Don't know? Ask a rock climber. (Time allowed for finding and questioning a "trad" climber.) See, was I right or was I right?

I realize this activity is out of context with the other activities in this book. But, I just couldn't resist passing along what I think is a dynamite adventure idea.

Falling Down without Going BOOM

There are several reasons for including how-to-fall instructions as part of growing up, not the least of which is achieving that goal. Unfortunately, fall and roll instructions for children just don't rate up there with Little League or piano lessons as part of the parental paradigm and schools (other than some sports) definitely do not touch on the joint, skin, and bone saving art of transferring the energy of a fall into a shoulder roll.

Learning to fall should be basic training for young people, and I'm not talking about the frequent

Gumby-like tumbles of a toddler protected from real harm by bones that bend, guardian angels, and an efficient immune system that operates 24/7. Most people (any age) don't know how to handle a fall effectively in order to minimize or eliminate injury. Unless a person plays a fall-down sport (soccer, football, lacrosse), the awareness of what to do with your falling kinetic mass is so experientially out of context for parents, schools, and responsible organizations that the availability to learn and practice is not on the curriculum horizon. "Be careful; don't get

*on belay—Come on Down is not a game and should not be considered as such. Safety on this activity requires hard skill know-how and expertise. Do not attempt this activity without experienced help or personal training on how to belay.

hurt" has become the mantra of the ages, a not-to-be-ignored demand that translates to adherence, or else.... During my generation the evening admonition was simply, "Get home before dark."

Learning to fall* with some measure of control . . .

1. increases the safety margin for participants in risk-oriented activities such as after-school sports, bicycle riding, walking to school, getting out of bed, . . .

2. decreases the possibility or extent of injury as the result of a simple fall.

3. develops increased confidence in handling whatever the world throws at you on a daily basis.

Injury resulting from forward or backward moving falls—those exhibiting lateral momentum—usually are caused by friction on the palms and body (abrasions), or by sudden absorption of the impact by the hands resulting in scraped, sprained, or broken hands and wrists.

A proven way to escape or minimize injury in a lateral moving fall is to use a modified forward or backward shoulder roll. The falling and rolling techniques remove the impact from the wrists, dramatically reducing the potential for injury. The shoulder roll is spontaneously initiated as the result of a lateral fall combined with some forward, sideways, or backward movement (trip, push, jump). With no momentum in any direction other than DOWN (a plumb-line fall), an attempted roll is comically superfluous, and I don't mean funny.

Human Ladder

Human Ladder is a good, functional trust activity when sequenced well. Check out the objective and rules below, then give it a try. Also check the caveat!

Objective

To "walk" (crawl) on hand-held dowels that are so positioned between two rows of holders as to offer a vague approximation of a horizontal ladder.

Rules and Concerns

• Use stout (1.25" × 3') hardwood dowels as rungs. You will need half the number of rungs as people in the group. These rungs can also be used for the activity Balance Practice, page 113.

*fall—I'm not talking about falling out of a third story (or any story) window, or falling some distance out of a tree. When I say ". . . fall with some measure of control" above, I'm referring to the forward, sideways, and backward falls that result from tripping, being pushed, stepping off a curb, not watching where you are going, i.e., the erratic movements and motion that make up everyday living.

- The dowels (Human Ladder rungs) are held between two people who are of approximately the same height and strength. Admittedly a highly subjective criteria, but at least be aware.
- Participants are paired (see bullet above) and offered one rung of the Human Ladder. Several pairs, standing opposite one another in two lines, hold their single rung twixt partners, forming the ersatz ladder. See illustration.
- A climber starts at one end of the ladder, proceeding slowly from one rung to another, eschewing contact with the ground.
- Rungs can be adjusted for height* and angle between climbers.

- As soon as the first pair's rung has been used, and the climber has moved on to the next rung, that first pair can peel off from their starting position and reorient themselves as a "rung" at the far end of the ladder—don't forget to bring your rung with you. In this way the ladder's length can be extended indefinitely.
- The direction of the ladder can obviously change or vary as to the standing orientation of the rung holders.
- The Human Ladder should not be attempted until the participants have had a chance to participate in other less-intimidating trust exercises and games.
- Speed "climbing" should be avoided.

*height—*Caveat:* Individuals have a tendency to overestimate their own strength (ergo also the strength of the pair), and end up holding their shared rung too high, particularly in relation to the height of the next subsequent rung in the series. Sudden release of a rung can cause injury to the climber and rung holders. Other than damaging contact with the ground, strained muscles and ligaments are also a possibility.

I Trust You, but . . .

I can't remember if I made up this trust activity, or learned it from somebody, but I sure have used it a lot over the years. This trust-oriented activity can be used outdoors, but I've always appreciated the obvious walled-in consequences offered by the confinement of a gymnasium.

Objective

To provide the opportunity for each participant to jog the length of a gym with their eyes closed (or blindfolded) with the anticipation of being humanely brought to a stop before crashing into the bleachers or wall.

Caveat If participants in this exciting demonstration of commitment and trust do not take

PLYNN

what is happening seriously, injury can result. The following guidelines are not just suggestions.

Procedure

- Postpone use of I Trust You, but . . . until the group has had the opportunity to participate in other trust-building activities, (e.g.,. The Trust Fall/Dive, Spotting, The Sherpa Walk).
- Walk your group to one end of a basketball court and explain the procedure and rationale for participating in I Trust You, but . . . . Take your time and cover the necessary safety procedures, demonstrating as you go.
- Make special note of how important it is to make sure that no one is taken advantage of when their eyes are closed. I understand it's a summer camp ritual to pull a funny prank on someone if they are blindfolded, but that type of shenanigan is absolutely not allowed in this context.

Rules and Safety

- Explain that each person will have the opportunity to jog the length of the gym with their eyes closed and be compassionately stopped at the far end, before making contact with anything that could harm them. Blindfolds are optional.
- Participants' hands and arms should be in the bumpers up position for the entire jog down the gym floor.
- There will be three joggers at a time making the trip. The remainder of the group (spotters) will be standing at the far end of the gym with their backs toward the wall, facing the joggers. This is not a strict shoulder-to-shoulder positioning for the spotters, rather a comfortable spacing (no closer than 12" apart, and no further than 18"). The spotters should also assume the bumpers up position.
- Note that I keep using the term jog rather than run. Demonstrate what the speed rate of a jog constitutes, i.e., not fast. The safety of both joggers and spotters depends upon understanding that jog does not mean run.
- Locate at least two spotters on each side of the court in case the joggers become disoriented and begin following a curved path right or left; it happens on a regular basis. These sideline

spotters should be constantly ready to move in order to intersect a wayward jogger.

- Demonstrate how a spotter should stop a jogger at the end of their jog. Position the spotter in the bumpers up posture, with one of their feet positioned forward to get them out of the **domino stance.** As the jogger approaches, the spotter and jogger make gentle palm contact with both hands as the spotter simultaneously takes one step backward, affording a gradual slowdown and stop. Pair up and have each person practice being both jogger and spotter. Watch this practice carefully. If there is any fooling around, take a break and further discuss what you are trying to accomplish with this dynamic trust activity.

- Tell everyone that if they hear you yell "**STOP!**", the eyes-closed people are to stop their forward movement immediately. Before they can react to what you just said, shout "**STOP!**" as loudly as you can, then quietly say, "Just like that." This is your facilitator's fail-safe mechanism—be ready and willing to use it.

- Ask the spotters to be as quiet as possible as the joggers make their way down the court; this adds considerably to the challenge.

- Take three volunteers down to the other end of the gym and have them spread out, facing downcourt, toward the spotters. Visually look downcourt to check the spotters' positions and say, "Bumpers Up." Tell your three joggers to close their eyes, put up their bumpers, and jog.

- Watch carefully as they jog downcourt. Do not take your eyes off any of them until the last one has been stopped, as things can go wrong quickly. Congratulate them all and join in the applause. Ask for the next three volunteers.

- Here is another chance for you to apply the concept of Challenge by Choice, however it is important for all to realize that CbC is not a "get out of jail FREE card." CbC allows freedom of choice as to when and how participation will occur.

I Trust You, but . . .

As part of my ongoing on-the-road responsibilities, I was scheduled to work with a group of physical education teachers for six consecutive weeks, one three-hour meeting per week. During that time, I was supposed to provide them with all the information they needed to know about presenting an adventure program to their high school classes. In retrospect, a completely unrealistic task; at the time, "Sure, I can do it."

It was the second meeting and I was introducing the activity I Trust You, but . . . to about 9–10 teachers. Up to this point they had been very receptive, even enthusiastic. Because of the small group I was having them jog down the gym by twos. It was during the second set of joggers when the incident occurred. (I can't call it an accident, because it wasn't.)

One of the joggers was a big man with an ex-football player look and demeanor; kind of intimidating, but a decent guy, no problem. As he approached the line of spotters, one of the spotters, also a big man, stepped forward, bent over, and drove his shoulder into the chest of the sightless jogger. He went down like he'd been hit with a baseball bat, holding his rib cage. I usually always have something to say, but I was speechless, as was everyone else.

The guy on the floor was angry at first, until he recognized who had hit him. His face broke into a pained grimace that I think was supposed to be a smile and he said, "You really got me that time." The other guy laughed and said something innocuously stupid that I don't remember but the two of them continued laughing together, oblivious to the shocked group. They had played football together years before and this "tackle" was part of their twisted camaraderie.

As it turned out, the person who was hit ended up with two broken ribs and I lost the confidence of that group for the remainder of the six-week training session.

The PDQ

During workshops, conference presentations, and other educational settings, I've discovered that a session, facetiously dubbed "The Play Determinant Quotient" (PDQ), serves as a useful deinhibitor, results in copious self-deprecating laughter, and clearly illustrates the facilitator's role as occasional actor and co-participant. As you (leader, teacher, facilitator) demonstrate this bizarre potpourri of nostalgic shenanigans, consider the programmatic value of introducing play in the guise of pedagogic evaluation.

Indicate to your very attentive listeners that you are going to introduce, by demonstration, a progression of "things to try" and that you would like each member of the group to attempt to duplicate your manipulations, sounds, shakes, turns, etc. Explain that each demonstration represents a test (pop quiz in this case?) that is to be scored individually—correct, each person grades his or her self—on a pass/fail basis, and that the early tests will be easy compared to the later assessments. Pass/fail in this context means you can either do it, or not do it . . . no partial credit.

Admittedly, all this preliminary patter is to develop interest and psych the group for trying something new, mysterious, a tad alarming perhaps, and with a bit of pizzazz. Try to balance the initial tone and content of your presentation so that your listeners aren't quite sure if you are serious or putting them on.

The Tests

I chose the following "tests" because they are wacky and <u>I can do (demonstrate) them.</u> As the person presenting the tests, it is necessary that you be able to demonstrate what you want the participants to try. If the following tests seem too difficult or too . . . whatever, make up your own pseudo assessments. Think back to when you were a kid and try to remember what you did to amaze the kid next to you in class . . . while the geography teacher was droning on about the demise of Constantinople.

Test #1—Remember, we're starting easy and that you are demonstrating each "test" before asking the participants to make their attempt. **Hold up your dominant hand and snap your middle finger.** You will probably notice 100% success on this one, and if you don't, it's not necessary to say anything or point out the poor guy or gal who never learned how to snap their finger. It is important, right now, for everyone to realize that they really are "grading" themselves and that you are not going to reveal who can and who can't snap their finger. **Hold up your non-dominant hand and snap that middle finger. Return to your dominant hand and snap all your fingers in sequence.** Keep up a patter of congratulation and praise, but don't single out anyone.

Test #2—**Insert a stiff right index finger into your mouth and attempt to make a popping sound by levering that rigid digit out of your mouth with lips pursed.** Have you ever seen someone attempt to do this, generating only a wet, sploochy sound or none at all? It's funny and entertainingly useful, as expert *poppers* attempt to help the hapless *sploochers*. People helping one another? Absolutely. But this is a test . . . **Try the left index finger.** Good-naturedly emphasize the failures and jokingly remark on outstanding efforts.

Test #3—I'm not going to try and depict this next manipulation, at least not "by the numbers." It's an age-old, two-handed digital maneuver used to delight young children (and young minds) by **opposing palms, juxtaposing and intertwining the middle fingers, rotating the palms against one another in opposite directions (as the fingers seem to find their way), causing the middle fingers to eventually and metronomely flip-flop in opposite directions** (see photo). It's amusing to watch and fun to help someone try to accomplish this fairly intricate, well-known (by my generation anyway), and functionally useless movement.

Remember, you are presenting a number of maneuvers that will purposefully result in occasional

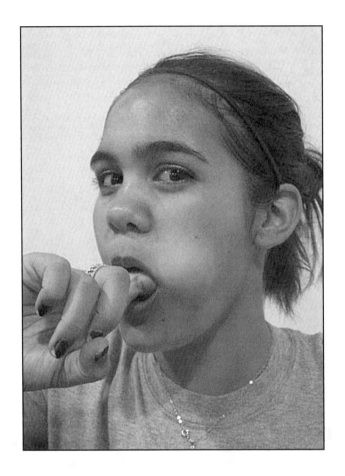

Test #4—**Touch the tips of your two index fingers together so that the point of contact twixt fingers is located about 14" in front of your face.** To pass the test you need to see (yes, visually see), a small link sausage balanced between your two fingertips. I like this particular test because there is no way to verify if a person passes or fails, it's all in their perception.

How are <u>you</u> doing with this? Did you see the sausage? If not, try looking at the floor or wall past your touching fingers, i.e., let your fingers go out of focus. Better? I hope so; it's a good looking sausage. As a bonus, pull your fingers slightly apart (1/4") and the sausage will float in mid air.

Really!

Test #5—**Cup your hands and blow across (like across the top of a bottle) the small aperture formed between the second and third joints of the thumb.** If done well and correctly this produces a hollow hooting sound that is the newfound delight of practicing youngsters and anathema to their beleaguered parents. It's also, as you have already probably discovered, difficult to accomplish. I told you the tests would get harder. In a group of about 30, you'll be lucky to get 3–4 people who can "hoot."

and obvious failure. If failure and fun can be combined, then the ole, often denigrated, trial and error technique of learning takes on a new look, as long as the error part isn't atrocious, (catastrophic).

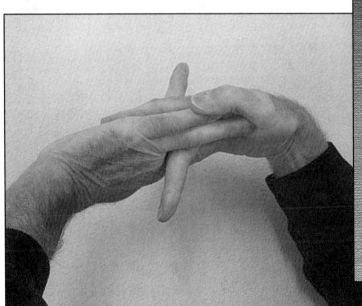

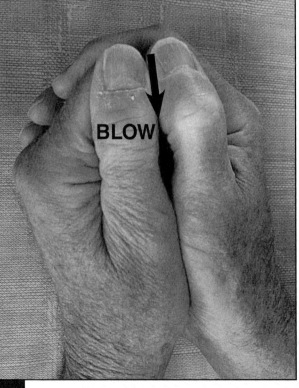

BLOW

PDQ

As the result of PDQing with a group, sometimes I just can't help demonstrating weird things I can do over and above the actual PDQ "tests." Maybe it's part of being an only child (look-at-me syndrome) because around the house it's just you and the parents, and parents aren't ordinarily impressed by weird things you can do with your anatomy.

Anyway, someone in a long-ago workshop was talking about rolling their tongue as a potential test, which most people can do; it's a genetic trait. After most of us rolled our tongues, nodding at each other with curled tongues extended in affirmation of our shared skill, I asked if there was anyone who could touch the tip of their tongue to their nose . . . because I could . . . and did. A couple of people tried and as I remember, couldn't do it. A young woman, who up to this point had not said much, spoke up indicating that just touching the tip of her nose was not difficult, and forthwith stuck her tongue UP her nose and even wiggled it around a bit—very impressive, very gross. The group was flabbergasted, applauding enthusiastically. I asked if she would mind being photographed; she wisely demurred.

The above "tests" are obviously not tests at all, rather an ongoing invitation to play, and amidst that play to experience acceptable failure, knowing that your conscientious attempts are more significant than your performance. Don't just let that concept float out there like a helium balloon . . . up, up, and away! Make sure that everyone knows and believes that initially a solid attempt is more important than the result of that attempt. If you can convince your group that it's not only OK to fail occasionally but necessary in order to complete the experiential learning cycle, then you have accomplished more than just having fun and sharing laughter.

Other "tests" for you to choose from:

Whistle loudly through your teeth.

Touch your tongue to your nose.

Roll your tongue or rotate your tongue upside down.

Play a tune by cupping your hand under your armpit and, well . . . you know.

Crack your nose by actually snapping a hidden thumbnail against an upper incisor.

Extend your thumb; a two-handed stunt.

Sherpa Walk

This follow-the-leader, action-oriented walk is probably the longest duration trust activity (other than marriage) I've ever taken part in. As such, participating in a Sherpa Walk requires remaining sightless for at least half an hour. When sequencing permits (high established trust), impel the participants into a sightless, constantly changing, challenging environment.

Objective

To set up a fantasy situation that requires two randomly chosen guides to safely lead a sightless group through a pre-planned "adventure" walk.

Set Up and Rules of Operation

- Tell the group they will be going on an extended guided walk and that during this time their eyes must remain closed. Assure them they can talk as much as they like and that they will be in constant contact with one another. Also indicate that spotters will be in attendance on the walk to maintain their safety.
- Considering most of the group will be asked to keep their eyes closed for at least half an hour, the facilitator should assure the group that no one will make fun of, or take advantage of, anyone with their eyes closed.

- For years I insisted on blindfolds for this activity. Typically, however, when people tie on a blindfold they do so with the intention of peeking out the bottom to see what's going on, and/or to gain an advantage. I chose then, some time ago, to ask people to simply close their eyes if a sightless challenge presented itself; peek-by-choice so to speak.
- Ask the group to close their eyes and, with bumpers up, to mill around for about 30 seconds.
- After they have stopped (confirm their eyes are still closed), tell the group that you are going to choose two people from their number to act as guides for the upcoming sightless walk.
- After receiving a tap on the shoulder from you, the two guides should separate themselves quietly and discreetly from the group, joining you some distance away.
- Before explaining to the guides what their responsibilities will be, tell the group (eyes still closed) that you will be gone for about five minutes while talking to the guides. Suggest that they take this time to discuss how they will travel as a sightless tourist group.

- If you are presenting Sherpa Walk to a young group, or any immature assemblage, don't leave them alone. Let them know a responsible aid will be in attendance during the short time you will be gone.
- Lead your two guides through the walk that you established earlier, indicating they will need to come up with an alternate means of communication with these "tourists" in order to guide them through the various ups and downs associated with this guided adventure.
- Explain to the guides, and eventually the tourist group, that they are not allowed to do or say anything (language, inflections, nods, hip thrusts, etc.) that the group will initially understand, but they can make whatever sounds they like: whistles, clucking, clapping.
- Guides are not allowed to touch any members of the group.
- Leave the guides alone for a few minutes so they can establish how they are going to guide and communicate with a group that does not initially understand anything they say, and vice versa. (Remember—even though they obviously

PLYNN

understand what the group is saying or asking, they cannot respond to their questions because in their role as foreign guides they don't speak or understand the tourists' language.) During these few minutes while the guides are talking to one another, return to the group and offer them the following story as to why they are there and undertaking this adventurous trip together, or any other highly fabricated scenario that fits the challenge.

You need to relate a story line that gives the upcoming sightless bash some reason for being. For example, fabricate a humorous and slightly plausible scenario that involves a basis for them to be blindfolded (national security), a reason for not recognizing their guide's language (foreign country), and justification for not being able to touch them (recent exposure to a highly contagious pathogen).

After having lightheartedly presented the necessary background information to the group (You don't just walk around "blindfolded" for no reason!), tell your travelers that two guides are here to lead them through a restricted area (allowed to be seen ONLY by locals), to where the tour bus will pick them up.

- Assure the group that you, and one other proctor, will be silently attending this walk to provide spotting in case of any potentially risky moves. As you see the guides approach, say "The next semi-human voice you hear will be from your guides. Goodbye for now and I hope to see you soon."
- As you walk along, with what has become a very verbal and animated group of travelers, watch for potential danger and put yourself in a useful spotting position if necessary. Most eyes-closed people are unhesitatingly trusting. Temper challenge with compassion. If it appears that the group is hesitating and consistently complaining about the physical challenges on the walk, signal to the guides to detour around the more challenging scheduled obstacles.
- Watch and listen for situations that will be valuable to relate during the post-walk debrief.
- After announcing their arrival at the "bus terminal," say those words they have been waiting for "open your eyes." Do not try to make any salient points at this juncture, just let the group look around and share with one another their at-the-moment emotions and observations.
- When conversations have slowed, ask the guides to take the group back through the route just passed, allowing them all (guides and tourists) to share reactions and sensations of what they felt at the time as they passed through the various physical obstacles.
- Finish up with a sit-down debrief session in a comfortable area—shade, no bugs, minimal distractions.

Debrief

Talk about anticipation, fears, location, leadership, trust, anger, high points, peeking.

Caveat   While proctoring a group through a Sherpa Walk many years ago, I spontaneously indicated to one of the guides to change route and take the group over and down an approximate six foot vertical landscaping incline rather than the gradual three foot incline immediately to the right. It was a disaster. No one got hurt but the diminishing of trust was painful and permanent. Stick with the plan unless you absolutely KNOW what the end result will be.

Spotting

There are times when the difference between a short fall and a possible injury is an effective spotter, i.e., a person trained and experienced enough to know where to position him or her self to be most effective, and further, how to blunt a person's fall without injuring that person.

Effective spotting involves having one or more trained individuals in position to catch a participant who is teetering on the edge of balance, or has tilted beyond retrievability and yielded to gravity's pull. The "catch" refers to supporting the upper portion of the falling person's body, with most concern directed toward the head. Attempting to heroically catch the whole body (Superman catch) is difficult and dangerous and most likely will result in injury to both parties.

A trained spotter offers constant attention to the person for which he/she is responsible, attempting to anticipate their movements and positioning. Efficient spotting is the result of hands-on training, not attention to text or listening to (not listening to) a lecture. For someone who has not seen it happen, it's hard to appreciate how quickly a person can switch from a balanced, confident position six feet off the ground to a prone, pained position on the ground.

Use spotters generously when the situation indicates their need, but avoid using so many ultra-concerned spotters (usually a sign of inexperience) that they get in each other's way, or in some cases, actually prevent the participant from disengaging from a low cable. Give the performer a chance to succeed or fail, being aware that it's not appropriate for spotters to offer physical aid to maintain a person on the cable. Physical support of a participant is well-intentioned theft of that person's challenge; make the catch, be verbally supportive, otherwise hands-off.

Caveat That elusive feeling of trust which develops gradually within a group can be easily diminished or lost by horseplay or inattentiveness. Guard against these lapses, recognizing that it takes longer to redevelop group trust than to establish it in the first place. Most of the time your role as facilitator involves watching and mentally recording what's going on with a group for later discussion. If there is a breech of safety, your role of observer immediately segues to safety supervisor—say something NOW to alleviate the unsafe situation.

Self Spotting

To gauge the initial proficiency level of the group, I used to ask students to form a semi-circle (on grass) facing me and, in turn, to demonstrate a fall to the ground as if they had been tripped or pushed. The majority would pitch forward onto the grass and catch themselves by extending their hands, palms forward, taking almost the entire force of the fall with vulnerable wrists and arms. Whenever a student spontaneously performed an efficient forward roll, you can bet they had previous experience with soccer, football, rugby, etc. I used this revealing how-not-to-fall demonstration many times over the years as an indicator of how many people do not know how to spot for themselves, i.e., how to safely handle a fall when the spotter became the faller.

Historical Aside

Unfortunately this effective demo is no longer salient; here's why. During the first few years of adventure programming with Project Adventure, we met with our assigned students three times a week for the entire school year. That amount of contact time with students seldom occurs anymore, except perhaps in some private schools. The extended student/instructor relationship that was enjoyed during the early PA years has been unfortunately shortened.

During those early years with Project Adventure I spent a considerable amount of time (days) working with the students on not only how to spot one another, but also how to spot for themselves, i.e., how to turn a fall into a forward or backward shoulder roll. In *Silver Bullets*, within the section on Spotting and Trust, I spent quite a few words detailing a spotting and trust series of exercises which took up a minimum of three class sessions with the full year PA students. I had hoped, at the time, that instructors would find the exercises and rationale about self-spotting and spotting for someone else, to be valuable and reproducible.

Those days, mentioned parenthetically above, just aren't available anymore. Times and priorities have changed; students' schedules are less flexible, administrators want more accountability, teachers are hassled to fulfill curriculum standards, and time for learning how to fall has fallen by the way side. So to save time and space in this book, I'll refer you (if interested) to *Silver Bullets*, pages 85–88, for details on what I've been referring to. If you are lucky enough to have extended scheduled curriculum time with your students, the pages are worth perusing, particularly Fall and Roll Exercises on page 87.

Squat Thrust

The activity Squat Thrust has been around for a long time, much longer than the early game days of Project Adventure. As blatantly competitive as the game represents itself, you might wonder why it was chosen to be included in a book that consistently underscores cooperativeness and communication. I can't give you a definitive answer other than people like it, the play itself is not only historic but nostalgic; participation requires a level of unselfconscious touch. It's a grand prelim to the activity Cooperative Competition, . . . and I'm good at it. Also, I have to admit, I get a little tired of the absolutely-no-competition-under-any-circumstances attitude of some gentle folks. So I occasionally slip in a funn-oriented, usually one-on-one, competitive skirmish that allows some level of being physical and usually results in a win/lose finale that can be talked about. Competition is part of our society and world, like it or not, so I'd rather there be some intelligent conversation concerning the pros and cons of winning and losing rather than hiding behind a veiled, and often denigrated, desire to be the best at something.

Objective

Two people, in a squat position facing one another, attempt to push/manipulate/trick one another out of their squatting position.

Rules

- The only physical contact allowed between the two squatters is palm to palm. Touching any other part of your partner's anatomy immediately ends the contest. The contest begins with both people making and maintaining palm contact for at least two seconds.
- The distance between squatters is up to the squatters, but there's not much action if squatters can't reach one another.
- Each squatter must be balanced on the balls of their feet. If either person moves one of their feet or drops to their heels, he/she loses. Get used to losing, it happens. Does it matter? If you make a big deal out of winning (applause, recognition, trophies), yes, so don't do that. After a loss (with the loser usually supine on the grass, feet in the air), have a laugh, take your opponent's proffered hand, get to your feet, and have a go at someone else who also ended up on their back. Or, if you are interested in a rematch, suggest best two out of three.

- To play the game well, there is almost a zen quality you must attempt to achieve. I'm being kind of facetious, but concentration and anticipation work wonders toward staying off your back. Strength is not necessarily an advantage.

Consideration

Since one of you is eventually going to end up on your back, choose a clear surface for play, i.e., no rocks, sticks, logs, chairs, tables. Grass is good . . . asphalt, not so good.

• •

Trust Fall

Love it or hate it, it's the quintessential, ground level, trust exercise. Jim Schoel, one of Project Adventure's founders, was the originator and strong proponent of the Trust Fall as most of us know it today. There are not many games, initiatives, or trust exercises that initiate such strong feelings, opinions, and even passionate emotion.

I have facilitated and utilized the Trust Fall exercise probably hundreds of times over the last 35 years. During that time I've seen my share of injury and loss of trust, but that was mostly during the early years when the person falling was still thrusting his/her hands in their pockets, or crossing arms on chest to keep from flailing their appendages. But, I'm getting ahead of myself.

Objective

To talk about, set up, and demonstrate a method that allows a person, standing at a height of about 4 to 4 1/2 feet, to fall backward, safely, into the arms of a disciplined crew of catchers, then to offer this controlled fall opportunity to everyone in the group.

Procedure

What I'm about to outline in detail for you works—the details will keep both the person falling and the catchers physically safe. Be honest with yourself about this exercise; if, for whatever reason, you feel tense and anxious about the outcome, don't use it. There have already been too many instances in which well-intentioned recreation leaders, parents, and friends who have introduced the Trust Fall as a "fun" thing to do, end up getting someone hurt because they "forgot to . . ." or "only left out one thing." Get some hands-on training from a recognized adventure training group and use the following presentation as a review of what you should then already know.

- Bring the group together and explain the whats and whys of the Trust Fall. Front load the experience so that there is not only a sense of impending challenge, but a strong sense of why they are being asked to participate in this demanding exercise. This is not a stopwatch event. Take the time (planning and sequence) to make everyone's attempt a quality experience, and so you don't have to rush to get finished by lunch.

- Take time before the students arrive to choose a safe site. What constitutes a safe site?

1. Something solid to stand on that is about 4' 6" high and will easily accommodate two people.

2. Something that is easy to ascend; climbing up to a platform should not constitute part of the challenge.

3. Is concrete or asphalt OK underfoot? Yes. There should be absolutely no possibility in your mind (and eventually theirs) that anyone will EVER be dropped onto that surface. If you don't think the group can and will solidly catch whoever falls, do not use this event.

- Ask all participants (catchers and fallers) to remove all potentially harmful objects from their person (pencils, wristwatches, keys, pocket knives). You may end up with a pocketful of these items.

- The Trust Fall is partly a distillation of spotting skills previously practiced, i.e., this activity should not be attempted until basic spotting skills have been talked about and practiced; a sequencing consideration.
- Bring the group to the chosen site and arrange the spotters (everyone) in two shoulder-to-shoulder lines facing one another, so the first pair of catchers are located directly below (plumb line) the front of the Trust Fall platform. Catchers should be close enough (vis-a-vis) so when they extend their hands (palms up, elbows bent) the tips of their fingers should be located about halfway between their partner's wrist and elbow. Extended hands of both partners should be alternated all the way down the catching line . . . and keep your heads back.
- Do not allow catchers, facing one another, to grasp hands or wrists in order to provide a firm, solid landing. Think about it, knocked heads will result. To wit: Physics 101—"For every action there is an equal and opposite reaction."

Trust Fall

This story was related to me some years ago by the parent of a female middle school student. Apparently the young girl had been part of an adventure-type program at her school, during which time the teacher/instructor had presented the Trust Fall as, logically, a trust building exercise.

The parent was talking to his daughter one afternoon, asking about what she had been doing in school that day. She told him about the Trust Fall, but said that she had decided not to try it. Somewhat disappointed, the parent questioned her about the whats and whys surrounding the exercise, thinking that she had opted out prematurely. Nonplused about her decision to not participate, she told her father that she was tenth in line to fall but was concerned about being dropped. He asked her if any of the students had been dropped that day and her response was "Yes." He asked how many. She said, "Nine of them."

- Each spotter should extend one leg forward about 18", and keep both legs slightly bent to cushion the catch. Extend either leg to make the spotting stance strong and to keep from stepping on your opposite spotting partner's foot.
- There should be a minimum of eight catchers. If a particularly heavy person is falling there should be stronger catchers in the prime catching positions, i.e., more people might be needed. (The 2nd and 3rd pair of catchers are called "prime catchers" because they handle most of the falling weight.) All catchers should stand shoulder-to-shoulder (**velcro stance**), as a "tight" catching line is more efficient.
- If you have 15 to 20+ people available, i.e., many more catchers than necessary, allow everyone to be part of the catching line anyway, so after the fall is completed the entire line can pass the caught person to the end as a way of extending trust. Accomplish passing a person with care, as being dropped even from this comparatively low height, will immediately diminish whatever trust has been established. Appoint someone at the end of the line to be responsible for holding up the participant's torso while his/her feet are being lowered to the ground. Stabilize the person vertically before letting go.
- Passing a person down the line can be done either with bent arms in the catching position or, more boldly, by lifting the person overhead and passing him/her from hand-to-hand at that height. If you choose the latter lift technique, have two people assigned as spotters to walk along the outside of the spotting line.
- Ask for a volunteer to fall and choose the lightest individual from the usually 2–3 that raise their hands, as there's scant value in choosing the heaviest person. Offer the catching line some success before you release the 225+ pound DF (designated faller). If no one volunteers, do not succumb to the temptation of volunteering yourself. The smiling group looking up at you has no idea what the dynamics of an in-your-face fall represents. That, coupled with a novice's prerogative of doing everything wrong, might be enough to result in a very hard landing; not speculation . . . fact! Bring the group back together and go over ground level spotting skills, then try again. If you are scheduled to be with the group for more than one day, come back at another time.
- Considering that you have a volunteer . . . place yourself in the catching line as part of the third pair (prime catchers) in case everything goes wrong. If you receive only minimal help catching, considering that a light person is falling, your catching efforts alone can prevent injury. After the students have successfully caught a few fallers, remove yourself from the spotting line, keeping a close eye on what's happening.
- If two facilitators are available, the second staff person should be on the platform with the person about to fall, making sure from that vantage point that all procedures are being followed and to simply "be there" for the person about to fall. A last second admonition to "fall stiff" might keep the falling person from sitting (a tough position to catch).
- If the head and shoulders of the faller reach the catcher's hands and arms before his/her feet do, the platform is too high. If someone complains that the falling height is too high, don't hesitate to offer a lower starting height. Falling from the end of a small, field bleacher provides a series of heights to choose from.

- Before a person falls, some ritualized level of communication should take place between the catchers and the person falling. Example:

  Faller (the person falling begins the sequence)— *"Ready to fall."*

  Catchers (in unison)—*"Ready to catch."*

  Faller (just before initiating the fall)—*"Falling."*

  Catchers (the faller waits for this final command)—*"Fall."*

- If the faller's hands and arms are not somehow restricted from spontaneous explosive movement, someone will eventually flail out with hands/arms/elbows during the fall and do damage to one or more of the catchers. THIS is the most dangerous part of the Trust Fall and has resulted in numerous injuries. I strongly suggest that you slip a rubber deck tennis ring over both hands of the faller so that the ring rests on his/her wrists; easy on, easy off, and effective. Putting hands in pockets, grabbing pants, or crossing arms over your chest does not work.

- After everyone has had a chance to fall and the students ask, "How come you haven't tried this yet, don't you trust us?" it's time for your show of calculated confidence. If you are not planning to fall because you do not trust the students, then do not use this exercise. (You may have other valid physical reasons for not falling that can be honestly shared with the students.)

- Allow students in the catching line to regularly alternate their positioning as different people take their turn falling, so they can eventually experience the responsibility of being a "prime catcher."

- This activity provides the ideal example of when Challenge by Choice is best presented and honored. Cajole—yes; coerce—no. The following quoted paragraphs are from the 1985 text of *Silver Bullets*, reproduced here because the catch phrase Challenge by Choice had not yet been accepted* and because I don't think I can say it any better 25 years later.

"Make an attempt to achieve 100% participation during this activity, even if participation means simply standing on the platform and looking down at the line of catchers. From this point, "the position of potential," it's often easier to go ahead and fall than to climb down. To quote from a former student who had been avoiding an attempt, 'That's not fair Karl. You know if I stand up there I'll do it.'

On the other hand, very little is achieved by demanding that a student stay up there until he/she makes a desperate attempt, in which case, trust is diminished. Participation in this and all activities must result from the student's own decision and not because of the instructor's impelling personality and certainly not from any cute coercion tricks. Also, I feel that a student should not be left standing on a platform for more than a few minutes. The choice to perform or not should be entirely up to the participant, but a decision must be made to either go or not go after a reasonable period of time."

*accepted—I started using the catch phrase Challenge by Choice in the summer of 1982.

Trust Dive

If you can bring yourself to fall backward into the arms of people you trust, why not try a dive forward? Why not indeed? Let's give it a try, but first . . . there are some things you need to know.

Procedure

Almost the same set up as with the Trust Fall, except:

- Ensure that the diving platform is solid and secure enough to preclude what was mentioned above concerning an "equal and opposite reaction." The platform is not sustaining just the weight of two people, but their weight in addition to a substantial lateral shove.
- Diving from the take-off platform should be from a height of about 2–4 feet. Dives from the top step of a six-step bleacher can be accomplished, but you are moving from perceived risk to real risk if you choose that level of challenge.

- Either end of a set of field bleachers provides a variable and usually solid take-off platform. The diver can choose height and distance by moving up or down the bleacher steps. Remember the dive is done off the END of the bleachers, not in the middle. Other usable take-off points include the back of a pick up truck tailgate, a tree stump, a low porch, and a well-positioned boulder.
- The diver is truly diving forward, but not like diving into a pool. Indicate to the diver that he/she should aim for an invisible trapeze hanging above the heads of the paired catchers. Discourage dives "into the pool," a much more difficult body position to catch. Encourage diving with arms extended forward and with the body as straight as possible, i.e., no pike position.
- Arrange the catchers in two lines like the Trust Fall arrangement, but ask the catchers to make a half turn toward the diver. This swivelled positioning will allow an increased ability to absorb the momentum of the forward-flying diver.
- As a catcher, if I am standing on the left side of the paired column facing the diver, after I make the half turn I will be doing most of the catching with my right arm. Alternate catching sides of the column to prevent over-use injury.

- Caveat catchers! Keep your head back as the diver comes toward you.
- The catchers can either pass the diver down to the end of the catching line (as in the Trust Fall), or simply lower the diver's feet to the ground and help that person stand before releasing contact.
- To increase the commitment of the diver, remove the first two paired spotters, i.e., extend the distance of the diver to the catchers. Let this be a choice that the diver makes; all you are doing is suggesting. By this time, the students should know that you would not suggest attempting something dangerous. Choosing to remove the first pair of spotters, and sometimes the second pair also, is not as risky and dramatic as it might seem, but if the students see it that way, so much the better. Even if the dive comes up way short (I've never seen it happen), only the diver's feet will make contact with the ground.

Winker

Winker is a "filler" activity, i.e., don't count on more than 10 minutes of willing, useful participation. And from a sequencing standpoint, don't use Winker as an "introductory" activity. Playing an eye contact game like Winker is easier when previous play and sharing time together has been experienced.

Face another person and locate your faces approximately 18" apart. Close your eyes, all two of you. One of the players counts to 3, and on 3, both players do one of the following:

- open their right eye only
- open their left eye only
- open both eyes
- keep both eyes shut (If you don't hear anything after a couple seconds . . . open up and check.)

The idea is to do the same thing your partner does with the objective of seeing how many tries it takes to be congruent or, once you get in tune with your partner, to see how many times in a row you can wink, blink, or stare concurrently.

Rules and Considerations

- Winker is a no-communication communication activity, so there's no talking, head jerks, finger spelling, animal sounds, etc., allowed, just pure, existential awareness . . . and repetition.
- Let the participants do their own thing; don't hover.

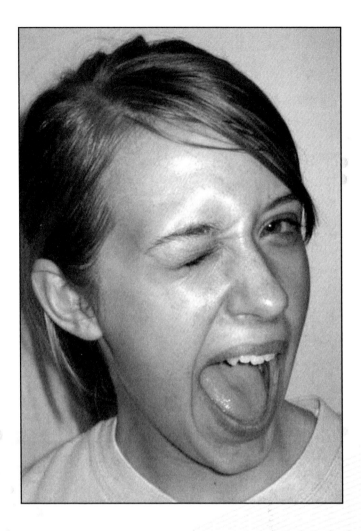

- Some people can't operate one eye at a time. Tell that person that this apparent disability is actually an indication of having outstanding peripheral vision. That's not true, but it might make them feel better for the short duration of the game.

Change partners a couple of times until it's time to move on to another activity and depending on the group's simpatico, it may be sooner than you think.

Quotes That Emphasize the Value of Play

Does the rubric above, "Value of **Play**," make you cringe? Does reading the words *fun*, **play**, *laughter*, *frolic*, *zany*, *crazy*, *games*, *enjoyment* cause you to cover the page to ensure no one thinks you take any of those words seriously? Check out the following quotes about fun and **play**, then think waaay back to when **play** was as natural as breathing, slip on a pair of tennies, and reintroduce yourself to:

"PLAY—Let it be an environment that is accepting and forgiving; and let there be real pressures, and let it make definite and clear-cut demands, and let the demands be flexible; and let there be no formal punishment or long lasting ostracism; and let there be friendship and hope of praise; and let there be abundant physical contact and physical exertion; and let the environment offer a sense of skills and a variety of behaviors that lead to greater pleasure . . . and greater security; and let the awards be immediate and intrinsic to the activity itself."
George Dennison

"All work and no **play** makes Jack a dull boy."
James Howell

"**Play** is the exultation of the possible."
Martin Buber

"**Play** so that you may be serious."
Anacharsis 600 BCE

"You can discover more about a person in an hour of **play** than in a year of conversation."
Plato

"In every real man a child is hidden that wants to **play**."
Nietzsche

"The right to **play** is the child's first claim on the community. **Play** is nature's training for life."
Frederick Froebel

". . . we take chances, risk great odds, love, laugh, dance . . . in short we **play**. The people who **play** are the creators."
Holbrook Jackson

"In the early formative years, **play** is almost synonymous with life. It is second only to being nourished, protected and loved. It is a basic ingredient of physical, intellectual, social and emotional growth."
Ashley Montague

"**Play** is the finest system of education known to man."
Neville Scarge

"**Play** is the art of bending reality to fit one's existing level of cognitive functioning."
Jean Piaget

"**Play** is where life lives. Where the game is the game. At its borders we slip into heresy. Become serious. Lose our sense of humor. Fail to see the incongruities of everything we hold to be important. Right and wrong become problematical. Money, power, position become the ends. The game becomes winning. And we lose the good life and the things that **play** provides."
George Sheehan

"It's fun to do things you are not made to do. I was **playing** when I invented the aqua lung. I think **play** is the most important thing in the world."
Jacques Cousteau

"To **play** means to accept the paradox of pursuing what is at once essential and inconsequential."
Joseph Levy

"Trying to define **play** and its function is like dissecting a frog to see why it's alive; both get killed in the process."
Anonymous

"All other species **play** to **play**. We're the only species that **plays** to win. Maybe that's why there are so many losers."
Lily Tomlin

"It seems paradoxical that although most people love having fun and enjoy humor, they are often resistant to its use. Perhaps the greatest resistance by people to the use of humor is the ingrained sense that work is work and **play** is **play**. Our puritan ethic subscribes to the idea that work should be hard, serious, important, direct, and efficient. Humor and fun suggest a lack of focus, a misuse of time, and a lack of attention to what is really important and to be rewarded. Not only is humor related to silliness, wasting time and laziness, but it is often seen as a measure of immaturity."
Napier/Gershenfield

"I have the feeling that all of what we do that counts is just love and work and **play**. And for me, because it makes the other two even better, the best of these is **play**."
Alan Alda

"We may be on the brink of an actual seller's market for wild and free-wheeling creativity for the clever, the goofy, the whimsical and **playful**. If ever there was a time to cultivate one's own audacity, foolishness and wit, this is it."
Success Magazine

"Being silly is a form of **playing,** yet so difficult for most adults. Silliness is something we should be doing for ourselves. Like laughter it can be contagious and good for the soul."
Joan Kolsbun

"We don't stop **playing** because we grow older, we grow old because we stop playing."
George Bernard Shaw

"**Play** is the anodyne of aging."
Clavidicus (32–69 AD)

"In the rush to give children every advantage—to stimulate them, to enrich them—our culture has unwittingly compromised **play**. Research indicates all that 'wasted time' was not such a waste after all."
Alex Spiegel of NPR

"As big, well fed animals, we have a propensity to become bored. Evolutionists tell us that **play** was put into our lives to prevent boredom."
Leonare Tere

"If, as a society, we have erred in this century (20th), it is in our failure to realize the importance of **play**; recognizing **play** as the primary activity for confirming our existence and affirming our worth."
I. Kusyszyn

" . . . instead of **playing** pirate with a tree branch they **played** Star Wars with a battery powered light saber."
Howard Chudacoff

"The spirit of **playful** competition is older than culture itself and pervades all life. Ritual grew up in sacred **play,** poetry was born and nourished on **play,** music and dancing were pure **play.** The rules of warfare, the conventions of noble living were built up on **play** patterns. We have to conclude, therefore, that civilization is, in its earliest phases, **played."**
Huizinga

"The younger generation do not want to be 'monitored', 'managed', 'conditioned' or 'programmed' in their **play** behavior. Those terms are the antithesis of **play** behavior."
George Leonard

"The great man is he that does not lose his child's-heart."
Mencius (372–289 BCE)

"**Play!** Where's the magic? We <u>have</u> technicians . . . we need magicians."
K. Rohnke

"Work consists of whatever a body is obliged to do. **Play** consists of whatever a body is not obliged to do."
Mark Twain as Tom Sawyer

"There is a certain type of person who refuses to grow old, who tenaciously but also naturally clings to childhood all their life. They are relentlessly inquisitive, buffoonish, cocksure, compulsively spontaneous, optimistic, gullible, impetuous, reckless, exuberant, moody, occasionally ill tempered, charming, often corny, and who possesses an uncanny sense of **play.** They are the children who never got tamed, those who resisted adultration, considering that an adult is simply a broken down child."
Paraphrase via Roger Rosenblatt & Piers Anthony

Quotes That Emphasize the Value of Play

Glossary

Following are words and concepts that are either selectively esoteric (I use them frequently.) or completely unique (I made them up.). Some of the definitions are skewed toward my take on the adventure/experiential scene. The ELC and ELS definitions are by Gloree Rohnke (who is credited with establishing and defining the ELS!)

ACCT—**A**ssociation for **C**hallenge **C**ourse **T**echnology: www.acctinfo.org

adventure—Adventure is classically defined as "An activity of uncertain outcome, characterized by risk and excitement." A sub-definition might also include that adventure need not be life threatening and not necessarily physical. Sky diving might be adventurous for me, while someone else might perceive hunting for antiques as being equally adventurous. Uncertain outcome? Risk? Excitement? Depends entirely upon the person and how they define (perceive) risk and excitement.

Adventure Games—Offbeat games applying studiously different rules and play objects; often created spontaneously with rule changes fitting the Calvin & Hobbes paradigm and usually associated with an adventure/experiential curriculum.

Bag of Tricks—Quarterly adventure curriculum written and distributed by Karl Rohnke during the years 1979–1995. "Bag of Tricks" formed the basis and content for *Silver Bullets*.

The Big 4—Communication, Cooperation, Trust, and Fun—(THE immediate answer to "Why is my son/daughter playing games, looking silly, climbing trees, etc.")

1. *Communication*—There is usually no problem in getting people to talk but is anyone listening? Effective communication involves more attentive listening than talking.
2. *Cooperation*—Working together to achieve a jointly decided upon goal.
3. *Trust*—Without trust (physical and emotional), communication and cooperation are just impressive concepts.
4. *Fun*—And the last should be first. Without some level of enjoyment, people will not return for more of what you have to offer.

Wrap the first three bulleted items in a matrix of fun and you have a powerful, almost irresistible, educational package.

bight—That part of a rope length that exists between the working end and the standing end, also refers to the curve in a rope. The curved part of a jump rope is called the *bight* of the rope. If the curve crosses itself, it becomes a loop.

boffer—A commercial play-sword made from *Ethafoam*.

bumpers up—A means of self spotting, particularly when a participant's eyes are closed. The position: arms extended, elbows bent, palms forward in front of the participant's face.

calculated abandon—A means of operating within an adventure-based curriculum, based on experience and over-engineering of safety gear.

Calvin & Hobbes—A now defunct, at one time nationally syndicated cartoon strip, that featured a small boy and his make believe toy tiger. Whenever the two played a game, if the game became tedious or boring, they modified or changed the rules.

Challenge by Choice—A catch phrase I inadvertently created during the summer of 1982. It has since become a cornerstone of Project Adventure philosophy.

chutzpah—shameless audacity, brass

cognitive, affective, psychomotor triumvirate—Esoteric words for thought, emotion, and physicality, linked by the word triumvirate to impress. Used ad nauseam in academic theme papers and reports.

contraindication—To make inadvisable, i.e., don't do it; originally a medical term.

domino phenomena—Where one thing (invariably bad) leads to another, and to another . . .

domino stance—Standing with both feet parallel to one another so that your base of balance is concentrated in a comparatively small area. This is an unstable position for a spotter. Extend one foot forward or backward to solidify the base of support.

edutainer—Combination educator and entertainer (ref. edutainment).

ersatz—substitute

experiential learning—A term for how learners translate personal and shared experience through cultural and social filters into personal discovery.

experiential learning cycle—David Kolb's multiphased learning model. Learning begins during a concrete experience that becomes the source for thoughtful observations. The learner then builds connections from the proceedings of the experience and eventually develops theories of the possible implications over a range of circumstances. The final stage of this process asks the learner to decide on a course of action, then actively experiments with it in another circumstance or situation. The new concrete learning situation begins the cycle again.

experiential learning spiral—Learning, whether by designed or unintentional events, is a progression of connected phases interpreted from the learner's previous experiences. The ELS is a learning philosophy that represents the continued progression of connected events that make up an individual's or group's lifelong evolution of knowledge and understanding.

facilitator—*One who helps things to become more easily attained.* A facilitator in the field of experiential/ adventure education presents situations in an attractive manner; sets physical perimeters of operation, i.e., what you can and cannot do toward solving an initiative problem; establishes safety guidelines; mentally records information about the group's performance for later feedback and stimulating discussion; and occasionally supports the group's efforts as an enthusiastic "cheerleader." See *teacher* below.

failing forward—When someone fails at a task, learns something positive from the experience, and applies what they learned to their next attempt, they are failing in the right direction, i.e., forward.

flow state—Involvement in a skill-based activity where the participant is neither frustrated nor bored by his/her level of participation. There are various other stages of the flow state. See CSIKSZENTMIHALYI on the Internet.

Full Value Contract—A structure for creating behavioral norms that everyone in a class agrees to follow and that everyone in the class agrees to work on maintaining throughout the life of the class.

FUNN—Acronym for **F**unctional **U**nderstanding's **N**ot **N**ecessary.

FUNN First—A catch phrase to remind people how important it is to capture your audience (group) with fun before you attempt to pursue an agenda.

Goldilocks rule—It's not too big, too small, too hot, cold, sweet, sour, etc.; it's juuust right.

histrionic—overacting, theatrical, affected

i.e.—Abbreviated Latin for *id est*; that is, i.e.

impossiprobability—Rohnkeism for a situation that can't possibly occur . . . but could.

an initiative—A fabricated situational challenge.

kernmantle—Synthetic climbing rope that consists of a woven covering (mantle) and interior, parallel fibers (kern).

Klim—Used as a verb; to klim or be klimmed. Refers to doing something egregiously and flagrantly wrong while building a ropes course, but fortunately not getting hurt.

lottsa knot—Can't remember a particular knot? Tie "lottsa" whatever you do remember.

New Games Foundation—The company (no longer extant) best known for their catch phrase, "Play hard, play fair, nobody hurt." They published two very popular game books, *New Games* and *More New Games*.

origami—Origami is ordinarily a noun, but used here purposefully as a verb, i.e., *to origami* a sheet of paper is to crumple the paper into a ball.

over-engineering—When safety is paramount, to build or create something that is much stronger than necessary.

peek-by-choice—Most people when they wear a blindfold, try to arrange it in such a way that peeking is possible. Do away with the blindfolds and tell everyone to go ahead and peek if they need to, but try not to; make it their choice. Peek-by-choice is a functional example of Challenge by Choice.

pejorative—Tending to disparage or belittle.

perceived risk—Pseudo-risky situations that appear threatening to clients (ex. Rappelling).

rabid nugget—A made up word (older son Kurt is responsible) for a tennis ball. Used originally in the game *Frantic*.

raison d'être—Reason for existence.

ropes course—A historical term for a challenge course, i.e., what challenge courses used to be called.

scooch—For our purposes, it means "sliding by increments," particularly involving the gluteus maximus area of the torso.

serendipity—The faculty of finding agreeable things not sought for.

sociogram—A diagram designed to measure how individuals in a group feel toward one another; a terrible way to choose up sides for a game.

sotto voce—in a private manner, very softly, a whisper

teacher—*Someone who teaches, instructs* (to impart knowledge in a systematic manner). In contrast, facilitators do not teach. If the facilitator, even in good faith, helps the group solve a problem, the opportunity to learn from their struggles and minor failures is reduced. Be there to provide a supportive presence but allow the group to learn from experience. See *facilitator* above.

throwables—soft throwable objects used for games and initiatives. Spell check consistently tells me that *throwable* should be *throw able*; take your pick. Adding an **s** to throwable (pluralizing a nonexistent word) is really a dictionary no-no, so I'm including the word here to give it temporary validity.

travesty concept—Would it be easier to walk around the 12-foot initiative wall than go over it? Yes, but considering that your group is attempting to function within an adventure context, is walking around the wall challenging, adventurous, or creative? No, those choices represent a travesty. But, if the group decides to choose that easy walk around T*he Wall*, their apostasy provides an opportunity to talk about why their school (organization) has provided a day of opportunities to overcome fabricated obstacles

for the purpose of developing communication skills and learning to work together as a team. Basically, no challenge = no enjoyment (ex. playing tennis without a net). Either way, a debrief session is indicated.

trial and error—The quintessential experiential technique for discovering solutions as long as the consequence for error (failure) is not catastrophic.

troika—three of anything

unselfconscious touch—Practically unnoticed physical contact made with another person while playing a game or participating in an initiative problem. Considered important toward developing trust.

Velcro stance or Velcro circle—Imagine standing next to someone, shoulder to shoulder, with opposing Velcro strips on both your upper arms. If you ask a group to make a Velcro circle, you are asking them to make a tight circle.

vignette—A short literary sketch or description.

vis-à-vis—with regard to

world record—A stunning, dazzling, incredible incentive for trying harder. People love to set records so it might as well be a world's record. And who's to say it isn't, if the task is exotic enough. I set world records all the time.

zax—a slate-working tool, and absolutely the *BEST* three letter SCRABBLE word available in this particular parallel universe. (Only defined in an unabridged dictionary.)

zzyzogeton—other than *zax*, my favorite Z word. A large genus of South African leaf hopper (insect), also the last word in this glossary and Webster's Way-Unabridged dictionary; trivia folks take note.

Activity Index

About Karl Rohnke

Karl has been an enthusiastic "player" in the field of experiential/adventure education for more than 40 years. He served as Watch Officer at Hurricane Island Outward Bound in 1967 and instructor/chief instructor at North Carolina Outward Bound from 1968 to 1971. He left Outward Bound to become one of the founders of the Project Adventure program in Hamilton, Massachusetts, and worked there continuously until 1996. During his tenure at PA, he operated as president of that company. Karl is also one of the founders of The High 5 Adventure Learning Center in Brattleboro, Vermont.

He has authored more than 15 books that relate to the field of adventure/experiential education, including *The Bottomless Bag Revival*, *Silver Bullets*, *QuickSilver*, *Cowstails & Cobras*, and *Funn 'n Games*. He is currently semi/quasi/occasionally retired and lives in Galena, Illinois, with his wife, Gloree.

Guilin, China

About Project Adventure

Project Adventure, Inc.

701 Cabot Street, Beverly, MA 01915   978-524-4500
PO Box 2447, Covington, GA 30015 770-784-9310

www.pa.org

Project Adventure is a nonprofit, international teaching organization that is committed to providing leadership in the use of experientially programming to promote individual growth, effective organizations and healthy communities.

Project Adventure offers the following services. For more information, check out website at www.pa.org, email info@pa.org or call 1-800-468-8898 (Catalog/Publications)

Open Enrollment and Custom Training
Challenge Course Design and Installation
Program Safety Services
Publications
Equipment
Custom Youth Programs

First Edition *Silver Bullets* Cover Explained

In the spirit of historical perspective, I thought you might enjoy a detailed breakdown of Bob Nilson's creative and classic cover art for the original *Silver Bullets*. Starting at the Project Adventure banner on top of the mountain and continuing clockwise, by the numbers, here's a list of the depicted games, initiative problems, trust activities, and stunts. It's quite an artistic accomplishment when you think about it.

1. Tumbling paper cores from the activity Paul's Balls
2. A generic trust walk spotter's "save," or perhaps compassion, being displayed during the Blindfold Soccer game
3. Blindfold Soccer
4. Electric Fence initiative problem
5. People-to-People (ice breaker)
6. Sardines (a Seek-and-Hide game)
7. Cable Spool initiative (following Sisyphus up the mountain road)
8. The game Tubecide
9. Carabiner Walk
10. Trolley
11. The Amazon (initiative)
12. Rolling Raft Adventure
13. The A-Frame (initiative)
14. Self portrait of Bob Nilson sitting with sketching pad (Bob included himself in most of his illustrations)
15. Frisbee Tag (center front)
16. Bear Claw (initiative/ice breaker—center back)
17. It's obviously the Lone Ranger's trusty horse Silver bugging out on the intrepid masked man and his loyal side-kick, Tonto. I don't know what Bob was trying to depict other than just the humor of Silver taking a powder while a few sticks of dynamite are about to explode.
18. Zig Zag (low-ropes course initiative)
19. All Aboard (initiative) under the cloud
20. The Rope Push (Push-O-War)
21. The Unholy Alliance (4-Way Tug of War)
22. Back to the top and the Project Adventure banner

The END

Karl and Kali c1966

EXPAND YOUR PROJECT ADVENTURE LIBRARY

Since Project Adventure began in 1971, thousands of teachers, health care professionals, PE instructors, corporate trainers, recreation specialists and others have attended Project Adventure workshops. These people have come away rejuvenated and eager to take back to their own programs the power and magic of Project Adventure activities.

QuickSilver BY: Karl Rohnke; Steve Butler; Project Adventure Inc.
Adventure Games, Initiative Problems, Trust Activities, & A Guide to Effective Leadership

QuickSilver includes ten years' worth of new ideas: Icebreakers, Warm-Ups, Games, Stunts, Initiatives, Trust Activities, Closures and more. There's a plethora of programmatic play in these pages, enough to delight even the most avid game collector.

There is also a section on leadership, where the authors have combined their 43 years of experience to provide you with some insights into leading effective Adventure programs.

Whether you are an experienced or novice Adventure leader, or just looking for ways to bring people together in a fun, positive and meaningful way, QuickSilver will surely become one of your most valued resources.

Silver Bullets 2nd Edition   BY: Karl Rohnke; Project Adventure Inc.
An Updated Guide to Initiative Problems, Adventure Games, and Trust Activities

Revised in 2009, after 25 successful years, this 2nd edition of Silver Bullets brings time-tested wisdom to the problems, games, and initiatives. This edition, with the inclusion of new entries as well as revised classics, speaks directly to contemporary adventurers.

The activities have been used effectively by a variety of teachers, counselors, therapists, camp directors and church leaders who wanted to bring people together to build trust and to break down the artificial barriers between individuals and groups.

The curriculum is alive and engaging; it is sequenced and adapted by practitioners to meet the needs of each group it serves. These activities have been implemented and proven to improve self-concept, enhance the ability of members to take risks, and strengthen the willingness of group members to cooperate and work well together.

For whatever age, these "Silver Bullets" can make a difference in your program and the people with whom you work.

Order Today! _____
To order these invaluable resources, please contact Kendall Hunt Publishing Company:
Toll Free: 1-800-338-8290 | **Fax:** 1-800-772-9165 | **Email:** Orders@KendallHunt.com

Learn More _____
Learn more about these publications and the authors online at:
www.PA.org | www.KarlRohnke.com | www.KendallHunt.com